DREAM WORK

Techniques for Discovering the Creative Power in Dreams

JEREMY TAYLOR

With an Introduction by Ann Faraday

Paulist Press • New York/Ramsey

To
KATH

Library of Congress
Catalog Card Number: 82-62411

ISBN: 0-8091-2525-0

Published by Paulist Press
545 Island Road, Ramsey, N.J. 07446

Printed and bound in the
United States of America

Contents

CONTENTS

Acknowledgements

I would like to gratefully acknowledge my indebtedness to
Kathryn and Tristy Taylor, Edith Taylor, and Rita Buffett for
their unfailing patience, encouragement, candor, and support, to
Ann Faraday and John Wren-Lewis for their thoughtful and
illuminating responses to and criticisms of this book, and
particularly to Ann for her introduction, to Arthur Hastings for
sharing his copy of Kilton Stewart's Ph.D. thesis with me, to
Maxine Cavanaugh for providing me with my first experience of
professional dream work, to Dorothea Romankiw for providing
me with my first opportunity to do dream work with the
profoundly disturbed, to John Van Damm, George Johnson,
Linda Purrington, Nick Kessler, Paul Carnes, Katherine
Whiteside Taylor, Murray Landsman, Orloff Miller, John and
Patience Kowal, Til Evans, Ron Cook, Ian and Sandy Cameron,
Hank Bischoff, Austin Fox, Orville Murphy, Charles and Angie
Keil, Leslie Fiedler, Bob Kimball, Bob Forbes, Carol Edwards,
Junella Hansen, Paul Sawyer, Rob Isaacs, and Wayne Arneson
for their wisdom and encouragement in difficult moments, to
Rich Byrne, Larry Boadt, and Kevin Lynch for their invaluable
support in the process of publication, to Goolcher Wadia for
her skill and good humor, and to all the people who have
honored me by sharing their dreams and the details of their
waking lives with me.

Dr. Ann Faraday

Ann Faraday received her Ph.D. from the University of London for research into clinical variables involved in the recall of dreams. Her book, *Dream Power,* has been a perennial bestseller since its publication in 1972, and has been one of the most powerful influences on the burgeoning dream work movement in the English-speaking world. Her second book, *The Dream Game,* was first published in 1976, and has also become a perennial bestseller. Since the publication of these books, Dr. Faraday has traveled worldwide with her family, and currently resides in Australia.

Confidentiality

Apart from my wife, my daughter and myself, no living dreamer is identifiable in the pages that follow. I would urge my students, friends and clients whose dreams I have used to illustrate the arguments to read the whole text before choosing to identify themselves with the dreams quoted. It is possible that comments regarding the dreams that fall later in the development may be such that the dreamer may not wish to be identified with them.

A sense of trust and security is an absolute *sine qua non* in sharing dreams with anyone. Dreamers and dream workers should always remember this, and either agree formally to strict confidentiality in dream work, or to "anonymity" in any reference to dreams outside of the presence of the dreamer. I am particularly grateful to the many people over the years who have agreed to anonymity instead of strict confidentiality regarding our individual and group dream work experiences.

The Arabs are right—"Without water there is nothing."

True philosophy is not the
one that lays down certainties
and classifies phenomena; on
the contrary, it is the one
that discerns the reasons for
these categories and makes
clear how arbitrary they are.
Michel Thévoz

Introduction

Jeremy Taylor is a man with a mission. This became evident the very first time we met, at a dream workshop I was leading at the San Francisco Theological Seminary in 1977. As he spoke of his own personal and professional work with dreams over the past decade, in family groups, churches, schools, colleges, hospitals, prisons and with schizophrenic adolescents at Berkeley's St. George Homes, one special enthusiasm emerged again and again. He had come to see dreaming as the revelation of an inner creative process underlying all consciousness, a process wherein we transcend the conflicts which threaten the very existence of life on this planet today. So he had a vision of dream work as a tool not just for helping a few individuals toward greater self-awareness, but for changing the world.

Now he has translated that vision into a book. In the pages that follow, he describes practical, down-to-earth techniques for understanding dreams, drawing with disarming openness on his own experience—but at every point he uses the insights derived from dream work to illuminate the tremendous social, political, international, ecological and spiritual crises of our time. For example, he insists it was no accident that dream-sharing became the focus of the informal association of houseboat owners in Sausalito in their struggle against predatory developers. He tells their story as just one small illustration of "dream power" in action to create a gentler, more harmonious social order.

Since this is not a book about clinical psychotherapy (though I would urge therapists to take time out to read it), Jeremy devotes only a little space to the specifics of his work at St. George Homes, but he mentions one lesson from that work which to my mind expresses the very essence of his vision. For decades now, it has been a cliché of both professional and popular literature on dream psychology that schizophrenics have only banal, static and fragmentary dreams. Jeremy maintains this is a libel, expressing and reinforcing society's wish to dismiss these sufferers as alien, sub-human beings. He suspects that the heavy medication to which schizophrenics are commonly subjected has a freezing effect on their dream life, for at St. George Homes, where therapists make the extra effort of working without behavior-controlling drugs, he finds that even this most despised and rejected section of the human race shares fully in the creative process of dreaming.

As an extension of this principle, Jeremy sees in dreams the healing magic we so desperately need today to deliver us from racism, sexism and every other form of tyranny and exploitation, including war itself. For are not all these horrors rooted, psychologically, in the alienation by which one section of the population sees another as less than human, not worthy of the same kind of consideration they give to themselves? Even humanity's destruction of the natural environment, Jeremy believes, springs from our denial of our oneness with universal life, which allows us to treat the non-human world as "mere matter" to be manipulated and controlled.

Moreover such outward acts of violence go hand in hand with the inner violation of despising and rejecting parts of ourselves which our conditioning has taught us to fear as alien. In dream work, however, Jeremy sees the key to "loving the enemy" both within and without, since dreams reveal that the despised and feared "other" is actually a challenge to our own narrowness. His aim throughout this book is to show that when we establish conscious contact with our inner resources of creativity by understanding and listening to our dreams, fear and alienation give place to growth and compassion.

In fact Jeremy presents dream work as the missing link between the age-old religious ideal of love and its practical realization. One of my special hopes for this book is that it will find a hearing in the churches, where dreams are still widely dismissed as meaningless rambles, or seen only in terms of prophesying the future. Moreover I believe church people might profit from the style as well as the content of the book. When I have conducted dream workshops for churches, I have often come up against strong inhibitions about self-disclosure. It may come as an eye-opener that Jeremy, himself a minister, is prepared to give reality to his accounts of dream work by frank illustrations of its impact in his own personal life. A portrait emerges of a growing human being, "warts and all," and his openness says much for his contention that dream work overcomes the irrational fears that cause us to hide ourselves from each other.

He is also not afraid to risk intellectual controversy, for example with his bold claim that *every* dream, even the tiniest dream fragment, *always* has multiple levels of meaning. To be precise, he maintains that all the great dream theories of the past contain valuable elements of truth, and so urges us to look at every dream for a "Freudian" sexual meaning, an "Adlerian" struggle-for-identity meaning, a "Jungian" archetypal meaning, an "Edgar Cayce" physical-health meaning, an "existential" revelation of the dreamer's concern with death, a "psychic" meaning for the future, and a religious meaning in terms of higher spiritual realities! Both psychologists and laymen—and particularly dream group leaders—are likely to balk at this, but I suggest we should be missing Jeremy's point if we take it as a claim to some abstract metaphysical truth about dreams.

As such it would be strictly redundant, since it could never be either proved or disproved. For Jeremy, however, it seems to be more an act of faith, a *working hypothesis,* to encourage the examination of every dream from all possible angles to see what lessons it might have, instead of foreclosing on its creative potential by dogmatic obsession with only one kind of meaning. How he ever finds the time to allow all members of his groups to work on their dreams in this way I shall never know. But the principle is fair enough, so long as it doesn't tempt people, including group leaders, to think they know what another person's dream *really* means whether the dreamer can see it or not.

Of the many skills which Jeremy brings to dream work, perhaps the most outstanding is that of the poet, and when he embraces all the great dream theories of the past and urges us to apply them to every dream, he is really singing a song of praise to the infinite potential of the dreaming mind. On the same poetic principle, he draws with immense fertility on myths and legends from all over the world to illustrate the working of the creative process in human evolution on the global level. What makes this book unusual is that he can bring these poetic gifts to bear on the "minute particulars" of everyday life and contemporary social realities. Perhaps he has learned this lesson too from dreams, which are always utterly specific to the dreamer's present life even when they plumb the ultimate heights and depths of universal being.

Some of the most famous statements about dreams in the world's literature are the stinging denunciations of them made by another "Jeremy" well over two thousand years ago, when he saw his Hebrew countrymen being deceived by bogus fortune-tellers claiming to dream rosy predictions of the future in an age of crisis. If our latter-day Jeremy strikes an optimistic note about the future at a time of far greater crisis than was ever conceived by his biblical namesake, it is because mankind today has the prospect of a more truthful, creative use of dreams. This book is his testimony to the new art of dream work, an individual and collective task which he sees as one of the best hopes of solving the terrifying problems that confront humanity at this crucial stage of its evolution. I join him in urging you to start practicing this art now, before it is too late.

Ann Faraday
Tamil Nadu, South India
November 1982

Chapter I
WHY WORK WITH DREAMS?

> A dream that has not been
> interpreted is like a letter
> that has not been opened.
>
> *Talmud*

For the past four hundred years or so, dreams and dreaming have had a very bad reputation among Western intellectuals. In general, educated people have tended to dismiss dreams as either unimportant or totally meaningless. At best, dreams have been viewed as curiosities—the epiphenomena of neurosis—while at worst, they have been seen as "occult nonsense"—the meaningless products of disordered metabolism which some people use as an excuse for hysterical self-deception.

Current scientific research has done much to dispel these misconceptions. Starting in 1955 with the publication of Aserinsky and Kleitman's original research demonstrating that their subjects exhibited more or less regular periods of rapid eye motion (REM) during sleep, and that these periods were associated with dreaming, it has been repeatedly verified by independent researchers that all people dream, whether they remember these nocturnal experiences upon awakening or not. Thus those who say, "I never dream," are actually saying, "I habitually forget my dream experience."

The rapid eye motion studies have since been extended to animals, and it has been further demonstrated that all mammals and marsupials exhibit rapid eye motion in sleep. The association of this phenomenon with dreaming in human beings is so clear that

it is now generally accepted that all mammals and marsupials
dream. There is also a large and growing body of research with
other animals and plants demonstrating rhythmic patterns of metabolic activity during sleep (and analogous cyclic dormant periods) which are strikingly similar to the patterns of REM sleep in
more complex organisms. There is substantial reason to believe
that *all* living things may participate in the dream state. It is interesting to note that shamans and mystical thinkers of all persua-
sions have said for centuries that this is the case, and now
contemporary science has begun to verify it experimentally.

This research also demonstrates that the phenomenon of
dreaming must have an essential evolutionary value as well, since
despite the wide range of evolutionary choices and adaptations
that the mammals and marsupials have made, there is not a single
species that has selected for not-dreaming. In fact, this connection
between dreaming and the evolutionary development of increasingly complex organisms is so clear that the Hungarian psychiatrist, Sandor Ferenczi, came to the tentative conclusion that the
dream state is the "workshop of evolution." Ferenczi suggested
that human beings may have evolved in large measure because
our ancestors first initiated and explored the psycho-biological innovation of articulate speech in their dreams.

These substantiated facts and dramatic implications alone
would be sufficient to warrant a serious reexamination of dreams
and dreaming, but when we combine them with the fact that an
astonishingly large number of the cultural ideas and scientific in-
novations which have shaped our contemporary world were born
first as inspirations in dreams, it becomes even more clear that
dreams and dreaming are worthy of our serious and sustained attention.

Dreams have long been associated with creative inspiration
in the expressive arts, and this popular association has tended to
obscure the equally dramatic and consistent history of dream-inspired scientific and technical discovery and innovation. Descartes
first formulated the basic philosophical stance of Rational Empiri-
cism which undergirds the entire development of modern science
as the result of a vivid dream experience. Kekulé, who was inspired to understand that the molecular structure of benzine is
ring-shaped as a result of dreaming of a snake biting its tail, once

admonished his colleagues in basic research: "Gentlemen, learn to dream!" Albert Einstein, when asked late in his life just when and where the idea of the Theory of Relativity had first occurred to him, replied that he could not trace the earliest intimations back any further than a dream he had had in adolescence. He recounted that in his dream he was riding on a sled. As the sled accelerated, going faster and faster until it approached the speed of light, the stars began to distort into amazing patterns and colors, dazzling him with the beauty and power of their transformation. He concluded by saying that in many ways, his entire scientific career could be seen as an extended meditation on that dream.

These are not isolated examples. There are literally hundreds of similar accounts: Mendelejeff dreaming the structure of the Periodic Table of Elements appearing in the shape of chamber music; Niels Bohr dreaming of a pleasant day at the races and realizing that the marked lanes on the race track within which the horses are required to run were analogies of the fixed and specific orbits that electrons are required to follow in their circulation around atomic nuclei (leading to his formulation of Quantum Theory and subsequent winning of the Nobel Prize); Louis Agassiz dreaming the shape of the fossil form within the as yet unopened geode and articulating the only immutable law of scientific inquiry: "Go to Nature; take the facts in your own hands, and see for yourself. . . ."

My own favorite story of dream-inspired technological innovation is the story of Elias Howe inventing the sewing machine in 1844. Howe, after reaching the stage of exhausted frustration in his efforts to invent a machine that would sew, fell asleep at his workbench and had a "nightmare." In his dream he was fleeing from cannibals through the African jungles. Despite his frantic efforts, he was unable to escape them. They captured him, bound him, and took him back to their village where they tossed him into a huge pot of water to cook alive. As the water began to bubble up around him, his bonds loosened and he was able to free his hands. He attempted to climb out of the pot, but each time he clambered up over the edge, the natives would reach over the flames and poke him back into the cauldron with their sharp spears.

Howe awoke from this dream in a state of some agitation,

but one part of his mind that was not totally absorbed in the emotions of the experience articulated the thought as he came awake: "That's odd; all those spears have holes in the points." As he came more fully awake, he suddenly realized: *Holes* in the points! Holes in the *points*! That's it!" If you move the thread transport hole down to the point of the needle (where it is convenient for the machine, instead of remaining fixated on the needle as a hand-tool with the hole in the blunt end), then it is a relatively simple matter to design a machine that will poke the thread down through the layers of cloth, wrap it around another thread, and pull it back up again, all very rapidly and efficiently.

This has been the basic design of all sewing machines ever since. At this very moment, most of the people in the world are dressed in clothing put together with a machine that was invented in a dream. Howe's dream, and his creative use of it, transformed planetary society, releasing the pent up energies of the Industrial Revolution (which, prior to Howe's discovery, was stalled because even with Cartwright's spinning jennies and mechanically driven looms, all the work required to transform the raw cloth into salable goods was still skilled hand-labor). With Howe's invention, the economics of manufacture and distribution were freed from their pre-industrial, essentially medieval form, and the modern social, technical/industrial, economic, and political situation we currently live in was created.

We are still elaborating on the momentum of the technological/industrial revolution that was begun in that era. For me, the story of Howe's dream stands as a compelling reminder of the potential collective transformative power of the creative impulse in general, and its manifestation in the form of dreams in particular.

An examination of the role such dream inspirations have had in shaping society and world culture, from the most ancient times to the present, shows clearly that dreams are neither meaningless nor unimportant. Since the dawn of written history, and even earlier, dreams have served as a primary vehicle for human creativity and increasing self-awareness. Dreams have also been viewed traditionally as a means of communication with and revelation of "divine will" (regardless of the particular religious beliefs prevailing in any society in any particular historical period). The religions of the world all have ancient traditions of dream work woven into their sacred texts and oral traditions. A survey of these various traditions and a comparison of historical recorded dreams with our own dreams in the present moment show that dreams speak a universal language of metaphor and symbol.

All people dream in essentially the same fashion, and because all people dream, the energies of the creative impulse are increasingly available to anyone who takes the time to remember and work with dreams. When we make the effort to remember and record our dreams and playfully and meditatively explore and express their images and energies, this effort almost invariably reveals startling insights, creative ideas, and more conscious understanding of confusing emotions.

Dreaming is a universal human phenomenon which unites us all, even across the boundaries and barriers of age, sexual difference, racial background, social class, religious, political, and cultural attitudes, social and historical circumstances, and even profound mental and emotional disturbance. I have always believed that most of these mechanisms of "discrimination," of separation of the human community into "real human beings" on the one hand and "not-quite-human-beings" on the other, are self-deceptive prejudices that should be resisted wholeheartedly. However, I used to believe that there was at least *one* way such a discrimination could be made between "real human beings" (with whom I could communicate and identify) and "not-quite-human beings" (with whom the effort to connect and communicate was essentially pointless and counter-productive) and that was on the basis of profound psychological disorder. However, when I actually began to encounter and work with "chronic and incurable" schizophrenics and autistic people, I soon discovered that even this perceived barrier to human connection is ultimately illusory.

At the level of the dream, we are *all* one. I see now that this (to me) dramatic realization is in fact a commonplace, summed up in the popular opinion that "dreams are crazy." In all my years of work, I have been unable to discover any guideline by which the dreams of profoundly disturbed people can be distinguished from the dreams of "normal folks." I suspect that such a discrimination might be possible on the basis of comparing extended dream series, using such clues as repetitive settings, and the patterns of relative strength and activity of the "dream ego," etc., but I have consistently found it impossible to make such discriminations on the basis of comparing individual dreams. Over the years the only consistent difference I have been able to detect between "crazy people" and "sane people" is that the crazy ones are generally unable and unwilling (in varying degrees and proportions) to distinguish between the dream state and the waking state in the same fashion as the prevailing society.

In working with even the most profoundly disturbed and withdrawn people, I have discovered that dream work is an extraordinarily effective method of facilitating interior transformation of feeling and motivation, and consequent external behavior. Over the last fifteen years I have done dream work with a wide variety of individuals and groups in diverse settings including churches, schools, hospitals, prisons, and mental institutions. In every instance, not only have I observed both subtle and dramatic transformations of character and personality in the persons with whom I have worked, but I am also aware of similar developments and changes in my own life. The transformative power of dreams is inherent, and this power can be nurtured, developed, and enhanced dramatically by turning conscious attentions to dreams and working with them, either alone, or in company with others.

Summary: WHY WORK WITH DREAMS?

Scientific research demonstrates that there is no such thing as a person who does not dream. There is an impressive historical record of the way dreams have served as vehicles of creative inspiration. This record also demonstrates that dreams speak a universal language of metaphor and symbol. When the effort to remember, record, and reexamine dreams is made, it often results in startling insights, creative ideas, and more conscious understanding of confusing emotions.

Chapter II
DREAM WORK AND
SOCIAL RESPONSIBILITY

> The personal is political
> because a change in the
> intimate power relationships
> of our everyday lives is
> necessary for a free world.
> The political is personal
> because we need the power
> to determine our lives.
>
> *Sue Negrin*

There is another accusation that is often made against dream work by men and women of good will: that it is "navel gazing"— just another excuse to escape from the demanding realities of waking life into a "dream world" of irresponsible, self-centered withdrawal.

We live in perilous times. A litany of our collective ills and woes would fill a much larger book than this one. We stand in peril of total extinction, the extinction not only of the human species, but of most of the other complex organisms with whom we share the planet, and we have methodically manufactured these terrible perils for ourselves. We live each moment in the shadow of nuclear, chemical, and biological warfare, technological accident and planning failure, industrial eco-cide, economic collapse, civil strife, *and the attitudes of mind and heart that make these horrors possible.* Indeed, our collective circumstances are so ominous that

11

most people prefer simply to repress their unease and sense of utter helplessness in the face of these problems and not to think consciously about them at all, but think about them we must. We must have the courage to examine them with clarity and bring our best and most creative energies to the task of transforming and resolving them.

To begin this necessary effort of looking consciously at our darkest and most evil individual and collective potentialities, let me propose a simple mental exercise:

Imagine the planet as it is, but simplified, without a human presence. Imagine the rhythm of the night and day, the sky, the clouds and changing weather, the endless ebb and flow of the tides, the turning seasons, the myriad of creatures and organisms living in the sea, inhabiting the land, flying through the air—all existing together in a web of intricate, subtle, invisible, impartial natural forces—creating together a single, delicate, evolving eco-system, this whole bio-sphere spinning on into the eons of geological time and climatic change, beyond the life span of any individual organism.

In such an imagined world, even pain and death lose their horrific and "evil" quality. The rhythm of life and death, the drama of a predator and prey, the suffering of individual creatures, even the passage of whole species into extinction, are all spontaneous and natural, wholly innocent because they are wholly unconscious and thus incapable of either premeditation or remorse. Here we stand simultaneously in a metaphoric "Garden of Eden" and in the biological circumstances that contemporary science suggests gave rise to the development of human life. It is ironic that with such substantial agreement of metaphor, there is such acrimonious debate between "evolutionists" and "creationists" (but then, Clarence Darrow always said that the Scopes Trial was merely a bad-tempered conflict of style and personality).

Teilhard de Chardin spent his entire life struggling to remain true to both the rigorous demands of scientific investigation and his own deepest intuitions of religious meaning as he examined the multiple evidences of biological evolution. He came to the conclusion (like the Hindus and Buddhists before him) that time is a useful illusion, and that "God" is the ultimate end-point toward which evolution is groping (but since time may be perceived as ultimately illusory, it is possible to think of all events as taking place simultaneously, and in this sense, "God" may be understood as existing always, "in the fullness of time," drawing evolution forward into progressively more and more conscious manifestations of Him/Her/Them/Itself). In the face of ideas of this sort, the endless controversies over "evolutionism" vs. "creationism" can be seen for what they are—the products of prematurely closed systems of thought and belief.

Imagine once again the planet as it is, but without a human presence. From this "thought experiment" (as Einstein called such efforts of mind and imagination) it is clear that in one important sense, everything that is truly "evil" (including all the horrifying possibilities of global disaster and personal misery that we have wrought for ourselves) is the result of human consciousness and human intervention in the "natural order." In this important sense, it can be understood that, metaphorically, human consciousness itself is the "original sin," the source of all our anguish and misery.

"Sin" has been defined by all the world religions as "separation from God." In a metaphoric sense, "separation from God" can be seen as a model of the separation of individual human consciousness from the vast collective unconsciousness of the natural world. This is the initial existential condition of the species, and of all conscious human beings. Indeed, consciousness itself is the only thing that "separates" us from the spontantous, natural cosmos, while at the same time consciousness is our primary means of apprehending and reconnecting with our environment. When Judaism, Christianity, and Islam all assert that the predicament of humankind is the inevitable consequence of original sin, at one important level this is simply a description of the seeming separateness of individual human consciousness from the collective unconscious.

Our waking, lucid, "objective" human consciousness is partial and intermittent at best. Even in our most intellectually clear and emotionally exalted moments, our experience disappears into realms of "unconsciousness" in all directions at once.

Here let me propose another mental exercise. Try to be as aware as you can of *all* your experience in this very instant. Try to remain aware of all your unconscious bodily processes—your breathing, the food digesting in your stomach and intestinal tract, the blood coursing through your veins, the various states of tension in your musculature, your thoughts, your emotions, your visual perceptions of this page and the scene beyond, the sounds in the air around you, the meanings of these perceptions, the steady tug of gravity, the feel of the air against your face and in your lungs. Try to keep it *all* within the field of conscious awareness at once. No matter where your attention is turned, you will always have a sense at the edge of awareness that there is more. It is only because our consciousness is always partial that we have the sense of being "separate," the sense of being "once removed" from the harmonious flow and rhythm of the natural world. It is in this sense that conscious self-awareness "once removed" our first human ancestors (the "Adam and Eve" of Near Eastern tradition) from the "Garden" of collectively unconscious natural life.

At another, related metaphoric level, the "expulsion from the Garden" also describes the birth trauma. Each of us was once expelled from the Garden of the maternal womb into the experience of separate, "sinful" existence and toil. In this sense of biological metaphor, it is important to remember that we are all expelled from the Garden, *into* the Garden. The natural order, rhythm, strength, subtlety, beauty, and unity of the natural world is itself the root metaphor of the religious imagery of the Garden of Eden. In this important sense, consciousness is the original separation from unconsciousness that allows us to look around and realize in a self-aware fashion that we are deeply connected to the entire cosmos, and that the Garden is all around us.

The entire evidence of modern physics demonstrates this same ultimate connectedness. As Carl Sagan points out, we are all made of "star stuff"—the very atoms of our bodies were first created in the furnaces of the "Big Bang," in the pure energetic hearts of the stars, and our ultimate and intimate connections with all things extend even beyond the planet, out into the vastness of inter-galactic space.

Even though all the evils we face are of our own making, we human beings intervene in the natural order in ways which are both good and evil, destructive and productive, both malicious and altruistic, both intelligent and stupid, both creative and habitually uninspired. It is in this way that I come to understand nurturing the creative impulse to self-expression, growth, and change as an activity of ultimate moral value and importance, without which evil always threatens to overwhelm us.

(And at the same time, that is much too heavy and portentous—at bottom, nurturing the creative impulse is a metaphor of play, an activity undertaken for its own sake, for pleasure.)

It is in the premature closure of thought and experience that we imagine that "we know it all," that we try to make absolute and final distinctions between "our own best interests" and the interests of everyone and everything else. It is clearly this sort of premature closure to which Yeats refers when he speaks of horrors of modern life: ". . . the best lack all conviction/while the worst are filled with a passionate intensity. . . ." It is this basic attitude of premature closure which characterizes all "the passionate intensity" of the evil that we do—the bigotry and hypocrisy, the stupidities and cruelties. Counterpoised to the attitude of premature closure from which these evils stem is the attitude of openness to new thought and experience and as-yet-unconceived possibility which is at the root of all creative activity (including dream work).

In our more uncreative moments, we persist in the delusion that we have it all figured out, that we can make absolute distinctions between our own interests and the interests of "others" and of the planet as a whole. We act (or, more often, fail to act) on the basis of these prematurely closed notions, and then flee in astonishment and horror when the consequences of these actions/inactions rebound upon us in ironic metaphors of self-destruction (as they always *do,* because everything actually *is* interconnected through both obvious and subtle chains of cause-and-effect, structural interdependence, association, and synchronicity).

This might be termed "the Law of Irony": as long as consciousness is partial, irony is inevitable (so one might as well cultivate a taste for it).

Our current global perils are all specific examples of the Law of Irony at work in our collective lives. We alone have created these horrors for ourselves, and it is we alone who must devise ways of disarming ourselves and reconciling ourselves with our planetary neighbors and with the ecological realities of our ultimate interdependence.

It is only when we open our minds and hearts to new experiences and possibilities that we are able to act in ways to avert our self-destruction. The specific actions we undertake can only be productive to the extent that we recognize the true nature of our predicament, of our "original sin" of becoming conscious human beings in the first place.

In the same sense that all our personal and collective problems are created by our partial consciousness, so the solutions to these problems can only be found in extending the range of consciousness and innovative, creative action. The development of this increasing self-awareness is the first step toward the transformation we must effect—of our own lives and our collective perils simultaneously. In this kind of effort to nurture the creative impulse and develop effective strategies for preserving human life on the planet, dreams can be most illuminating.

I first came to dream work in the company of my wife, Kathryn. We started sharing our dreams with each other and our close friends many years ago for the interest and pleasure of it. We discovered that the dreams mobilized energies for growth and change in us that were immense. As we struggled to rid ourselves of the oppressions of sexism, the dreams proved increasingly useful and valuable in revealing the self-deceptions and unconscious motivations that made that struggle so difficult, and that made the changes and growth so rewarding when they were achieved.

I did my first formal, group dream work in the course of my alternate civilian service as a conscientious objector. I had occasion to propose, during a consciousness-raising seminar focused on racism, that we all share our dreams in which black people appeared and concentrate our attention on them. The energy for growth and transformation of personality and unconscious attitudes and fears that were released by this work was truly astonishing, even to me. The dream work was effective in bringing deep-seated unconscious ambivalences to light, and the work was further effective in transforming them, because each of us was forced to "own" both the negative and positive images of black people in our dreams as representations of aspects of our own personalities (regardless of the waking life experiences that were also brought up in association with the dreams).

It was in this way that I came to realize that dream work was potentially far more important than simply one tool among many for consciousness-raising around racism. It became clear that dreams could be used to increase consciousness self-awareness around *any* issue, and, what is more, that dream work could be effective in releasing dramatic energies for growth and change within. As this growth began to take place, it also became clear that one further consequence of this work was to develop deep and lasting bonds of trust and mutual affection and respect among the people who shared the experience of working with dreams. As a community organizer I realized that dream work could bring people together across all the barriers of race, age, sex, class, *et al.* to join in the work of changing society. I came to understand that dream work has the potential to be deeply "radical," not only in the original sense of *radix,* getting to the "root" of things, but also in the political and social sense of dramatic transformation of collective fears, opinions, attitudes, and behaviors.

Over the years since this initial experience, I have had a chance to watch the longer term results of dream work among people who are actively involved in social and political action. I have seen the intracollective support systems developed by dreamers, and the effectiveness, creativity, and sophistication of their organizing efforts grow and deepen.

Most importantly, I have seen dream work strengthen the commitment and resolve to change, both personally and collectively. I have seen dream work overcome the inevitable depression and sense of despair that occasionally overtakes everyone engaged in attempting to promote change in a society that fears and resists changes. The deep sense of community which group dream work creates continues to sustain and nurture the individual creativity and courage, without which collective change is impossible. I have also seen dream work open up prematurely closed political and strategic ideas. I have seen "religious" people awaken to the necessities of political and social action, and I have seen "atheist" activists become aware of a new spiritual dimension to their lives and work. I have seen the understanding that "the personal *is* political" grow into styles of action and communication which are more imaginative and which awaken conscience and courage in an ever-increasing circle of people. During dream work I have seen people who imagined that they were "uncreative" discover their own creative and expressive powers and transform their lives and feelings.

It is these experiences which have kept me focused on dreams and dream work ever since, while at the same time continuing to work for the goals of social justice, reconciliation, peace, and creative, non-violent change that have always been at the center of my life.

Dreams come always in the service of promoting wholeness. They have an inherently opening effect, always bringing to consciousness those aspects of our own being which we have closed out of our waking experience.

It is this inherent "radical," open, wholeness-seeking quality of dreams which explains in large measure why even those religious and philosophical traditions that emblazon dream work (Judaism, Christianity, Islam, Freudian psychology, *et al.*) have all virtually abandoned the actual practice of paying serious attention to dreams, despite their acknowledged traditional importance. Sustained dream work always calls into question the fixed beliefs and ideologies of prematurely closed experience and thought (even when dreams were the initial inspiration of those beliefs and ideologies). Once an idea or religious intuition becomes frozen in an institutional form, the continued criticism and creative innovation offered by dream work becomes "heresy," and dreams themselves become suspect, persecuted, and ultimately repressed and ignored.

The basic problems of individual and collective life have never changed. The problems we face in the twentieth century may appear initially to be different from the problems of previous generations, but honest examination reveals that they are simply the age-old problems of human consciousness itself—greed, malice, and stupidity—magnified to world-shattering proportions by the increasing power and efficiency of our contemporary technology and social organization. We are the "sorcerer's apprentices" who have called up powers we cannot control—the powers of consciousness itself. One inevitable, positive result of our "sorcerer's apprenticeship" in consciousness thus far is that now we can no longer escape the knowledge that interior lives and our external circumstances reflect each other—that planetary ecology and psychology are inextricably intertwined, and that the solutions to our personal and collective dilemmas must be sought simultaneously. Throughout our history as a species the dream has been a primary vehicle for the evolution and unfolding of human consciousness and increasing self-awareness. In the contemporary struggle to evolve ourselves, in this "race between education and disaster," as Bertrand Russell called it, we can no longer afford to ignore the creative potential inherent in each individual—a potential embodied in our dreams, and released consciously when we remember and work with our dreams.

Summary: DREAMS AND SOCIAL RESPONSIBLITY

Our collective perils are real and pressing. We have manufactured them for ourselves, and we must look at them consciously and clearly in order to find ways of disarming ourselves, reforming our institutions, reconciling ourselves with our planetary neighbors, and with the ecological interconnectedness of all beings. Dream work can enhance and energize these efforts by breaking down our prematurely closed prejudices, opinions, ideologies, and world views. Group dream work can also create a community of support and understanding which can sustain us in the efforts to remake global society in a wiser, more humane and just form, as well as offering specific creative insights and ideas to accomplish this vitally important task.

Chapter III
EIGHT BASIC HINTS
FOR DREAM RECALL

The realization that there *was* a pattern to my life, one which made sense, came about in a curious way. Shortly after moving into the Villa Seurat I had begun to record my dreams. And not only the dreams but the associations which the act of transcribing them induced. Doing this over a period of months, I suddenly began to see, "To suddenly see," as Saroyan says somewhere. A pregnant phrase—to anyone who has had the experience. An expression which has only one meaning: to see with new eyes.

Henry Miller

None of this exciting work with dreams can begin, however, until they are first recalled. Most adults do not remember their dreams, although almost all of us have one or two dreams in our lives which are so vivid and strange that we can recall them with ease, even years later. I believe that the primary reason for this general lack of dream recall in most people is simply the modern prejudices against dreams which have already been mentioned. When these prejudices are overcome, when we make the step of deciding that we do actually care about our dreams and what they are saying, there is usually a marked increase in dream recall.

However, no matter how clear dream memories appear to be on first awakening, unless the additional effort is made to record them in some fashion, they almost invariably disappear from memory within a few minutes or hours. Thus it is important to follow up on the initial decision to remember dreams with some practical action to record them.

There are many ways of doing this. They all involve preparing the means of recording dreams before going to sleep and to leaving them close at hand so that they can be used immediately upon awakening. There are several "gadgets" that can be rigged up to facilitate this process: tape recorders with sound activated controls, ordinary tape recorders, light-pens, and the like. I have even read about researchers in England who have developed a prototype bio-feedback machine that is activated by REM sleep, and that awakens the dreamer with a low tone when the REM period has come too close!

Here it is worth mentioning the dream deprivation studies: experiments carried out in the 1960's in sleep laboratories where sleepers were allowed to sleep in all the sleep phases except REM sleep. Whenever a sleeper entered REM sleep, he or she would be awakened by the researchers. The results of these studies were that the more often the REM periods were interrupted, the more rapidly the sleeper would enter the REM state upon returning to sleep. When these disruptions of the dreaming cycle were continued over a period of days, the subjects would begin to exhibit rapid deterioration of mental capability and emotional stability, eventually hallucinating when awake, *even though all other phases of the sleep cycle were allowed to proceed uninterrupted.* Thus it was made clear that dreaming is essential to mental and emotional health, whether dreams are remembered upon awakening or not. Although more recent studies of REM deprivation have yielded less dramatic results, the symptoms of increased irritability and per-

ceptual error were noted, and these symptoms are similar enough
to the symptoms of *delerium tremens,* that there is now a substantial
body of medical opinion that holds that the "d.t.'s" are a direct
result of the suppression of REM sleep by increased levels of alcohol in the blood during sleep. Alcohol, marijuana, cocaine, barbi-
turates, and muscle relaxants all have a negative effect on the
amount of time spent in REM sleep, and an even more negative
effect on subsequent dream recall. I mention this here because it
is clear that if a bio-feedback machine like the British prototype
were to malfunction, even only slightly, the effects might be much
more deleterious than a simple interruption of a night's sleep.

I have several acquaintances who swear by the tape recorder
as the initial means of dream recording. However, experience has
shown that for serious dream work, a written record is essential
primarily because the problems of indexing and retrieving material on tape become so difficult and cumbersome, the more material
you accumulate. The people for whom the tape recorder has become the best means of capturing dream memories are characterized by two things in my experience: they most often sleep alone,
and they are relatively skilled typists. Their practice involves
speaking their dream memories into the tape recorder over the
course of the night, and then transcribing them with a typewriter,
usually the same day as the dream, and almost always within a few
days. The main reason they seem to prefer this seemingly cumbersome process is that it is during the "extra step" of typing the
transcription that the "aha's" and flashes of insight come most
consistently.

I myself find this process too cumbersome and annoying to
my sleeping partner, so I have settled on the "light-pen" as my
main tool for capturing dream memories initially. These pens are
little flashlights with pens attached that only illuminate the portion of the page where you are writing. There are several light-
pens manufactured commercially, but I have found them all
unsatisfactory. These pens were first developed to facilitate hospital personnel making entries on patients' charts at night without
waking them up. At first they were available only through medical mail-order houses and hospital supply outlets. Recently, however, they have become available generally and are sold at most
department store stationery counters. The main difficulty with

these commercial light-pens is that they are quite expensive (I don't believe there is one available for under ten dollars) and (because the ball-point cartridges must be quite short to accommodate the batteries and bulb in the barrel) they run out of ink very quickly. When this happens, you usually discover that the place where you purchased the pen does not carry refills, and that you must write directly to the manufacturer, pay almost as much as you paid for the pen itself, and wait six to eight weeks for delivery. All this is quite unnecessary, since a superior light-pen can be put together quite easily with components readily available in almost any drugstore.

The design that works best for me is to take a "penlight" flashlight and fasten a metal ball-point pen refill cartridge to it with smooth plastic electrician's tape. This offers a much longer period of time of uninterrupted use before replacements are needed, and when they are required, they can be obtained inexpensively almost anywhere.

The simplest method, of course, is just to put pencil and paper right next to your sleeping place. Whatever method you try, it is important that it be easily accessible to you without having to get up, or even wake up and move around too much.

Once you have prepared and situated the physical means of noting and recording your dream recollections, it is also important to focus your intention before going to sleep. There are a wide variety of such pre-sleep rituals. In my experience, all the effective ones have one thing in common—a clearing away of ambivalences about the negative images that may come in dreams and a clear and wholehearted affirmation of the desire to remember and learn from the dreams.

Some people have become very enthusiastic about pre-sleep rituals which involve asking a specific question or making a request for particular kinds of dreams. Such techniques have an ancient lineage and history in the "dream incubation" rituals practiced all over the world to attract healing dreams and dreams of divine inspiration. Contemporary pre-sleep rituals vary widely, from a simple affirmation as you roll over to go to sleep that you will remember and understand your dreams, to elaborate ceremonial meditations engaged in before going to bed, and in bed before finally going to sleep.

When you have made your external and internal preparations for your night voyages of discovery and gone off to sleep, you may awaken during the course of the night with dream memories. When this happens, it is almost always a good idea to awaken enough to make notes. I do not recommend awakening fully and recording the whole dream in the middle of the night (unless it is one of these "big," unusual, or extraordinary dreams that simply will not let you get back to sleep until it has been recorded and ruminated over). Most often, a few key words or images jotted down with the light-pen or whispered into the tape recorder will be sufficient to recall a much fuller and more complete memory of the dream experience upon awakening in the morning. Occasionally, the deteriorated handwriting or the sleep-clogged voice on the tape will be too garbled to make any sense of in the morning, but most usually the notes recorded during the night will stimulate a much more detailed recollection upon final awakening.

Even for people who fix on writing as their means of first capturing dream memories, I would recommend trying the tape recorder method at least once. It is almost always a shock and an illumination hearing one's own voice "objectively" for the first time on a tape recorder. By the same token, it is often even more surprising and illuminating to hear one's voice clogged with sleep. Just as the handwriting disintegrates in sleep, so does the voice, and many different voices can be heard.

There is another pre-sleep and waking ritual which also deserves special mention. Many people are put off by the prospect of disrupting their night's sleep with even the occasional, partial awakenings that note-taking requires. To preserve the entire night's sleep unbroken, many of these people have centered on a meditative practice that involves focusing the mind and memory before sleep, and upon awakening. This technique requires that you recall your whole waking day, backward, as your last act before going to sleep. You lie in your sleeping place and say to yourself, "Here I am lying down, going to sleep. Here I am making sure everything is set to record my dreams in the morning. Here I am changing into my nightclothes; here I am washing; here I am brushing my teeth; here I am putting the cat out, etc.," moving *backward* through the day's events until you get to ". . .

here I am waking up this morning remembering my dreams." Then you go to sleep and do not trouble yourself with taking dream notes, even if you do drift awake with dream memories during the night. Then in the morning when you first awaken, you repeat the process, only this time it is the night's sleep that is reviewed backward: "Here I am waking up, here I am asleep having a dream, here is the dream (pause to write notes); here I am asleep not dreaming; here I am dreaming an earlier dream (pause again to write notes), etc." People who are practiced in this ritual will sometimes catch as many as four or five dreams a night with this method, without ever waking up over the course of the night at all.

Sometimes, even with the most elaborate rituals and preparations, people will still awaken with no dream memories. When this happens, there are still things that you can do that may trigger memories of your "lost" dream experiences. The first thing to try in such a circumstance is to move slowly and meditatively through the series of body postures you habitually are in over the course of the night. Everyone has a more or less unique but repetitive series of body postures which he or she moves through in sleep, and simply moving your body back into these postures will often stimulate a recollection of a dream, probably dreams had while lying in that particular posture earlier in the night.

If this exercise does not immediately produce results, it is often helpful to imagine and visualize the faces of the people with whom you have the most emotional connection, or to whom you have the greatest emotional response in waking life. Often one or more of these faces will appear in your mind with a background or a setting which you were not consciously imagining. This is usually a piece of a dream, and focusing on it can usually recall a much fuller account of the dream. You can also achieve similar results by visualizing the places where you live and work, the places where you have lived and worked in the past (particularly childhood homes), favorite natural settings, particular qualities of lights, etc., since these are also elements that are quite likely to appear in the dreams you are trying to recall.

It is also a good idea to check your diet for B-vitamins if you are having continuing difficulty recalling your dreams, despite serious efforts to do so. B-vitamins appear to be important in the bio-chemistry of dream memory for some people, as well as being helpful in dealing with stress. B-vitamins are water soluble, and so they are leached out of virtually all prepared and packaged foods. Even if you are eating leafy green vegetables fresh from your own garden and are preparing them by boiling or steaming, the chances are the B-vitamins are mostly gone by the time you actually eat them. For this reason, most people in industrialized countries appear to have B-vitamin deficiencies. There are several good commercial B-complex vitamin supplements available, especially those that provide a portion of vitamin C in the mix. Since the B-vitamins are water soluble, they do not build up in the body. "Overdoses" of B-vitamins may result in increased urination, but the dangers of cumulative toxicity from body storage that exist with other vitamin supplements apparently do not exist with the B-vitamins.

Finally, having someone or a group of people you care about with whom to share your dreams almost invariably increases dream recall. I am convinced that one of the major reasons why most adults do not regularly remember their dreams is that most adults have no social reinforcement to do so. Most often in society, dream reports are greeted with derision and boredom. However, when a social context which is supportive is created, the motivations for having a dream account to share with friends or loved ones is greatly increased. Even taking a class or joining a dream group composed of strangers is likely to have the effect of increasing dream recall.

Over the years that I have been exploring and teaching techniques of dream work, I have had the experience several times of people joining the group who habitually do not remember their dreams. Many of these people will begin remembering one dream per meeting, usually on the morning of the day of the meeting. When these people have been given the opportunity to share and work on more than one dream per meeting, their recall has tended to increase accordingly.

Summary: EIGHT BASIC HINTS FOR DREAM RECALL

1. Simply deciding that you really are interested in your dreams and desire to remember them is the single most important step in dream recall.
2. Decide what means you will use to record your dreams, and prepare and place everything necessary right next to your sleeping place, so that you can use it easily—without having to get up, or even having to wake up or move around very much.
3. Focus your attention on remembering and understanding your dreams before going to sleep. These pre-sleep, "incubation" rituals can be as simple or elaborate, as specific or general as you desire.
4. If you awaken during the course of the night with a dream memory, jot down a few key words or images. Most often, this will be sufficient to stimulate a much fuller recollection of the dream upon awakening.
5. If you do not recall any dreams upon awakening, try moving into the various habitual body positions you use in sleep. Often, this simple action will trigger a dream memory.
6. If you still do not recall anything from your dreams, try imagining the faces of all the people you have the strongest emotional response to in waking life. Often one of these faces will appear in scene or setting; this is often a dream memory, and once grasped can serve to bring more of the dreams to consciousness.
7. Check your diet for B-vitamins. They appear to be important in the chemistry of dream memory for some people, and are useful in dealing with stress.
8. Consider sharing your dreams with someone you care about. Consider joining or forming a dream group. The social reinforcement of having other people with whom to share dreams most often has a significant impact upon dream recall.

Chapter IV
FURTHER THOUGHTS ON
RECALLING DREAMS

> Having eyes, see ye not?
> And having ears, hear ye
> not? And ye do not
> remember?
>
> *Mark 8:18*

The reasons why we remember, or fail to remember, our dreams on any given night are varied and complex. Research has shown that there are rhythmic patterns of dream recall in each person, associated with the circadian rhythms, the pressures of the work-week, fluctuations in physical health and emotional life, social reinforcement, diet, etc.

Statistical studies of remembered dream content, such as those carried out by Calvin Hall, all suggest that women "dream in color" more consistently than men. I am convinced that in very large measure this is a function of dream memory, rather than of primary dream experience. There is an archetypal resonance between color and the life of the emotions. My experience leads me to conclude that the skewed statistical result of women reporting "technicolor" dreams with greater frequency than men, a significantly greater proportion of whom report that their dream life is in "black and white," is a secondary and subtle function of sexism. It is clearly the case that most women are trained and socialized to pay more attention to both the realm of aesthetics and to the life of the emotions to a far greater extent than most men. I believe that

28

this general tendency of women to report "dreaming in color" more regularly than men reflects on a statistical level, the general tendency of women to pay conscious attention to the realms of feeling, and to the visual and aesthetic impact of waking life.

This conviction is substantiated by the experiences I have had working with people (mostly men) who say initially that they "only dream in black and white." Very often these "black and white dreamers" will eventually report a dream in which a color suddenly appears. Most often, red is the first color to be "seen" (or, as I believe, remembered) as the exploration of inner life through dream work begins to have its subtle, alchemical effect. In many of these cases, once the first color has appeared, the whole range of color soon becomes clear and the dreamer no longer "dreams in black and white," except on rare occasions. My subjective observation in all these cases has been that as the dream work proceeds and as the dreamer becomes more conscious of the previously ignored inner world, the life of the feelings and the emotions comes much more to the surface of conscious awareness in waking life, and that the progressive "coloration" of the dreams is a reflection of the progressive "coloration" of waking life by the introduction of the previously repressed and ignored element of emotional life. This is also one of the reasons, I believe, why red is most often the first color detected in the transition from "black and white" to "color" dream memories—red is archetypically the color associated with the strongest emotions (rage, lust, love, passion, "blood," and strong, spontaneous feelings of all sorts). In this sense, it is not surprising that red should be the first color to appear, and that in both dreams and waking life it should be associated with warmth, strong emotion, and danger simultaneously. Based on these speculations and experiences, I am now convinced that everyone dreams in color (in the same sense that everyone dreams, whether dreaming is remembered or not), and that as dream work makes people more conscious and aware of their interior lives and feelings, this repressed element of the primary dream experience tends to surface in the evolving pattern of dream recall.

Freud devoted much effort to unraveling the intricacies of repression as a reason for selective memory, both of waking experiences, and of dreams. His work has popularized the notion that if you do not remember your dreams, there must be something "inside" that is so scary and repugnant that you simply do not wish to admit to consciousness in any form. In my experience, repression certainly is one of the reasons why we fail to remember our dreams, or parts of our dreams, but I have found that it is not as common a reason as one might suppose, particularly among people who come to dream work voluntarily out of curiosity, openness, and a desire to explore their interior lives and enhance their creative potential.

In my experience, even the most successful and practiced dream recallers will consistently remember only two or three dreams a night, while the REM research shows that over an eight hour period of sleep, we regularly dream perhaps five or six times. The research suggests that although the time spent in REM sleep varies, as does the time elapsing between REM periods, the average is one sustained period of REM every hour and a half or so. This makes it clear that even the most successful dream recallers usually forget at least half of every night's dream experiences.

For a long time I was deeply puzzled by this apparent anomaly. I was also puzzled by another seemingly anomalous pattern of dream recall in dream groups which I participated in: often the group members who seemed most enthusiastic about the work, and who appeared to be the least repressed and self-deceived about their own lives and dramas, would suddenly stop remembering their dreams just after joining the group. They would begin to feel awkward and embarrassed, and begin to suspect themselves of massive unconscious self-deception and fear of self-revelation in the group, even though they were not consciously aware of any such feelings. I would ask as searching and probing questions as I could about the precise experience of failing to catch any dream memories upon awakening, and over and over again I would hear wistful and frustrated stories of awakening directly from a vivid, colorful, and emotionally pleasant dream, and having the memories completely disappear in the split second between being asleep and dreaming, and awakening enough to begin to reach for the recording materials.

My experience with loss of dream memory due to repression is that it is almost always associated with emotions of fear, anger, repugnance, and unhappiness. These accounts simply did not fit my experience, yet the dreamers themselves were increasingly suspecting themselves of massive repression. Then one morning my wife awakened with a similar experience, coming awake from a vivid dream having already remembered to make notes, and having the seemingly clear details of the dream disappear entirely in the split second before opening her eyes. Later in the morning, however, she had a sudden flash of memory that she was able to put into words; in her dream she had been in an immense crowd of people, outdoors. Her experience had been of multiple consciousness, all existing simultaneously—her experience had been the simultaneous individual experiences of every single person in the immense throng. She had looked simultaneously out of each person's eyes, and heard with each person's ears, and been moved by each person's feelings, and thus had had no one viewpoint or "ego" from which to recall the experience.

Having myself had the experience of participating in dreams from the simultaneous experience of several figures at once, and having struggled to capture those experiences in my dream journal, I could imagine the difficulties of recalling such a dream experience at all!

It became increasingly clear that one of the reasons why many of the "best" dream recallers were losing their dream memories might be that they were the victims of their own enthusiasm. I began to see that the subtlety, complexity, and basic dissimilarity of waking experience to deeper and more archetypal dreams and experiences within dreams might in itself be cause of forgetting.

As a result of my continuing investigations into such "unremembered" dreams and parts of dreams, I am now convinced that the *primary* reason for forgetting the majority of our dream experiences is that they take place beyond the basic structures we use to organize our waking personalities and consciousness: most particularly the sense of "self and other" and the sense of linear time. These are clearly the two basic defining coordinates of our common waking experience. However, I know in dreams we enter into experiences where these basic categories of conscious life simply do not apply. I have had many dreams where several different narratives take place simultaneously, and where I am several different "people" at once, as have many other dreamers. In the realm of archetypes, in the "collective unconscious," or "objective psyche," it is clear that the experiences of time and self-awareness are very different from the experiences of waking life. There is a level at which the archetypes are clearly "timeless" and "transpersonal," and when our individual dream experience enters those realms to any depth, the basic categories of waking consciousness and memory simply are inadequate to record those experiences (beyond the vivid if generalized sense that we *were* dreaming).

I believe this also begins to explain the even more common dream experience of hearing something, or reading something, or simply understanding something in a dream with great clarity, and then discovering when recording the dream that the specifics of what was heard, or read, or otherwise comprehended have completely vanished from memory. My strong suspicion in the majority of cases is that such experiences are an indication that at that point in the dream, a much greater archetypal depth or resonance is shaping the dream.

In many ways, these dream experiences suggest the experiences reported by shamans, mystics, and yogic adepts of "ego-loss" and "merging with the One" during meditation. Religious descriptions of "returning to God" and "mystical union" are very similar to descriptions of this loss of particularized identity in dreams. In that sense, I now believe that everyone "dissolves" into the collective every night and simply does not remember it. This, I believe, is one of the main reasons for the great restorative and recuperative powers of sleep. Certainly the dream deprivation studies dramatically demonstrate the central role dreams have in the maintenance of mental and emotional equilibrium, and it may well be that the impossible-to-remember dreams play an even greater part in that restorative function than the remembered ones.

It is also interesting to note that the descriptions offered by religious mystics and yogic meditators often use the metaphor of "dreamless sleep." Many yogis assert that "the one who has achieved enlightenment ceases to dream." Experiments in India carried out with yogis who made this claim demonstrated that in sleep these adepts still exhibited rapid eye motion, even though the experiences they reported on being awakened immediately after these periods were not what we would necessarily recognize as dreams. Most often, they reported experiences of "oneness" and "merging with the light." I suspect that the achievement of certain levels of meditative discipline in waking life may create patterns of dreaming where virtually all the experiences in sleep are at profound, archetypal depths, and thus the subjective, waking experience is of "no longer dreaming."

However, I also believe that startling and important as such meditative achievements are, they are available to and experienced by everyone each night (only without the quality of will, intention, and meditative discipline that meditative adepts bring to their achievement in the waking state). I am also convinced that the effort to capture these ineffable, transpersonal dream experiences in words and images is always worth undertaking. Even though the effort to capture that which cannot be spoken in words is always doomed to failure, it is the history of those failures that inspires our deepest convictions and beliefs.

I am also convinced by experience that the "yoga of dreams"—the application of increasing conscious intention and attention to the world of our dreaming—can bring similar spiritual, emotional, and intellectual attainments to those claimed by other waking meditative and yogic disciplines. What is true of the waking exercise of attempting to be equally aware of *all* our experiences simultaneously is also true of our dream experiences—no matter where we focus our attention in the dream, there is always at the edge of awareness a sense that there is more. The exercise of meditative discipline in the remembering and recording of dreams can lead to increasingly clear awareness of more of our subtle experiences, both asleep and awake. When one achieves success in developing meditation discipline, this often results in dreams in the midst of which the dreamer realizes he or she is dreaming. This extraordinary state of consciousness is called "lucid dreaming" and will be dealt with at greater length in another chapter.

Dream work can be a profound spiritual discipline, as well as a means to psychological self-awareness and creative inspiration and energy. Indeed, in many ways, these are merely different ways of describing that same process—the process of increasing "individuation," as Jung termed it.

Summary: MORE THOUGHTS ON RECALLING DREAMS

Many physical and social factors influence dream recall. We sometimes forget our dreams because their content is too disturbing and challenging to our current idea about ourselves and the world. "Repression" of repugnant material is only one of the ways this manifests, however. Another reason for forgetting dreams may well be that the categories of linear time and separate ego consciousness with which we organize our waking experience are simply irrelevant to the dream experience, because it resonates with the "timeless" and "transpersonal" realm of the archetypes. The effort to capture and record dream experiences which are without an experience of linear time and without a single ego viewpoint is in itself a spiritual discipline that can expand consciousness dramatically.

Chapter V
WHY ARE DREAMS OFTEN SO HARD TO UNDERSTAND?

> To me dreams are a part of
> nature, which harbors no
> intent to deceive, but
> expresses something as best it
> can. . . .
>
> *C. G. Jung*

In my experience, the dream does not mask or hide but does its best to reveal. Why then are dreams generally so obscure and opaque to waking consciousness? It is because every dream has multiple meanings, and multiple levels of meaning woven into a single metaphor of personal experience. It is the multiple, many-layered quality of dreams that makes them so often appear obscure and devoid of meaning on first awakening. However, when we take the time to work with our dreams, they most often reveal enough of their multiple significances to surprise and enlighten us and demonstrate that they are far from meaningless.

This purposeful, paradoxical, many-layered quality of dreams is modeled in the paradoxical quality of verbal puns. A pun exists because at least one word has more than one possible meaning and implication in the context in which it is used. In the dream, *everything* has more than one meaning, and the entire dream is the product of the spontaneous effort below the level of conscious self-awareness to weave all these different meanings into a single experience. This experience is obscure and ambiguous because all

35

the implications and resonances of all the multiple levels of meaning are still present to one degree or another in the finally remembered dream. Initially the experience appears to be "meaningless" only because waking consciousness has not unraveled the hints and implications of multiple meaning that are already present in the structure of the dream.

Here we encounter one of the major reasons for the plethora of competing dream theories and ideologies held by psychologists, therapists, religious leaders, medical researchers, occultists, anthropologists, gamblers, *et al.* Each one of these perspectives focuses on some general aspect of dreaming, and individuals in each "camp" become convinced that the element they are most interested in is *really* what dreams are all about. Their research demonstrates that this element is indeed always present in dreams, and having demonstrated this to their own satisfaction, they then proceed to announce that their particular theory answers all the remaining questions about dreams and dreaming, and that somehow they have demonstrated that all other theories about dreams and dreaming must be wrong, because theirs is clearly right. This is simply foolishness, masquerading as science, or, even worse, as revealed truth.

I have studied and practiced a wide variety of dream work techniques, and I can testify on the basis of my own experience that there is not one of them which does not reveal a part of the truth about dreams. Every time a dream work authority says "the dream is always thus and so," he or she is usually right in my experience, and every time a dream work expert asserts "and this is all a dream can ever be," he or she is invariably wrong. This is because the dream and all elements within the dream are "overdetermined," that is, the product of multiple factors merging and melding to create the metaphor of experience which is finally remembered as the dream. Thus when Freud focuses on the sexual/wish/desire element of dreams, he discovers that such factors are always present as a major component of the dream experience and its meaning. But when he asserts that this fully explains the nature, function, and purpose of all dreaming, he is clearly in error, and is forced to ignore and deny the reality of many common dream experiences because they do not easily fit his theoretical model. Unfortunately this same premature closure of thought and experience characterizes the vast majority of work on dreams, from the most rigorous and scientific to the most "fuzzy" and occult. In fact, it is the obvious inadequacy of most of these theoretical models that has given dream work much of its bad name over the past several hundred years. We are now entering an era where the exciting possibilities of scientific dream investigation, together with the dramatic insights and creative possibilities opened up by individual and group dream work, are coming together to create a new understanding of the importance and potential benefits of paying attention to dreams and dreaming.

At the level(s) of the unconscious where the dream is formed, it is "understood"—the many meanings that merge to create the experience of the dream are known and recognized. Conscious dream work consists of bringing to consciousness what is already "known" about the dream below the threshold of conscious self-awareness. The dream comes into our waking experience with its many meanings inherent, but not yet consciously recognized. Dream work consists of a wide range of strategies and techniques for lifting this already inherent knowledge and understanding up into consciousness.

This revelation of meaning inherent in the dream always comes with a "flash," a "tingle," an "aha," a "felt-shift"—an interior knowledge that something is true and on-the-case. Whatever you choose to call it, or however you experience it, this interior and initially wordless sense or "rightness" is the only reliable touchstone of dream work. Only the dreamer himself or herself can *know* with certainty what meanings his or her dream may have. Other people may have wonderful theories that work a lot of the time, wonderful intuitions that are uncannily accurate a great deal of the time, marvelously empathic understandings that are almost always accurate, but only the dreamer can *know* what a dream means. This knowledge is always initially in the form of a wordless "tingle," although often it is usually followed by an ability to articulate some of the connections and meanings in words.

If the dreamer himself or herself does not have a "tingle," then it simply does not matter whether what is being thought or suggested in relation to the dream is right or not. There is only one exception to this general rule that I have been able to think of, and that is in the relatively rarefied case where a wholistic health practitioner is using a person's dreams as an aid in diagnosis and treatment.

Having said all this, it is important also to say that the "tingle test" (as Ann Faraday calls the interior knowledge that something is true in relation to a dream) is only a positive test. The absence of a tingle does not necessarily mean that an idea or a piece of suggested work related to a dream is wrong or erroneous; it may simply mean that for whatever reason, the dreamer is not recognizing the truth in what is being said and shared in that moment. Only the dreamer's own interior confirmations of truth about a dream are ultimately valid.

Repression sometimes accounts for the absence of a "tingle" even when what is being said is true. However, once again, repression seems to me to account for a relatively small proportion of "lost tingles." By far the greatest proportion of "lost tingles" appear to be due to peculiarities of type-function and the deep desire on the part of the dreamer to retain a sense of autonomy and self-directedness in his or her interior explorations. For introverted types the verification of proof and truth requires aloneness and a reduction of intrusive, external stimuli. For such a person, a suggestion about the possible meaning of a dream coming from another person, or from a group of people, often simply cannot be verified until that person is alone and can test the insights against uninterrupted interior experience.

Whatever the reasons for the failure to recognize the truth in what is being offered and suggested about one's own dream, it is my experience that "the truth will out," and that sooner or later, if what was said was indeed true and on-the-case, the dreamer will come to recognize it. Many times I have had the experience of working with someone's dream and getting no tingles from the dreamer, only to discover later that what was said and suggested turned out to be very productive. Sometimes someone will come to a dream group with a dream that defies the efforts of the entire group to evoke any tingles. Often this person will return to the group later with another dream which is very similar in important ways to the first dream (a dream exhibiting similar settings and involving similar emotions and similar figures). When this later dream is worked on, the dreamer often verifies with tingles the very same insights and ideas that were greeted with no confirming feelings the first time they were offered. It seems reasonable to suppose in such a circumstance that the ideas and suggestions were not that off-the-mark to begin with, and that it is the ability of the dreamer to acknowledge and admit to consciousness the truth in what is being said that has changed, and not the inherent meanings of the dreams themselves.

In the midst of work on your own and others' dreams, it is important to bear in mind always that the only thing that matters is whether or not the dreamer himself or herself has a confirming sense. It is also always useful to bear in mind that when one has evoked a tingle confirming a suggestion about a dream, it is only one meaning among many that is being confirmed. In my experience, it is always impossible to reach the end of the possible meanings and layers of significance of any dream.

Keeping those two basic principles always in mind while dealing with dreams—(1) only the dreamer can know what a dream means, and (2) there is no such thing as a dream with only one meaning or layer of significance—means that dream work is much less likely to become an instrument of tyranny in your life. Because dreams are so multiply significant, and because they always touch down into the unplumbed depths of unconscious emotion and feeling, there is a real danger that dream work can contribute to giving away one's own power and sense of self-determination to the "expert" or the "authority." Ironically, even when the authority is "correct" in his or her pronouncements about the meanings of someone else's dream, this does not prevent the tyranny of truth from having its counter-productive effect on the dreamer who gives up autonomy and enters into a tyrannously dependent relationship with the dream authority. This kind of relationship is ultimately destructive to all parties involved and can best be avoided by keeping these two principles in mind while working. In this way, you are much less likely to become so dazzled by the first set of tingles you have that you fail to explore deeper and perhaps even more significant layers of the dream's full meaning. Conversely, you are much less likely to take on the role of external authority for someone else and overpower him or her with the depth and subtlety of your insights or the dazzling profundities of your theories.

Some work with an image from a dream of mine may serve as

an example of some of the ways the multiple meanings of dreams can be woven into a single symbol. Some time ago I dreamed that everywhere I go in the course of my normal business I see a huge block of French cheese standing incongruously in the scene somewhere. I never see the cheese move, but everywhere I go, there it is, and I have the thought in the dream that I am being "shadowed" by it. Just as I am waking up, I see it again, and I ask myself: "What's *that* doing there again?" Immediately an answer pops into my mind with the often embarrassing force of a genuine "tingle." The image represents a visual pun at one level on the phrase "big cheese," and represents my vaguely obsessive desire to be influential, rich, and famous—to be a "big cheese." In this sense, it is certainly a "shadow" and the pun on the Jungian name of the archetype of the "dark, scary unknown" is also clearly there. In musing over these initial insights obtained in the process of awakening, I also realized that it is a *French* cheese because, as with many varieties of French cheese, it is only a matter of taste and aesthetics whether you think I have "charm and robust character" or simply that I "stink!" At another level it is a pun on the image "block"—this desire for success is a "block" to be overcome and transformed, and simultaneously it is also the "uncarved block" of Zen tradition, an image suggesting creative potential and meditative self-awareness. Continued reflection and work with the dream reveals multiple, interlocking levels. At one level, the size of the block of cheese makes comparison to a tombstone, and at this level the dream embodies and implies concerns about death and related spiritual matters, far removed but not at all disconnected from the immediate levels of significance related to drives for achievement in waking life.

Continued reflection and playful expression of this image and its energies leads to further tingles at related levels of meaning. It is truly impossible to come to the end of any work on even a single image out of a dream, let alone an entire dream narrative, or a continuing series of dreams.

Summary: WHY ARE DREAMS OFTEN
SO HARD TO UNDERSTAND?

All dreams have more than one meaning and more than one level of significance. It is this quality of multiple significance that makes dreams appear obscure and without meaning upon first awakening. Virtually all the "schools" and "camps" of dream work have important insights to offer about one aspect of the process of dreaming or another. Unfortunately, most of the debates among these schools over which one is "correct" are examples of premature closure rather than serious efforts to discover more about the complex and multi-leveled truth about dreams. When the effort is made to remember, record, and work with even the simplest dream, it most often reveals some of its multiple levels of meaning. When working with dreams it is important to bear in mind that all dreams have multiple meanings, lest one become too fixated on one meaning, or one set of meanings at one level. It is also important to remember that only the dreamer can know with certainty what significance a dream may hold. Without a confirmatory "tingle" from the dreamer, it makes no difference whether an idea about a dream is right or not. Remembering these two basic principles is the best and most reliable way to see that dream work does not become an instrument of tyranny.

Chapter VI
SEVENTEEN BASIC HINTS
FOR WORKING
WITH YOUR DREAMS
BY YOURSELF

> I share all my readers'
> prejudices against dream
> interpretation being the
> quintessence of uncertainty
> and arbitrariness. But, on the
> other hand, I know that if we
> meditate on a dream
> sufficiently long and
> thoroughly—if we take it
> about with us and turn it
> over and over—something
> almost always comes of it.
>
> *C. G. Jung*

Because of the evanescence of dream memory, it is important to make a written record of your dreams, no matter what means is used to first catch and record them. Usually, this is best accomplished by having a bound journal in which the dreams are recorded and kept. However, if you use a typewriter as your primary writing tool, a bound journal is obviously not very practical, although many dreamers who use the typewriter eventually have their typescripts bound to preserve and honor them. The issue of "honoring" the physical place where the dreams are recorded is an important one. The more care and energy one puts into working with dreams and expressively celebrating their ideas, energies, and images in waking life, the more likely it is that the dreams will reveal more of their potential insights and gifts for living. If you record your dreams on stray scraps of paper and do not keep your dream records in an orderly fashion, it is likely that the quality of your dream memories will reflect this state of affairs (as they reflect all others) and be scattered and dim and seemingly incoherent. Conversely, if you spend time to beautify the journal or file where you keep your dream records, and if you make other expressive representations of your serious interest in and respect for your dreams, the more the dreams will tend to respond to that attitude in you and give you more beautiful, illuminating, coherent, and immediately meaningful dream experiences.

I am a great believer in decorating the dream journal with images drawn from the realm of dream and myth. Not only does this most often have the effect of promoting mutual respect, harmony, and cooperation between the conscious and unconscious, but as you develop a library of dream records over the months and years, the visual images with which you decorated each one while you were using it begin to serve as aids to memory and as metaphors of one's evolving life dramas.

It is important, when you make your notes and write out the accounts of your dreams, to try always to do it in the present tense. The use of the past tense is a distancing mechanism, and serves more often than not to create a barrier between the waking mind and the dream experience. This distance militates against the generation of tingles and the exploration of the possible meanings of the dreams. Sometimes there will be experiences in the dream which are themselves memories of earlier events; the habitual use of the present tense in dream recording facilitates the making of clear distinctions and accurate accounts of the experience of time in the dream, whereas the habitual use of the past tense tends to obscure and obliterate these subtle and meaningful elements of the dream experience.

It is also important to title the dreams as you write them. This is crucial for going back and reviewing the dreams and discovering the larger patterns revealed by the cumulative series of dreams. Without titles, this process of review can be very cumbersome and frustrating. It is also the case that the moment of picking a title is often a moment of insight. I came to understand this most vividly when I first attempted to review the dreams I had recorded over the first three years of concentrated dream work. I soon discovered that this was actually a process of going back and titling the dreams so that I could then get a sense of how they had developed and changed over that first three year period. Now that it is habitual to title dreams, this "extra step" is not at all cumbersome or time-consuming (although the effort to reread and title the dreams of the first three years was itself a process that took more than a year).

There are also interesting things to be learned from the ways that our understandings change regarding the titles of dreams and how adequately they reflect and evoke the memory of the dream. I worked with a woman once who realized that her first tendency was to title her dreams with phrases which were humorous and self-deprecating. Upon reviewing these dreams later she often discovered that there were elements of the dreams which were much deeper and more positive than her initial title suggested, so she developed the practice of subtitling her dreams days and weeks later. These "second" titles almost always were more serious and self-affirming, and more ultimately evocative of the dreams themselves. This process of increasing awareness of her deeper and more positive energies also seemed to be reflected in her waking life.

Always remember, you are the only one who can know with certainty what meanings and significance your dreams may hold. The "aha," or "tingle," or whatever you feel like calling it in your own experience is the only reliable touchstone of dream work. Remember that the "tingle test" is only a positive test; the absence of a tingle does not necessarily mean that an idea or expressive possibility is "wrong." Time and continuing attention to the dreams themselves will most often correct any "errors" of this sort that are made along the way.

This is an important aspect of dream work that deserves to be emphasized. The dreams themselves have a "self-correcting" tendency and always bring symbols and experiences which reflect a more complex and "objective" view of the situation, within and without, and tend to reveal the self-deceptions of waking consciousness with gentle (and sometimes not-so-gentle) persistence. Even the worst nightmare has as one major reason for its existence the correction of some imbalance in waking perception, attitude, or behavior. The very emotional strength of the nightmare experience is in itself an assurance that it will make an impression on the conscious mind and stay in consciousness long enough to be remembered at least a little while, whether the dreamer is actively engaged in recording and paying attention to dreams or not. This spontaneous self-correcting quality of dreams makes dream work unlike many other meditative disciplines which have a tendency to want to "discipline" the expressions of the unconscious into certain formalized patterns. The link with the unconscious is strengthened and the spontaneous curative and harmonizing influences of unconscious nature are enhanced through the active cooperation of self-reflective consciousness. This is not to say that formalized meditation is not conducive to increased awareness of the unconscious. My experience is that a combination of dream work together with the practice of some other formal meditative discipline in waking life is conducive to dramatic enhancements of both experiences.

Do not put any habitual limitations on the ways in which you record and interact with your dreams. Remember when you are recording your dreams that present tense prose narrative is only one alternative. It is almost always productive to draw sketches in your dream journal of any images which are clear enough to render. Several visual artists of my acquaintance maintain dream sketchbooks which have in some cases become their primary means of recording dreams, as well as being goldmines of creative inspiration. Many people extend their dream work into new areas by recording their dreams as poems. It is well-known that many of the greatest poets of the species sought and received much of their best work in dreams. When such expressive meditations are engaged in with some regularity, even the initial process of drawing and writing and recording the dream becomes the place where many insights and tingles come. It is a reciprocal process, and as the skills of writing and sketching are stretched and developed in the regular practice of recording the dreams, the dreams themselves tend to deepen and resonate more fully with waking consciousness.

In addition to recording the dreams in both visual and poetic form, it is also almost always productive to explore and express the more obviously charged and important images in dreams. In all cases, the "artistic merit" or "aesthetic worth" of the eventual product is not the primary issue. The primary issue is the deepening insights into and understandings of our unconscious interior life, together with the pleasure which these expressive meditations can bring. It is also true that the crudest and most "unaesthetic" expressions of dream imagery often have a haunting and compelling quality, while the dream images of skilled artists are among the most beautiful artistic creations we possess.

As you begin to pay attention to and record your dreams, it will most often be the case that along with the more fully remembered dreams will also come snatches and fragments of memory that seem "hardly worth recording." For a long time I paid very little attention to dream fragments, but an experience doing group dream work caused me to change my attitude radically. Several years ago, a young man who did not remember his dreams joined the dream class I regularly teach at the Starr King School for the Ministry in Berkeley, California. He had read enough to know that he did in fact dream, and that dreams carried important information that could improve decision-making and psychological health and growth, so he joined the class in hopes that it would offer him new ways of getting in touch with his interior life. All of these were perfectly reasonable expectations but still he did not recall any of his dreams, except occasionally the wispiest fragments.

One evening well on into the academic quarter he came to class once again with nothing to report, despite his interest and attention, and our collective encouragement. Because he had not had dreams to share and work on, his participation in and his experience of the class had been qualitatively different from everyone else's. He had not been the focus of everyone's interest and attention while he worked on a dream, and thus he had not yet felt and verified for himself the positive transformative energy of that experience. This evening I decided to wait no longer, and I began to encourage him to "make up a dream"—to fantasize in class what a dream would have been if he had remembered one. I suggested this to him because it is clearly the case that the ultimate source in the unconscious of all experiences of interior imagery and spontaneous emotion is one. The imagery and feelings of dreams are ultimately the same as the images of imagination, creative reverie, meditation, and peak experience on the one hand, as well as the delusions of neurosis and psychosis on the other. The manifestations of these unconscious energies in dreams are more spontaneous and obviously complex and overdetermined than the manifestations in the other waking states of daydream and reverie, but even the most consciously evoked products reveal the same unconscious dramas and multiple meanings when examined with the same care and attention with which we examine dreams.

This truth is given most charming shape for me in a scene from Cocteau's film *Orpheus.* The main character enters an ornate Victorian greenhouse to paint a night-blooming flower under the full moon. He sets up his easel and begins to work furiously to catch the fleeting effects of light, but each time he starts to sketch, the drawing turns into a face, rather than a representation of the flower. His frustration mounts with each failure until suddenly Orpheus appears (with a wonderful special effect long pre-dating the "transporter" on *Star Trek*). Orpheus laughs at the main character and says words to the effect: "When will you artists ever learn that the only thing you are capable of is self-portraiture!"

It was in this spirit that I suggested to the young man that he make up a dream on the spot that we could all work with in the same fashion as a genuine dream from the land of sleep. Although he understood the principle, he still did not want to make up a dream because it "felt too much like cheating." In the course of the discussion he did say, however, that he had had a twinge of memory from his morning's dreams—there had been "pastel colors." When asked what colors, he responded that he had no specifics—only a vague memory of "pastels."

Although I could not imagine a more inadequate fragment to work with, I decided on grounds of group-process alone that it would be a good idea to go ahead and work with it. We proceeded and another student eventually asked the young man if there was any association in his mind between the word "pastel" and the word "pastoral" (the technical name for such connection of such homophonically similar words is "clang association"). The young man got a strange smile on his face and admitted with some resistance that there was indeed an association. He finally recounted that when he had been asked the question, he suddenly knew that his commitment to training as a minister and to "pastoral life" was "distinctly pastel." He was forced to admit the self-knowledge to consciousness in that moment that he was in theological school primarily to satisfy parental expectations rather than as an expression of his own deepest desires and commitments. Having once admitted this to himself, it became impossible to pretend once again that he did not know this about himself. (He left school soon afterward and took up a career in banking.)

I was very deeply struck with this piece of dream work. He had shared only the most insubstantial fragment of a dream, yet it had carried in it a metaphor of his deepest and most pressing life problem in that moment. It was more like a tiny poem edited out of a much larger pile of rough drafts than it was like a fragment of a broken pot or torn corner of a painting. I became very excited about the implications of this extraordinary little dreamlet and the subsequent work with it. I started to ask for fragments rather than "whole dreams" to work on, and soon discovered that the initial experience of working with the young man's dream was by no means an accidental or isolated case. Virtually all the fragments we shared and worked on had the same quality of condensation and metaphoric precision. Even the "dreamlets" we failed to elicit tingles from seemed to me to be meaningful. The failure to evoke a tingle in the dreamer was much more a criticism of our own process of work than it was an indication that the fragments were in fact "meaningless."

From such experiences, I have come to value fragments as highly as longer narratives and to understand that the structure of the memory of a dream is as laden with meaning as the specific content of the memory. Dream fragments, more often than not, reveal themselves to be highly condensed and "edited" versions of the night's dreaming. More often than not, we remember only fragments of dreams when our waking life is particularly busy and stressful. I used to think somewhat grimly that this was primarily the result of wavering attention and general frazzledness. I now know that although there certainly is an element of losing the memories because of uncenteredness, it is far more importantly the result of a distinctly cooperative effort on the part of the unconscious to provide "edited copy" for our attention.

In this connection I am often reminded of Thomas Wolfe's ambiguous boast that he used to send his manuscripts to the editor in a moving van, and the editor would return them in a taxi. It is as though the unconscious were doing a similar thing for us in those stressful moments, saying in effect, "All right, we realize you don't have hours to spend writing down and ruminating over your dreams today. Here's a little poetic telegram that carries the main messages. Just carry it around with you and glance at it when you have a moment, and you'll probably 'get it.' " In this sense, the "fragmentary" quality of the memory itself carries meaning, as do other seeming anomalies of dream memory.

Anyone who has kept dream records for any length of time has probably had the experience of remembering a piece of a dream and not knowing exactly where in the narrative to put it. Does it go here? Or earlier? Or later? Or . . .? Often such seeming failures of memory are the occasion for annoyance and a frustrated desire to "remember it right." However, my experience with such "floating fragments" is that they tend to be like more isolated dream fragments remembered alone—that is, internally complete and carrying metaphors evocative of the main themes of the longer dream of which they form a part. My experience is that in virtually all cases, such floating fragments appear to be in large measure the result of the "editing process," captured "in process." I suspect that if one were to awaken even more stressed and more willing to turn conscious attention to the problems of the day, rather than to the memories of the night, these "floating fragments" would likely be the only things remembered.

This is admittedly difficult to demonstrate, but it is clear that there is a tendency of such fragments to reveal the major themes and tensions of the more complete narrative. In this sense, I believe that the original seeming anomaly of memory is in itself meaningful. It appears to be a positive assertion on the part of the dream memory that in fact the "fragment" can go in any of the places where you remember it might have fallen, and that it goes in all of them simultaneously because it is a metaphor of the basic themes of the dream—a "hologram" of the larger narrative.

In this same sense, all anomalies and "slips" in the process of recording dreams are significant in my experience. If one makes a "slip of the pen" while writing a dream, or a "slip of the tongue" when sharing a dream with other people, these slips are an indication that at precisely that instant, the vital process of the dream has taken over and forced a "mistake" which metaphorically reveals *more* of the multiple layers of significance present at that moment in the dream than the "correct" word would have conveyed. Often people will write "whole" when they mean "hole," and make similar kinds of slips; these "errors" are themselves often more revealing of the true import of the dream than the "correct" narrative would have been. For this reason it is always useful to note such slips when they occur, and to preserve them in the written record instead of erasing them or crossing them out.

This principle of multiple levels of meaning combining to create a seeming anomaly also applies to those strange words and phrases that often occur in dreams. These strange words and phrases almost always reveal themselves to be little compressed metaphors of the larger meanings of the dream. The same is often true of numbers and series of numbers in dreams. Sometimes the individual letters will have the weight of whole words, in the fashion of a rebus. "4C" may likely have a level of meaning where something is "foreseen," etc. My experience suggests that all seemingly "meaningless" words and phrases and numbers in dreams have much the same quality of "floating fragments"— they usually condense the themes of the dream into a compact form with multiple associations and ironies.

Repetitive, recurring dreams also appear to have this quality of presenting a particularly apt metaphor of some on-going life drama at the center of psychological life for that person. Here again, the structure of the memory itself carries a message, as a separate question from the specifics of the dream, which themselves also carry multiple levels of meaning and resonance. All dreams come at some level as a response to the immediate experiences of waking life, so when a particular dream recurs over a long period (often over an entire lifetime), it is the case that is relevant to the dreamer's immediate life experience, each time it recurs, and there is some repetitive psychological drama or situation being acted out over and over again to which the recurring dream refers. These repetitive dramas may range from simple and positive acknowledgment of increasing maturity and growth, to indications that there is some unresolved interior conflict which repeats in frozen, ritualized form until it is at last dealt with and its energies transformed.

Let us look for a moment at the dramatic and specialized case of recurring nightmares of combat veterans depicting the horrors of their war experiences. Records of such "symptoms" and the treatment of men with dreams of this kind extend back in the annals of the Veterans' Administration to the period of the Spanish American War (1898). The cumulative evidence of these and similar records appears to be that when the veteran who is plagued by such recurrent nightmares is finally able to *fully* recall and speak clearly about the details of the waking-life combat experiences, then the repetitive nightmares are released from their obsessive, unchanging form and tend to continue in a more "normal" fashion. I take this to be in large measure a confirmation of the principle that all dreams come ultimately for the purpose of promoting wholeness in the dreamer, bringing to consciousness anything and everything that has been repressed or otherwise excluded from consciousness, because without this material the dreamer cannot be truly whole.

I believe this is also the reason behind many dreams where "old problems" emerge—problems which we believed we had at last resolved and transcended. When we have dreams of old, previously pressing and unresolved problems of this kind, we all have a tendency to become disheartened and to question whether all the work of interior exploration and transformation has in fact been of any value at all. How can we still be dreaming about *this* when we had worked so hard and changed so much in the struggle to overcome the problem? It now seems to me in a great many cases where such "old problem" dreams return after a long absence, it is in the name of acknowledging wholeness. Whoever we are at any given moment is the result of the totality of our previous experience. We are the people we are as a result of the problems we have resolved and the difficulties we have overcome, and

the dreams come to integrate these important old dramas into the
make-up of the "new person" we have become as we have grown
and changed. I often think of the image of a receiving line—the
"new administration" has been elected and installed in office, and
all the old characters and dramas come out in relatively orderly
fashion to "shake hands" and give and receive acknowledgment
of the latest orderly transfer of power. There is, I believe, always
an element of challenge in this encounter with old dramas, as
though they were seeing if the new administration were at all likely to relinquish any of the changes and gains already made, but to
the extent that the resolutions to such old difficulties are genuine,
there is no real indication in such "old problem" dreams that the
work must be done over again in the same fashion; rather they
should be remembered and honored consciously as part of the history that has shaped our current senses of ourselves and our
world.

From these examples it will be clear that paying attention to
the form of memory itself, as well as to the content of what is remembered, is an important part of dream work.

Even when one is also working with a group, or with one
other person, it is always alone with oneself that the work of integration is accomplished. In this work it is important to stay aware
of where our creative edges and uncertainties lie. It is only at the
edges and through the holes in what we imagine we know that
what we do not yet know and have not yet imagined or conceived
can enter our consciousness. Thus the more rigid and internally
self-consistent our world-view, the more likely that this premature
closure of thought and experience will inhibit the flow of dream
memories, flashes of insight, and the creative impulse as a whole.
The best dream work is carried out in this context of openness
and an acceptance of irony, paradox, ambiguity, uncertainty, and
multiple possibility.

We each need to think, pay attention, extend our inquiries
into new areas, read a variety of materials regularly, and remain as
open to what we do not yet know or understand. We must try always to exercise the imagination at the places where our experience becomes ambiguous and difficult to make sense of.

It is always worth remembering that despite our vast variation and individuality, we are one species, united by these subjec-

tive experiences of partial consciousness. Everyone is in the same boat. We share one planet on the outside, and one archetypal drama on the inside; we are one folk. In this way I have come to understand the basic radical message of Christianity. "Love your enemies" is a statement of psychological truth; we must learn to love our enemies because it is the only thing that works in actually bringing about change, both in ourselves and in the world.

In our dreams and dream memories, we seem to be viewing a reality as separate from ourselves as is the reality we experience when we are awake. Yet it is clearly the case that these interior landscapes and dramas are all composed of our own interior energies, and are thus at one important level representations of aspects of our own interior life and being. Yet the images seem separate. We accept this as the convention of the dream world, and do not realize that we do the same thing in waking life.

The technical name for this self-deception is "repression/ projection." I mention it here because it is the single most difficult obstacle to solitary dream work. The dream itself is an example of the completely compelling, "real" quality of our projections. We "invent" the experience of the dream, yet we perceive it as though it were a separate reality which we "inhabit" in the same fashion that we "inhabit" the seemingly objective reality of waking life. However, the dream proves nightly that we are capable of deceiving ourselves in this regard with convincing illusions of separateness from our internal experience.

When we deny something, some energy or potential within, we do not destroy that energy or potential; on the contrary, by denying it a place in the pool of light shed by our conscious attention and forcing it to live its life in the dark, we free it to roam around and act at will, beyond our conscious awareness and control. In this way, our repressed emotions and energies begin to influence our seemingly "objective" perceptions of the outside world when we are awake. We begin to believe that we "see" the very things which we are denying in ourselves as the exclusive property of others around us. This is a distortion of perception, an hallucination if you will. However, to our waking consciousness it is almost completely convincing, even though in all but the most mystical phases there is a twinge of anxiety and uneasiness associated with the seemingly "objective" perception of evil in others.

Usually we recognize that we have been dealing with projected forms of our own repressed energies only after some unusual
"set-breaking" when the projections have been withdrawn and
we have acknowledged whatever it was in ourselves that we were
previously denying and pretending was not present as an element
of our nature. Often this withdrawal of projection only comes after some painful mistake or blunder has revealed to us that we
were deceiving ourselves. Such experiences, prompting the withdrawal of projections and the acceptance of one's own fallibility
and humanity, are often available in a less painful fashion through
dream work. Such realizations are very much like awakening
from a nightmare and realizing it was "only a dream." However,
the consequences of the evil we acted out ourselves in the state of
repressed/projected self-deception do not disappear as quickly as
the "waking dream" that caused them.

Our history and our personal experience are filled with examples of such phenomena. Our negative projections are most
visible to us in the form of those people whom we most dislike
and with whom we have the most difficulty communicating and
"getting along." It is this psychological mechanism that is at the
root of virtually all our collective problems, from war and racism
to the ecological crisis and sexual oppression. In every case we
deny some aspect of our interior life and nature and then begin to
see it everywhere around us in others. The canards and accusations of racism for example are always detailed portraits of the
very energies within, which are denied and then ironically released in the hysterical effort to deal with the "others" who are
viewed as less-than-fully-human, because they exhibit the very
things we have denied the humanity of in ourselves.

It is this denial of our own humanity in the act of repression,
this refusing to consciously acknowledge our less attractive traits,
which allows (and ultimately requires) that we deny the humanity
of others in whom we perceive these same energies. When we release the projections and accept the reality of the interior energies
to waking consciousness, we *perceive* differently, and the reality we
inhabit is transformed.

Let me offer a comic example. In a recent *Broom Hilda* car-
toon in the *San Francisco Chronicle,* Broom Hilda and her friend,
Irwin the Troll, are on one of their rare visits to the city. They

stroll down streets filled with graffiti, they make superior comments to each other about how glad they are that they don't live here in this squalid environment. They even go so far as to ask rhetorically why people would want to destroy their own environment in this fashion. Then they come to a wall which has no graffiti on it. Irwin promptly grabs a can of paint and brush and writes "DO NOT WRITE IN THIS SPACE" in big letters, all over the wall.

We can each recognize ourselves in this comic vignette, and at the same time we can recognize the basic drama of repression/projection. The dreamer projects the scenes of the dreams all night, and in the same, self-convincing way we project our repressed interior energies while we are awake.

In most cases, the situation is further complicated by the fact that we usually choose people who actually have the same elements in their character similar to the ones we are projecting on them. An angry person, for example, who denies his or her anger from consciousness (often in metaphors of "spirituality" and "service") will begin to perceive everyone around as angry, and genuinely angry people will be seen as dangerous maniacs in need of strong measures to control their fundamentally irrational, "not-fully-human" behavior. To offer another, less humorous example of the ironic way in which repression and projection works, one need only look at the history of the assassination of Mayor Moscone of San Francisco, and his colleague, Supervisor Harvey Milk, by a third member of the City Council, Dan White.

Prior to the assassination, Supervisor White was an avid supporter of the death penalty, saying on several occasions that the death penalty was the only adequate deterrent to the unbridled expression of criminal behavior in the population as a whole. During his tape recorded confession after the murders, Supervisor White said that he knew he would be called upon to pay for his action with his own life and that the knowledge that he would be caught and punished allowed him to proceed (even though he was eventually convicted of acting with "diminished capacity" and thus not subject to the death penalty). Thus, in an ironic, but far from accidental way, it was Supervisor White's belief in the rightness of the death penalty that gave him "permission" to kill. Virtually all murder, from the "heroisms" of war, to the depredations of crime, to capital punishment, is the result of this drama of repression/projection where one's own full humanity is denied, and the victim is viewed as less-than-human. In this deep and important way, murder and suicide are psychological equivalents.

The shape of the repression/projection drama is visible in both of these examples, humorous and fictional, tragic and historical. What is true at the level of individual psychology is also true at the collective level of human society. It is collective repression/ projection that allows our enemies in war and civil strife to be viewed as "not human," and thus the appropriate targets for action which, if it were practiced against us, we would denounce as "inhuman." In times of war, the governments involved invariably mount propaganda campaigns to encourage the population to see the "enemy" as inhuman, so that the full potential for effort can be released in the war effort. It is only after the fact that we become aware of the ways in which governments waged war on their own populations to support their military ventures.

The Christian admonition to "Love your enemies" is then at this level a psychological necessity. We must learn to love our enemies, both as a practical necessity for planetary survival, and as an exercise in self-knowledge and self-recognition. The "others" whom we hate and fear are, at one level, invariably mirrors of our own repressed energies and potentials. There is no "correct ideology" which can prevent this drama of self-deception. The communist's description of the "capitalist warmonger," the racist's description of the "nigger" or the "honkey" or the "wop" or the "howley," the sexist's characterization of a "chick" or a "pig," the agist's mind set about the "kids" or the "old fogeys"—in every example, the characterization of general classes of people without regard for individual variation forms an ironic mirror of the very things which are rampantly and dangerously unconscious and active in the life of the person making the characterization. Each night our dreams bring us face to face with our projections in the form of dreams, and dream work seriously undertaken always results in an increased awareness of how very much we are alike, especially like the very people whom we most dislike and fear. Ecology, history, psychology, and religion are all entwined in this dance of individual and collective repression/projection, and we must learn to love our enemies because it is the only exercise capable of actually transforming our experience.

In the same sense that only the dreamer can know what a dream means, it is also the case that only the person doing the repressing and projecting can recognize and change the situation. The work can only be done within, but at the same time the structures of pre-conscious self-deception are so well-constructed that the dreamer is in many ways the one in the least advantageous position to recognize the dramas of repression/projection with any clarity.

However, there are exercises that can be undertaken alone which can shake us out of our habits of mind and our pre-conscious patterns of repression/projection.

One of the most powerful of such exercises is to re-experience the dream in as vivid imagination as possible while awake. Sometimes this can best be accomplished by writing an imagined dialogue in a journal, or by simply imagining with one's eyes closed. It is almost always productive to re-experience the dream from the point of view of some other figure than the dream ego (the point of view from which the dream was first recalled and recorded). Such exercises are most often called "gestalt work" or "active imagination" in the literature.

Such exercises are always possible because, as has already been mentioned, at one level every image, event, and feeling in a dream is a metaphor of interior life and gives symbolic shape to aspects of our own personalities and characters. For this reason, it is always possible to re-experience a dream or fantasy from the point of view of some other character (or object). Let me offer an example of such work.

There was a young woman, let us call her Margaret, who came to class one night with a rip-snorting nightmare. In her nightmare she is at a dance. Most of her fellow students in theological school are present at the dance, playing and having a good time. She stands at the side and observes them somewhat critically. All this dancing and merry-making seems like a trivial and unworthy occupation for people who are supposedly devoting their lives to religious leadership, and Margaret feels that she is rather above it all. At the same time, she has a nagging worry that she really ought to be home studying and not wasting her own time with such frivolities, that if she doesn't spend her time studying she is likely to flunk out. Driven by these simultaneous feelings of superiority and insecurity, she decides to leave the dance and return home. However, when she gets outside, she is surprised to discover that she is not up on "Holy Hill" (on the north side of the U.C. Berkeley campus where the theological schools are clustered); instead she finds herself on a garbage filled street in the industrial area of Emeryville, surrounded by dark, looming warehouses. She pauses for a moment, unsure of what to do next. Suddenly she spies in the shadows off to her left a young, burly black man. As soon as she lays eyes on him, she knows that he is a rapist and murderer and that he intends to kill her. He comes forward toward her, and in her panic she does not turn back into the dance where you would expect her to find security and safety in the company of her friends and classmates, but instead flees in panic down the dark street. She hears the black man pursuing her. She hears his footsteps coming closer and closer behind her. She is expecting him to grab her from behind as she pops awake in her bed, sweating, heart pounding . . .

Margaret was obviously agitated all over again by the strength and vividness of the dream as she recounted it, and it was clear that the first order of dream work was to touch her physically and center her more fully in the warmth and security of the present moment. After that was accomplished, the usual verbal approaches to the dream did not seem to evoke any tingles, beyond the fear and upset of the original experience, so I suggested to her that she re-experience the dream in waking imagination, only that this time she see and experience it all from the point of view of the young black man rather than her original point of view as dreamer.

At first she resisted, saying that he was "too scary," and that she "couldn't be *him*," but soon she gained enough confidence to give it a try. She closed her eyes and was amazed (as most people are) at how easy it was to re-enter the dream, and how easy it was to see it from the point of view of the black man. Almost immediately she showed a curious smile (a smile I have come to recognize—it almost invariably accompanies an embarrassing tingle). When asked, she responded that when she saw herself emerging from the dance, the thing that struck her most forcibly was how "prissy" and "silly" and "uptight" she looked. And at the same time, she went on, she also saw herself standing next to the lighted doorway to the dance and saw that she looked quite "cute" and "attractive." In the consciousness of the young black man, she stepped forward to invite herself back into the building to dance and saw the look of fear and hysterical racism come across her face. She watched herself turn and flee into the night and was aware of thinking as the black man: "Hey, this chick's in no condition to travel! I'd better follow her and see that she doesn't get into any trouble!"

Margaret returned from this meditative reverie amazed at the content of the experience. She was visibly less upset. Her upset was rapidly replaced by confusion and curiosity. We continued to work on the dream, and she began to tingle to a series of self-understandings, beginning with a hesitant admission. She said she realized not that she had "made a mistake" about the nature of the work in theological school—she had assumed that the primary hurdle would be the pressure of academic work and study, but now that she had actually arrived and oriented herself to the new experience of being a divinity student, she realized that she could handle the academic work with relative ease, and could in fact "party every night" and still make a respectable showing academically. However, what she had not properly anticipated was that despite the relative ease of the academic work, far greater demands were being made upon her to articulate her own deepest convictions and bring a strength and authenticity to her interpersonal relating that was beyond her previous social experience.

This increasing authenticity and personal strength at first seemed beyond her powers, and she had retreated into a persona (a consciously chosen image of herself) of "the good student," the "goody two-shoes," in whose mouth "butter would not melt." This image was "safe," but increasingly restrictive. What she came to understand as the dream work continued was that the black man was an image of her own masculine energies (what Jung termed the "animus")—a kind of self-assured, street-wise, sardonic, clever, strong, "unfeminine" energy in her being which she feared, and yet which was increasingly popping up in her interior experience. As she went through this effort of discovery and integration, her physical demeanor changed radically—instead of perching on the edge of her chair, she arrived in it fully and sat with her feet flat on the floor. Her already mobile and intelligent face took on a look of increased relaxation and self-assurance that was most dramatic. As her self-revelation continued and she realized that she was not rejected or disliked by members of the group as more of her true self emerged into freer expression, she felt a flush of exhilaration and energy. By the time the dream work was over, she appeared greatly transformed.

This dream and Margaret's work with it are dramatic and instructive in many ways, and I shall have occasion to return to it again. I offer it at this point as an example of the revelations that can be engendered through imaginative re-experiencing of a dream, particularly from a different point of view from the "dream ego."

In addition to such active imagination, drawing, and other experiential techniques for exploring the dream, there are also a number of simple exercises for working with the recorded dream narrative. For instance, it is almost always productive to go back over the narrative, paying particular attention to emotions and feelings, and to list the sequence of emotions experienced by the dream ego and observed in other characters in the dream on a separate sheet, divorced from the specific events and imagery in the dream. Often, when this is done, patterns of repetitive feeling will emerge that will be recognizable in waking life as well. Conscious recognition of such previously unconscious, repetitive patterns of feeling is often the first step toward transforming them and freeing one's creative life energies to find a more satisfying and creative expression in waking life.

Similarly, it is almost always productive to imagine how a dream might have continued if you had not awakened when you did. This is particularly productive with nightmares and similar dreams where the emotional tone of the experience is fearful, frustrated, or apprehensive. To the extent that every image and event in a dream reflects at some level an image of some aspect of our own character and being, the conflicts with dream characters almost always represent interior conflicts and ambivalences, no matter what other levels of meaning they may have with relation to exterior, waking life people and events.

Thus, the exercise of "dreaming the dream onward" in active

imagination and creating a more positive and harmonious outcome can have the effect of promoting such reconciliation and harmony within. To some people, such exercises seem like foolishness and "mere fantasy." However, just as we recognize that the dream is a major determinant of our mood and energy level upon awakening, so our waking mental and imaginative life shapes and influences the dream and the interior, unconscious dynamics that form and shape the dream.

Consider in this regard the ancient Hindu/Buddhist teaching story of the Snake in the Road. A man is walking down the road when suddenly he sees a huge snake in the dust in front of him. The snake is truly enormous, and the man quakes with fear, sweat breaking out over his body and his knees shaking. But the snake doesn't move. The man peers at it more closely and sees that it is not a snake at all, but rather a rope with a knot tied in the end which has fallen in sinuous curves onto the road off a passing wagon. The man straightens himself and walks onward with a firm step, hoping that his foolishness has not been observed by anyone.

In the hands of the Eastern sages, this story serves to suggest that "all is illusion," that all the seemingly "real" and "objective" experiences of waking life are analogous to mistaking the rope for a snake. However, seen from the perspective of Western science, the story serves equally well to demonstrate the primary importance and reality of *imagination.* If we were to attach all the sensitive measuring devices of Western medicine to the man in the road, we would be able to measure and verify the biological consequences of his mood change—the increase in respiration, the change in galvanic skin reaction, the levels of adrenalin in the blood, the changes in heartbeat and blood temperature, muscle tonus, etc. To the extent that we are of necessity only partially conscious at any given moment, what we imagine to be reality constitutes reality for us. In this vitally important sense, to imagine is *everything.*

As we alter our interior energy balances through the use of active imagination, we influence the whole system in a very real way. The exercises which "manipulate" the dream experience by extending it into fantasy have this effect of altering interior energy dynamics, and often the influence of such waking work can be seen in the spontaneous night dreams which follow it.

Continuing with the exercise of remembering the dreams, writing them down, and playing with them in various ways generates increasing volume of material. Provided you have been titling the dreams, it now becomes possible to take a longitudinal view of one's dream life and to detect larger patterns of growth and development. There is a tendency "not to see the woods for the trees" when one is in the midst of regular recording of dream experiences. However, when it becomes possible to review the dreams of weeks, months, and years in a single attention, often the result is a revelation of seasonal patterns of mood and behavior, cyclic dramas of growth, and consolidation of previous growth.

My own meditations in this regard have been enhanced by keeping a second, separate journal where the dream titles are listed in order down the right-hand page (together with their dates and page references), while on the facing page I list what seem to me to be significant experiences in my waking life. It has been my experience in going through this "index of dreams" that I realize in retrospect that the waking events which reveal themselves to be the most significant and important in relation to dream life are sometimes not the ones I initially recorded at the time. All these ways of working alone with just the dream record can be most productive, but in the last analysis there is nothing as productive in my experience as sharing your dreams with people you care about and working together to discover what they mean.

Summary: SEVENTEEN BASIC HINTS FOR WORKING WITH YOUR DREAMS BY YOURSELF

1. Make a *written record* of your dreams, no matter what means you use to record them initially.
2. When you record your dreams, do so in the *present tense* (reserving the past tense for what is experienced as memory *in the dream*). Make sure always to note the date and day of the week of the dream.

3. Give your dreams *titles* when you write them down. Not only is this crucial in going back and reviewing your dreams over the months and years, but the moment of picking a title is often a doorway to insight.

4. Remember, you are the only one who can know what meanings and significance your dreams may hold. The "tingle," or "aha," or "flash," or "felt-shift," or whatever you feel like calling it—*the inner knowledge that something is true and on-the-case—is the only reliable touchstone of dream work.*

5. However, the "tingle test" is only a positive test. The absence of a tingle does not necessarily mean that an idea or experience is wrong—only that it may be; it may also be that for whatever reasons, you may not be prepared to acknowledge some aspect of the whole truth about yourself in that moment.

6. Do not put any habitual limitations on the ways you record and interact with your dreams. Prose narrative is only one alternative. *Draw pictures* of your dreams. Experiment with different ways of recording and exploring your dreams. Try recording with *poems.*

7. *Give expression* to the images, ideas, and energies of your dreams in as many different ways as you would like to explore. The more expressive work that is done with a dream or a compelling dream image, the more likely it is that the dream will reveal more of its meanings and insights and gifts for living. Cultivate whatever expressive methods you find satisfying.

8. *Do not ignore dream fragments.* The structure of the memory of a dream is often meaningful as the dream itself. Most often, the "fragment" is an image carefully edited by memory to make as economic and clear a symbolic statement as possible.

9. Read, think, pay attention to the full range of your experience in each moment, and try to make sense out of it as whole, in pieces, any way you can.

10. Remember that every dream has many meanings and many levels of meaning and don't be too dazzled by the first or second set of tingles you have.

11. Remember, everyone is in the same boat.
12. That is one of the best reasons I can think of to love your enemies—we *are* all in the same boat. We share one planet on the outside, and one archetypal drama on the inside, and we must learn to love our enemies because it is the only thing that *works*.
13. Re-experience your dreams in as vivid imagination as possible. Re-experience the dream from points of view of characters and figures. Write these imaginings down and reread them. Imagine different ways your dreams might have continued had you not awakened when you did. (Exercises of this sort are usually called "Gestalt work," or "active imagination" in the literature.)
14. Take the time to make your journals where you record and write your dreams visually beautiful and interesting. The more you honor and welcome your dreams and the insights they bring, the more likely they are to provide them.
15. Go back and look over all your dreams periodically. Be open to seeing new patterns and directions of development. Look over your expressive work at the same time. This work can be greatly facilitated by keeping a second journal where you list your dream titles on one page (along with dates and page references) and a list of significant events in waking life on the facing page.
16. If you practice any formal meditative discipline in waking life, see if you can remember to practice it in dreams as well.
17. Share your dreams with people you care about. Ask them about their dreams.

Chapter VII
DEATH IN DREAMS

> If you meet the Buddha on
> the road, kill him!
>
> *Zen proverb*

In my experience, all dream deaths are related at one level or another to the growth and transformation of personality. It is as though the old structure of personality which is being altered as a result of increasing maturity must die in order to make way for the new. Often this death is experienced as death in the dream. I believe that this is one of the main reasons why childhood is so often characterized by nightmares. Children change so quickly, and for them also the experience of growth is characterized by the experience of death and dying in dreams. Even happy childhood (not characterized by child-abuse and the horrors of war, famine, and civil strife) is characterized by nightmares, and most often these nightmares are associated with growth milestones. This appears to be the case even when in waking life these developmental achievements are the focus of positive parental attention and regard.

This raises an interesting point with regard to children dreaming of their parents' deaths. My experience is that, more often than not, the primary reason for such dreams is once again deeply connected to the metaphor of death as the necessary prerequisite for growth and "rebirth." When a child grows, that growth must also be paralleled by growth in the parents, at least to the extent that they grow to love the more mature child as much as or more than the less mature child. Most often, this

growth is pictured in the child's dreams as death, and although
the first thought may be that the dreams represent some deep, repressed resentment of the child against the parent—a "wishing
that they were dead"—my experience is that far more often the
primary significance of the dream is that the parents are growing
too.

This idea occurred to me many times in the course of working with the dreams of pre-school children, but never more force-
fully than one morning when my daughter came bouncing
cheerfully up into the loft where my wife and I sleep to share her
dream. She told us that she had just awakened from a dream
where she had been killed by a monster. She added that Kathy
and I had been there in the dream and that the monster had killed
us too. This information was delivered with great animation and
none of the fear or upset that one might have expected, given the
content of the dream. My daughter then proceeded to draw a picture of the dream for us. She gave us the picture, kissed us both,
and then bounded off to say good morning to the cats.

My wife and I were dumbfounded and amused by this, and
when we talked together about it, we realized that our daughter
had recently learned to tie her shoes, and there was a strong likeli-
hood that at some level this dream depicted the death/rebirth of
the little girl who didn't know how to tie her shoes. It seemed
likely that the dream also depicted the transformation through
death (and subsequent "off camera" rebirth) of the mother and
father who loved the little girl who didn't know how to tie her
shoes best in all the world, into the mother and father who loved
the little girl who knew how to tie her shoes best.

In my work with other pre-schoolers, I came to suspect that
dreams where parents were threatened with death but did not in
fact die were likely to be associated with the failure of the parent
to accept and celebrate the developmental achievements of their
children, and that children with such dreams and lack of parental
support for increasing maturity were very likely to revert to more
infantile behavior (apparently in an effort to retain the love and
acceptance of the parents, even when their infantilisms were the
occasion for seemingly negative parental response).

At one level, every dream figure is a shape expressing our

own interior energies. In the realm of the psyche, as in physics, energy cannot be destroyed—only transformed from one state to another. When a figure "dies" or "is killed" in a dream, at this level all that has happened is that the unconscious energies which assumed that particular shape in the dream are released and can now constellate again in some new form. These transformations of symbolic form and elaboration of thematic patterns in dreams can be seen with increasing clarity, the more dreams are reviewed in series.

By the same token, when we flee from death in dreams (barricading the dream house against the dark intruders, or fleeing from the dangerous enemies), we are often fleeing from inner promptings that it is time once again to grow and change.

In this connection, let me return for a moment to Margaret's dream of leaving the dance. You will recall that in her initial experience of the dream, she immediately "knew" that the black man coming forth out of the shadows to her left was a "rapist and a murderer." Her later imaginative meditative work with the dream suggests that her initial perception was a "mistake." In some ways it was—it is always a mistake to assume that the way one views any experience constitutes the whole truth about that experience—but in an equally important sense it was an accurate perception. To the extent that when she had the dream she was self-identified with the figure of the "prissy, goody-two-shoes" person of the dream, her perception that the energy taking the shape in the dream of the black man was "murderous," that is, intent on the destruction (and subsequent rebirth in new form) of that aspect of her total personality—to that extent her initial perception was quite accurate.

During the course of the active imagination exercise in which she "became" the black man and re-experienced the dream anew from this different point of view, the "rape/murder" of "goody-two-shoes" actually took place. It happened "off camera" as it were, during the course of acquiring the new conscious perspective on her life that the character of the black man provided.

Translated into more Jungian terms, one of the things that can be said about Margaret's dream is that at one level it depicts the abandonment of a particular Persona in favor of a more

evolved and expressive Persona embodying more energies of the
Shadow-Animus, including playfulness, assertiveness, and a kind
of "street-wise" sophistication and self-acceptance.

At another level, Margaret's dream is organically related to
Elias Howe's dream in that both of them are examples of the archetypal truth that the Shadow always carries with it the very
thing which is lacking from consciousness—the very thing that has
been "missing" and is required for the further growth and development. In the case of Elias Howe's dream, it is ironic but far
from accidental that the creative idea he is seeking is literally in
the hands of the darkest and most frightening and apparently
menacing and primitive figures in the dream. The same is true of
Margaret's dream, and ultimately the same is true of all dreams
and myths of the Shadow. One of the reasons why Shadow figures
are so persistent and inexorable is that they all have gifts to give
and they cannot be freed from their negative shapes and forms until the gifts are delivered.

Let me share a dream of mine in this connection. I am in a
field loading fodder onto a wagon with a pitchfork. I am wearing
a six-gun, as is my partner (Clint Eastwood in his "Man With No
Name" role). We are talking with one another as we work, remembering the scene which has just transpired where the owner
of the farm gave us the weapons we are wearing, and drank a toast
with us to mark our pledge to protect the farm from the marauders. These marauders are both Union and Confederate—both
sides are commandeering horses and supplies from local farmers as
they skirmish with each other, and Clint and I have agreed to de-
fend the farm from attack by either side. We are bragging about
our imagined valor, when suddenly a group of armed men on
horseback break cover from the woods off to our right and come
galloping toward us.

The moment I see them, I am transfixed with fear. The dark
riders are ugly and *serious* as they hurtle toward us. I can feel the
ground shake under their horses' hooves. I drop my pitchfork and
make a break for the cover of the opposite side of the field. I
know that Clint is disgusted by my cowardice, but I also know we
will both be killed if we stay, and a wagonload of hay is not worth
dying for—of that I am certain!

I make it to the brush at the edge of the field and plunge headlong down a narrow path leading down a bank to the edge of a river. There is a skiff drawn up on the gravel verge of the river, tied to a tree. I claw at the rope and free it. I push the boat out into the water and flop into it. I turn around and fumble with the oars. I look up and see Clint ambling toward me down the path. I call out to him in desperation to hurry. He comes down the bank and steps into the boat and I begin to row madly out toward the center of the stream. Clint remains standing and turns around in the front of the skiff, making rowing very difficult. I scream at him to sit down. I realize in the dream that I do not know how to swim, and if the skiff capsizes, I will drown. (There is an odd quality to this knowledge, because in waking life I quite enjoy swimming; in the dream I somehow reassure myself that I do know how to swim, "but not now, not here." This is lucidity of a sort, but since I do not consciously make the connection in the dream that the reason I don't know how to swim [even though I do know] is that I am dreaming, it cannot really be called a lucid dream.)

I scream at Clint again to sit down, saying that we will capsize otherwise. At this point, with his back still to me, facing the shore, Clint steps up onto the gunwhales of the skiff and starts to literally "rock the boat," heaving his weight back and forth from one leg to the other. I scream at him one last time to "STOP!" but he ignores me.

In my desperation I decide that even though he is my partner and friend, he has lost his mind and will kill me with his foolishness if I do not stop him. I draw my gun and point it at his back. I tell him I will shoot him if he doesn't stop. He is silent and rocks the boat even more. I tell myself that I have no choice. Then I pull the trigger and shoot him in the back. For one moment he arches his back, and then he falls backward at my feet in the skiff, his dead eyes staring up at me.

I am appalled at what I have done. I cannot bring myself to look directly at his dead face. At last I manage to heave the body up over the side into the water without really looking at it. The body floats face down near the skiff for a few moments, and then sinks as the waterlogged clothing pulls it down. I watch in horror as the body sinks.

For a long time I lie in the boat and float down the river. On

both banks men on horseback are looting and pillaging. I see the
smoke from burning fields and farmhouses. I hear shots, laughter,
screams, breaking glass, hoofbeats. The fire and carnage extends
as far as I can see on both sides as I float down the river.

Toward nightfall the skiff washes up on the shore of an island
in the stream. I climb out and hide the skiff in the driftwood that
has piled up on the point. I creep through the woods on the island
as the sun sets, until at last I come upon a small cottage down near
the shore at the opposite end of the island. It is dusk and I can see
into the cottage clearly because there are lamps burning inside. I
watch an old man and an old woman sitting down to their evening
meal. They appear to be tranquil and very much in love. They interact with each other with charming intimacy, seemingly unaware that I am watching them from the woods. I am obsessed
with the idea that this apparently safe and idyllic scene is a trap,
but there is no evidence of that, and since I am overcome with
hunger, I decide to risk going up to the house to ask for food.

It is now completely dark, and as I walk up onto the wooden
porch of the cabin, the old couple hear my footsteps and the old
man comes to the door and opens it to see who it is, just as I arrive at the threshold.

He greets me with surprise and openness and calls to his wife
that "a young man" has come fleeing from the war. They invite
me in and offer me food, which I wolf down hungrily. As soon as
I have eaten, I am overcome with exhaustion and tell them that I
must sleep. The old man tells me I am welcome to use the bed in
the adjacent room, and I rise from the table and stagger to the
tiny bedroom and collapse face-down across the bed and am immediately asleep.

Almost immediately I begin to dream. (I know I am dreaming while I am dreaming—so this is a species of lucidity, even
though I am still not consciously aware that it is a dream *within* a
dream.) In my dream, my subtle body separates from my "physical" body and I stand up for a moment and look at my own sleeping form prone on the bed in front of me. Then I turn and survey
my surroundings. I now have the ability to see through walls. I
look out at the old couple continuing to eat their evening meal
and talking to each other quietly about my arrival and the war in
general. I look out past the brightly lit tableau through the front

wall of the cottage, across the moonlit clearing down to the glistening waters of the river. On the far shore, the red glint of fires is eerily visible.

Suddenly, I see Clint's hat pop to the surface of the stream near the shore. As I stare in horror, it lifts slowly out of the water with Clint underneath it. He rises out of the water as he walks slowly and deliberately toward the shore and up on the bank, dripping bits of muck and water weed from his waterlogged clothing. As I watch this, the knowledge comes to me with perfect clarity that Clint is the son of the gentle old couple who have given me shelter. I am dumbfounded and horrified by this information, but I know it is true. I see Clint walking slowly up through the moonlit clearing toward the house. I know that he has become a zombie and that I am asleep on the bed, but I also know that flight is impossible—there is no escape from this relentless zombie. It is hopeless, but it occurs to me that, bad as it is, it might be a little better if the old people heard first from me that I have killed their son than if they hear it first from the gruesome zombie himself.

I rush back into my sleeping body and lurch to my feet. I burst out into the kitchen, startling the two old people. "I have something you must know—I have just killed your son," I blurt out. At that moment, we all hear the sound of Clint's boots on the wooden boards of the porch. We all turn toward the door, which swings open. There in the doorway is Clint's dripping zombie form. I reach for my gun which is still in its holster, but I think to myself, "What am I going to do? Shoot him again? What's the point—he's already dead!" I give myself up to death in that moment and slowly raise my arms in a gesture of resignation and acceptance. The old man and the old woman have risen from the table and are standing on either side of me, so that the four of us form a diamond shape. I expect Clint to shoot me at any moment. He moves forward, his dead eyes locked on mine.

I step forward. We meet in the middle of the room and I throw my arms around him in a strong embrace. He feels horrible and wet and dead, and yet as I hold him, I can feel warmth and life flowing out of me to him everywhere our bodies are in contact. I feel him becoming warm and truly alive as I embrace him. He raises his arms and embraces me, and I feel the power that animates us both flowing in endless abundance through and between us. The sense of release and well-being and wholeness rises in a crescendo of intensity. The strength of the feelings is so great that I pop awake in my bed with my heart pounding with relief and joy.

This dream came to me more than a decade ago, and it still reveals new resonances and meanings to me as I turn it over in my memory and imagination. Here again, the death of the Clint Eastwood figure led inevitably to a resurrection—a resurrection reflecting an integration of previously repressed Shadow elements into a new and more open and honest and less self-deceptive stance in the waking world. This dream came to me in the midst of my compulsory public service as a conscientious objector and coincided with an increasing realization that my opposition to organized violence in the world was fueled by an unwillingness to look at, consciously acknowledge and creatively transform my own anger and potential violence. The dream helped and continues to help me unravel my own shadow dramas in this regard.

In more classical Jungian terminology, the dream can be seen on one level as embodying a process of integration of elements of the Shadow in which the Mana Personalities (Wise Old Man and Wise Old Woman) appear, suggesting the shape of a Mandala. It is also interesting to note in this regard that in the experience, Gestalt, and active imagination work I have done with this dream, the Clint Eastwood figure has taken on distinct characteristics not only of the Shadow, but of the Trickster and the Willing Sacrifice as well.

What is true in the realm of dream is also true in the realm of myth. Myth and dream stem from the same ultimate source in the collective unconscious, and it is possible to understand myths as "collective dreams"—collective expressions of dramas that are universally human and thus are always experienced as personal, while at the same time they can be seen as repeating themselves endlessly in the individual and collective lives and dramas of all human beings.

The story of Conn Edda (lifted from Zimmer's *The King and the Corpse*) illustrates the same archetypal association between death and transformation of character and personality. Conn Edda's wicked uncle kills his brother, Conn Edda's father, and becomes regent until the time of Conn Edda's ascension to the throne at the age of majority. Meanwhile, he plots to destroy Conn Edda. Conn Edda (unlike his more sensitive and intelligent mythological cousin Hamlet) thinks little and suspects nothing of his uncle's true purposes, and idles away his youth in games and frivolity. As the time approaches for Conn to assume the throne, his uncle calls him in for an audience and tells him that he is appalled at the thought of turning over the throne to such a thoughtless wastrel. Conn Edda is essentially a kind and honest, if stupid, lad and is shocked and chagrined by the truth of what his uncle says. His uncle suggests that Conn should put away childish things and go on a quest in the hopes that it will make a man of him before it is time for him to become king. Conn agrees and goes off and changes into his armor. Later he goes to the stable to saddle up a horse, but his uncle stops him and tells him that because he has never bothered to learn horsemanship or acquire a horse of his own, he must now depart without one. Conn is shocked and ashamed again, and leaves on foot, dressed in full armor, with peasant children throwing clods and sticks at him from behind the bushes.

Conn trudges on until again a voice starts to mock him. He draws his sword in a rage, but can see no one in the empty fields around him. He eventually realizes that the mocking voice is coming from a plowhorse, standing alone, harnessed to a plow in the midst of a field nearby. Conn goes over and threatens the horse, but the horse continues to mock him and points out once again that Conn is not too bright to have gotten himself into this situation in the first place. Conn sadly admits the truth of the horse's jibes, and the horse offers to help him if Conn will cut him free of the traces of the plow. Conn complains for a moment that the horse is not very noble looking, and the horse points out that no matter how bad he looks, Conn will look better riding a horse than walking.

Conn cuts the horse free and they ride off. The story continues through many adventures where Conn proves himself to be brave and loyal and self-sacrificing, even though not very smart, and the horse proves itself to be extraordinarily bright (which one might expect from an animal that has learned human speech). The horse tells Conn what to do, and Conn carries out the horse's in-

structions bravely and without hesitation. Finally, having overcome each successive obstacle and passed each successive test of
wits and courage, they arrive at the object of their mutual Quest,
the castle of the King of Fairy Land (in other versions, the King of
the Land of the Dead).

The castle is surrounded by a moat of perpetual flames, and
there is no bridge. Conn asks brightly what to do now, and the
horse tells him to dismount and cut off the horse's head with one
blow. Conn is shocked and appalled and tells the horse that he
will do no such thing—he intends to reward the horse for his aid
on the Quest with a life of ease and luxury when they return tri-
umphant. The horse tells him to be quiet and follow instructions.
Conn again refuses and tells the horse that he cannot kill anyone
who has been such a boon companion and friend. Again the horse
mocks Conn and points out that despite his sterling qualities, he is
not too bright, and that it behooves him to do what he is told.
Conn eventually agrees and, with tears streaming down his face
(some of which are for the horse, and some of which are for himself at the prospect of having to go on to the final and most difficult part of the Quest alone), he begs and receives the horse's
formal forgiveness and then lops off the horse's head in a single
stroke. As the body of the horse collapses, the body of a youth the
same age as Conn Edda springs up. The youth embraces Conn and
tells him that there was a moment when he was afraid the Quest
would be lost.

Conn is dumbfounded and the youth explains that their desti-
nies are intertwined—he is the crown prince of Fairy Land and *his*
wicked uncle killed *his* father and condemned him to wander in
the land of the living in the shape of an old horse until such time
as someone would "kill him with love in his heart"—a seeming
impossibility, yet the only way to lift the curse.

With this, Conn Edda is transported into the Castle, together
with his Fairy Prince Double. Conn is then transported back to his
uncle's castle. He appears miraculously and the uncle is so
shocked he expires on the spot (like Theseus' father, Aegeus, and
Jason's uncle, Aegistus, under similar circumstances).

Here again, even more clearly, the death of the horse is only
the prelude to the reconstellation of the energies of that figure in
a new and more evolved and powerful form. The death is neces-

sary and is called for by the horse himself, making the horse a cousin to the Deer of native American myth, and ultimately to the figure of Christ, since they all give specific shape to the archetype of the Willing Sacrifice. In many ways, the *mythos* of Christianity offers one of the clearest and most evolved examples of the archetypal drama of the Willing Sacrifice. It is in this sense that Edinger and other Jungians refer to Christ "as an archetype of the individuating ego." In order to grow and change, the old must die and make way for the new, and in the world of the dream and myth, this death has the quality of literal experience. But the Christian promise is true, in this psychological sense at least—when death is accepted and fully experienced, it inevitably leads to an equally vivid and vibrant experience of rebirth. As Heraclitus said, "Nothing is permanent except change," and the archetype of the Willing Sacrifice is constellated when this truth is made a part of conscious living.

Summary: DEATH IN DREAMS

My experience is that death and the fear of death in dreams (and myth) are always associated at some level with the growth and transformation of personality and character. When we flee from death in dreams, we are most often fleeing from inner promptings that it is time to grow and change some more. This is also true of the images of death and dying in the world's mythology. The Christian *mythos* offers a particularly clear and developed example of the archetypal drama of the Willing Sacrifice for whom death is consciously understood as the necessary prelude to rebirth and transformational reconnection with the energies of the Divine.

Chapter VIII
TWENTY-ONE BASIC HINTS FOR GROUP DREAM WORK

> I believe that dreams are true interpreters of our inclinations; but there is art required to sort and understand them.
>
> *Montaigne*

Because dreams always merge many levels of meaning into a single metaphor of dream experience, it is almost always productive to share dreams with people you care about and ask them about their dreams. When the multiple intelligences and intuitions of several people are brought to bear on a dream or series of dreams, it is much more likely that the dreamer will be exposed to a fuller range of the dream's possible meaning, and will have a chance to "tingle" and resonate to a wider spectrum of the dream's multiple levels and layers of significance. This kind of collective, group dream work is most beneficial to the life of the imagination and can nurture a community of creativity.

When you share dreams with other people and begin to listen to their dreams, it is most important to remember the two basic truths about dream work: (1) only the dreamer can *know* what his or her dream means; (2) there is no such thing as a dream with only one meaning. When these two basic principles are borne actively in mind, the work has much less chance of degenerating into pointless argument, or of becoming the excuse or occasion

76

for either giving away autonomy or tyrannizing over others. When there is no "tingle" on the part of the dreamer, it simply doesn't matter whether the insight or suggestion that is being offered is true or relevant or not. The self-correcting quality of dream work, particularly group dream work, will sooner or later make it clear if some insight has been overlooked or prematurely rejected, just as it will tend to reveal when the tingles have been focused on elements of the dream which are distant from the dream's main theme or "message."

Some mental health professionals often are resistant to the idea of group dream work in general, and leaderless or "lay led" dream groups in particular, arguing that the realm of the dream is so charged with powerful unconscious energy that "amateurs" are in grave danger of doing themselves psychological injury blundering around in the world of dreams without a thoroughly trained guide. My experience is that this is simply not so. Even if it were to happen that a deeply disturbed person were to find his or her way into such a "lay" dream group, my experience suggests that such a circle of interested and compassionate fellow-dreamers is more likely to make appropriate referrals for continuing professional help than when these problems arise in other settings where such referrals and group support are not readily available. The dreams of even the most disturbed people come always in the service of wholeness, and my experience is that dream work never causes the disintegration of personality, although dream work may indeed hasten the development of such processes once they have begun.

It seems clear that lay-led and leaderless group dream work may eventually become a vital factor in promoting community mental health. It is clearly much better for serious and sensitive people to share their interior lives at greater depth and support each other in active self-exploration. Such people create a network of initial contact, support, and referral for truly disturbed people. At some point, such a group may encounter someone with larger and more dramatic problems than they care to deal with in the context of mutually supportive group dream work, but even when this occurs, it is my experience that the eventual outcome is almost always positive for all concerned.

The following suggestions for methods of work with dreams

in a group context are offered as a first step in developing such communities of mutually supportive dreamers. These suggestions form a coherent process which I have been working with for many years. However, this process is only a beginning, a "jumping off point." The particular methods and processes of group dream work vary widely, and many groups which have begun with the process described here have gone on to amend them and develop their own unique processes and ways of meeting the individual and collective needs of group members. As long as the two "rules" of dream work and the basic principles of mutually supportive group process are not lost sight of, such development of unique dream group forms can only lead to more creative self-expression and a deeper understanding of the nature and significance of dreams and dreaming.

First of all, it is almost always a good idea for groups that meet regularly to have a brief period of "touch in" at the very beginning where group members have a chance to tell each other how they are feeling at that moment, and what they know about why they are feeling that way. It is important to keep this initial touch-in brief and clearly focused on the life of the feelings and emotions. It is sometimes difficult to maintain this focus and brevity because the opportunities to share one's feelings with others are often very rare, and there is always a strong temptation to tell detailed stories about the events that are associated with the feelings. In most cases, a common consciousness of this danger and a shared commitment to hearing and working with dreams is sufficient to keep a group on course in this regard, even without a formal leader who takes responsibility for watching such group process dynamics and facilitating the movement from one place of sharing to the next.

Once the touch-in is completed, it is also a good idea for everyone present to engage in a meditation or centering exercise that quiets the inner tensions, both physical and psychological. Such exercises open the way more fully for the intuition to be heard. Dream work always involves intuitive energies raising from unconscious depths—becoming conscious of knowledge which is already present.

The particular form of the centering exercise should be

agreeable to everyone, and should evolve as the needs and perceptions of the group evolve.

The exercise which I would recommend using at the beginning and for as long as it proves useful is very simple. I have practiced this particular exercise for many years, doing it at the beginning and the end of almost every dream group in which I participate.

A CENTERING EXERCISE

Join hands in a circle. Close your eyes. Breathe easily and deeply. Relax. Search for spots in your body where you habitually hold tension. As you relax yourself consciously, imagine as vividly as possible that light is entering your body on the in-breath, and that darkness is exiting from your body on the out-breath, so that you become progressively brighter and more "self-enlightened" as you breathe. Exercise your imaginative powers to the fullest. If this visualization is not enough to occupy your full energy and you find your focus wavering and your mind wandering, try extending the visualization to include other group members. Try extending it to include any group members who are absent. Extend it to include seeing people's auras. Extend it to include seeing the chakra points become illuminated. Extend it to include everyone you love. Extend it to include everyone you think of as your enemy. Extend it to include everyone. Extend it to include all living things. Extend it to include the whole planet. Extend it to include the past and the future. Extend it to include *everything*. Go for your biggest and best vision in that moment.

I recommend this exercise for the space of ten to twelve breaths at the beginning and end of every formal dream group (and for informal ones too, when and where appropriate). This can be a very useful exercise to engage in any time, alone or in a group. It can be particularly useful in the midst of any hassled situation. If the hassle is so bad you don't think it's wise to take eyes off it for a moment, then try doing it with your eyes open. This exercise can have the effect of reorienting your interior energies and transforming your seemingly objective perceptions.

Whether one uses this exercise or not, it is good to do some sort of centering exercise at the beginning and end of sharing and working with dreams. Such an exercise marks and celebrates the time and place of the dream sharing as important and special. Such exercises also facilitate the adjustment of interior energy balances to allow the intuition to flow more freely.

This "breathing light" exercise has some claim to being the oldest formal "sitting" meditation in the world (as opposed to the older, shamanist, more active and expressive meditative forms of drumming, dance, and song). The best written piece on meditation that I have yet encountered is Claudio Naranjo's essay: "Meditation: Its Spirit and Techniques," particularly Part 4, "The Way of Surrender and Self-Expression" (included in *On the Psychology of Meditation* by Naranjo and Ornstein, Viking Press, New York, 1971, pp. 90–131).

Once the members of the group have "touched in" and shared brief statements about their emotional states in the moment, and the group has joined in a centering exercise, it is time to share dreams. Initially, it is best to simply go around the circle and share dreams without comment before any particular dream is selected for work. There are several reasons why this is a good way to proceed, at least at the beginning. First of all, it is important for anyone who comes to dream group with a dream to share to have a chance to share it. Failure to share a dream at a group meeting "because there isn't enough time," or "because someone else has a more pressing need for the group's attention," or for whatever reason, often results in a dramatic drying up of dream memory until the dream is shared. When the sharing of dreams which are not worked on is postponed to the end of the meeting, there often *isn't* enough time to hear them all.

Secondly, the sharing of dreams around the circle at the beginning allows everyone to hear and touch everyone else at the level of the dream—to reaffirm the deep bond that sharing dreams creates. For this reason, it is always useful for everyone present at a dream group meeting to share a dream at the beginning, even if it is a dream from some time ago, even from childhood, so that a subtle bond can be established and reaffirmed at each meeting.

By the same token that we actually understand our own dreams at the time when we dream them (at the level from which they spring and where they are composed), we also "understand" all the dreams of others that we hear, even though that understanding may be far from consciousness while we are listening. Thus, as a group continues to meet and people become more intimate and open and trusting, the cumulative effect of hearing at least one dream per meeting from everyone increases the depth and accuracy of one's insights and intuitions. This cumulative effect is subtle, but increasingly obvious over time.

When sharing your dreams with the group, it is always best to use the present tense as much as possible. If you are using the present tense when you record your dreams initially, this should soon become easy and not at all arbitrary. The present tense is much more evocative and engaging of attention than the past, and for this reason dreams shared in the present tense are significantly more likely to suggest possibilities to the people listening, and to awaken "aha's" in the dreamer. Indeed, sometimes you will notice that the dreamer shifts into the past tense without realizing it; this is often an indication that the symbolic and emotional content of the dream is particularly charged and significant right at that moment in the dream, and that the dreamer is unconsciously attempting to protect and distance himself or herself from the power of the dream at that point in the retelling. Most of the time it is useful to point these "slips" out to the dreamer when he or she has finished sharing the dream.

All inadvertent "slips" are associated with the intrusion of multiple meanings into the narrative in such a way as to create a seemingly anomalous "mistake" which in fact is more evocative and more true to the multiple layers of meaning in the dream than the "correct" statement would have been.

Let me offer an example. One evening "Jeff" was sharing a dream involved with climbing a huge tree. As he recounted the dream, he said that he had decided to "crime out on a limb." When this was later pointed out to him, he said it was a simple

blending of the words "crawl" and "climb," creating the "mistake" word "crime." However, it transpired over the course of
further work with the dream that it had significant reference to a
decision to have an affair with a woman other than his wife, and
Jeff himself came to see that the "slip" of saying "crime" was indeed a more accurate assessment of his deeper feelings about this
decision than he had consciously admitted to himself.

Such slips and anomalies are, in my experience, always meaningful, and it is always worth paying close attention to them.
However, a focus on someone else's "mistakes" as he or she
shares a dream can create a tone of criticism and judgmentalness
that is ultimately unproductive. It is always useful to pay attention
to the slips and mistakes of speech and writing (one's own, as well
as other people's), but care must also be exercised to bring up and
talk about these revealing anomalies in a way that is not too judg-
mental, threatening, gleeful, or picky.

It is usually best to refer to your written records, or to read
the dream account verbatim, to make sure that nothing is repressed or otherwise forgotten. Here it is important for everyone
involved to remember that every time we share a dream, we are
revealing ourselves more intimately than we ordinarily do. No
matter what the apparent content of the dream, it always reveals
more about ourselves than we consciously realize.

In fact, if someone has a "deep dark secret" that he or she
really wishes to keep hidden, that person should probably avoid
dream work altogether. This is a *caveat* I always offer to my classes
and groups at the very beginning. Although it is certainly possible
that any number of people have made it through these groups
with their deep, dark secrets intact, I am very much aware of numbers of people who made the attempt and failed. Without the help
of others, the dreamer is in a uniquely disadvantageous position
to determine exactly what meanings his or her dreams may hold at
any moment. I have had the experience many times of having
someone share a dream in a group and having someone ask with
surprise, "Have you just had an abortion?" or "Are you embez-
zling money from the place where you work?" or "Are you having an affair with someone?" or "Are you gay?" and the like, only
to have it come out that the answer is "yes," and that the dreamer
has been having several dreams about this secret which he or she

has been consciously not sharing, and only shared this one because it appeared not to be about the "secret."

Werner Wolf calls dreams the "mirror of conscience," and in the pursuit of wholeness the dreams always have a tendency to "reveal all," especially things which are being repressed and censored from communication with others.

It is important to remember this and to be as sensitive as possible to one's own feelings and the feelings of others. Never interrupt a person sharing a dream unless you have a compelling reason. Throughout all phases of dream work it is important to be as honest and conscious with one another as possible, to remain aware of group process and to speak the truth as you understand it, as fully as you can find words for. Treat each other with respect. This is obviously not a bad idea anytime, but it is particularly important when dealing with dreams and the intimate feelings evoked by dreams.

While a dream is being shared, pay attention to it with as much of your whole being as possible. To the extent that the members of a dream group are working consciously to extend the boundaries of their self-awareness and the limits of their perceptions of each other, then to that extent the work they undertake on one another's dreams will tend to reflect that effort. One of the most important things to understand about group dream work is that the flashes and tingles and ahas you feel are always signals of truth, but that it is always a truth about *oneself,* and not necessarily a truth about the other person's dream. Thus, it is always true that what is said about someone else's dream always reflects the personality and symbol structure of the person making the comment as much as or more than it reflects anything in the dream itself. For this reason it is often useful to preface any remark with the idea, "if it were *my* dream . . ."

At the same time, it is the case that we are all one folk, and that the dream speaks the same language to all of us, so that the comments and suggestions made about someone else's dream more often than not will awaken a tingle in the dreamer indicating that indeed they are not simply mere projections. Jung once made the comment that the *only* thing one can do with another person's dream is to share one's own dream about it. Even though we can do nothing but project ourselves into the understanding of other people's dreams, these projections often prove to be the source of insight for the dreamer.

Sometimes the size of the group will make time available for meeting insufficient to allow everyone to share a whole dream narrative and still have any time to work on any dreams. In such cases, many groups have evolved the practice of sharing only the titles of *all* the remembered dreams since the last meeting. Although this does not create as much of a connection at subtle depths as takes place when full dream narratives are shared, there is a different dimension of breadth gained by having a sense of the flow of dreams over a period of time. Some groups have evolved the practice of doing both, or of leaving the form of the initial sharing up to the discretion of each dreamer.

When any expressive work has been done in connection with a dream, it is also useful to share that at the same time you share the dream. Often someone will come to a dream group with a dream on which they have already done some work and about which they have already had some tingles. In these instances, it may be best for the dreamer to wait and share his or her self-generated insights only after the rest of the group has had a chance to work with the dream. If the dreamer's own insights are shared initially as part of the narrative of the dream, there is sometimes a tendency to "freeze" or fixate the attention of group members on what has already been discovered, rather than maintaining maximum openness to other possibilities. The style and personalities of the group members will best determine in any given instance what the best way is to proceed—either having the dreamer share all he or she has discovered about the dream immediately, or asking the dreamer to wait to share the interpretive insights until after the group has had a chance to work with the dream. Sometimes, if the decision is to wait, the dreamer has the confirming experience of having group members come independently to the same flashes of insight that he or she first discovered outside the group.

Once everyone in the group has had an opportunity to share a dream and/or a series of titles, then the people interested in working on a dream or dreams have an opportunity to request the group's energy and attention. A dream group leader is responsible for determining who should go first. In a leaderless situation, consensus is the best method. The number of times that each group member gets to work should be roughly equal over time. Care and sensitivity must be employed in making sure that more shy and retiring members of the group have as much of an opportunity to work as the more extroverted and aggressive members. If there is a leader, he or she should share and work with dreams in the same fashion as other participants.

Obviously there are exceptions to this last rule; if one is working professionally with an institutionalized population, it is often better to only share dreams and not to take up the limited time of the group meeting to work on one's own dreams, but even in such situations I have always found it most productive to regularly reassess this decision to limit my participation, and to ask even institutional groups to work on one of my dreams from time to time.

When a group works with the leader's dreams in the same fashion as they work with each other's, it provides the closest thing to an "objective" assessment of the group's development and skill that can be achieved. When I come to flashes of new insight as a result of work and help offered by a group I have trained, I know that the skills and sensitivities have been adequately taught. Imagine how the history of the psychoanalytic movement might have been altered if Freud had been willing to work with his own dreams as well as Jung's when the two of them were crossing the Atlantic together by ship to speak at Clark University.

When the decision has been made regarding whose dream(s) will be the focus of the group's attention, it is usually best to have the dreamer repeat the dream, even if it has already been shared as part of the initial go-round. Obviously, if the person selected is the last person to have shared, this is not as necessary, but even in this case there is often value to having the dreamer synopsize the dream again as a first step of group work.

When the dream has been shared, it is usually best to see if there are any questions of clarification about the narrative before other questions and suggestions for work are made. Most often, there is a smooth flow from questions about the narrative into other ways of working on the dream.

At this point it is important to remember again that the process described here is only one among many, and that the ways of working with dreams are limited only by imagination, nerve, and whatever constitutes the group's sense of propriety. The process of asking questions of the dreamer and making suggestions about what significance the dream might have "if it were my dream" usually constitutes the majority of the group's efforts. These verbal exchanges encourage full participation by each group member at every moment, while retaining the central importance of the dreamer's own tingles and responses. For this reason, it is my experience that these verbal techniques should form the initial foundation of any group dream work, particularly introductory and leaderless group dream work.

However, to become rigid or prematurely closed about the ways in which dream work may be productively undertaken is a great mistake. Let me suggest several other ways of work that I have engaged in and found to be reliably productive.

It is almost always useful to engage in further expression of a dream, particularly a dream which is charged with feeling. Drawing, painting, sculpting, writing prose and poetry, singing, dancing, making music, weaving, sewing, etc.—all the traditional arts and crafts can be brought to the work of giving further expression to the ideas and energies of the dream and discovering further insight in the process. Again, it is important not to become fixated on any particular means or mode of expression, although cultivating the expressive methods you find most satisfying invariably leads to improved skill with those methods. Some groups have experimented with a different medium or technique at every meeting. Whether these expressive exercises are carried out in the context of the group meeting or not, they are always productive solitary activities. One important way group members can support each other in these efforts is to make suggestions to one another about what particular expressive activities might be most likely to further unlock the meanings and release the best energies of the dream being worked on. Sharing the results of such expressive work with the group after it is completed can help unlock whole new levels and layers of understanding and insight.

Many group members often decide to decorate their dream journals as part of the expressive play and evocation of the best energies in themselves. Sometimes this effort is most successful and has the odd effect of discouraging other group members from following suit. Often people say, "Oh, you're an *artist.* I couldn't do that! I'm not an artist." This is most unfortunate, and sometimes it keeps people from opening to the experience of self-expression through visual images. To overcome this unfortunate effect of socialization in technological culture (in fact, *everyone* is an artist when the courage to engage in artistic self-expression is discovered), let me suggest collage as the ideal medium for dream journal decoration.

The existence of inexpensive, clear plastic "contact paper" (for covering shelves and the like) makes it possible to protect even the most delicate of collages, and to make dream journals which not only are strikingly beautiful but can be carried around and used regularly without becoming tattered. Dealing primarily with images which are already given in the printed media has the salutary effect of placing each group member in the same "artistic" universe and reducing unproductive comparisons of artistic talent, while at the same time offering an easily mastered medium of expression which encourages unique self-exploration and expression. People who have engaged in putting collages on their dream journals over any length of time all report that the moment of preparing the collage for the new journal is always a moment of great meditative energy and pleasure. An added side benefit of such expressive work is that the images on the covers of the various dream journals become a symbolic life history and serve to aid the memory and the consideration of one's life as an evolving whole. It is usually best to set aside a folder where images that catch the eye and the imagination can be filed away and brought out when it is time to prepare the next journal.

For several years I have used spiral-bound notebooks for my journals. I like them because they offer the maximum physical flexibility and can be folded open and laid flat beside my sleeping place. I have overcome the problems of the exposed wire of the spiral binding by using tape (book tape is best, duct tape is adequate) to make a "spine" that covers the spiral but is flexible and still allows the notebook to be opened and folded back on itself. This is accomplished by placing a sufficiently wide piece of tape against the binding, sticky-side out, and then taping this piece to the covers front and back with other pieces of tape. The "binding" is finished by a final piece of tape over the back covering any of the sticky surface of the first piece of tape that is still exposed.

My practice is to keep all my journalizing in one volume (dreams, accounts of waking events, ideas, poems, scrapbook items, etc.) and then to recopy the most important items (poems and ideas for creative work) into two other journals so that they are together and easily accessible. Journal practice is widely varied, and my experience is that no matter what style of journal you begin with, your eventual journal practice will evolve to be more or less unique.

Since at one level it is always the case that everything in the dream is a metaphor of the dreamer's own interior life, it is always possible for the dreamer to re-enter the dream in imagination and re-experience it from the point of view of other figures and characters (as Margaret did with her dream of leaving the dance). These "Gestalt Work" or "Active Imagination" exercises are almost always productive and can be done quite profitably in a group. However, my experience with such exercises is that they have a tendency to discourage active participation by other members of the group, as well as having a tendency to expand and fill whatever time is available. I am aware that much of the "tendency" stems from my own unwillingness to break into the Gestalt reverie of the dreamer and move the process along, but I know that it is an unwillingness I share with many others, and for this reason I usually refrain from any extensive Gestalt or Active Imagination work in groups that have not been meeting together for very long. After group dynamics have revealed themselves, and after every group member has had a chance to work on his or her own dreams at least twice, then the more adventurous and potentially time-consuming ways of work can be introduced and played with. In groups that have developed an atmosphere of trust, affection and mutual insight, members are more tolerant of each other. However, even in such ongoing groups it is important to keep the balance of attention to individual dreams relatively even.

Multiple insights among group members are often evoked by cooperating in a group dramatic presentation of a dream. Usually, this is best accomplished by having the dreamer assign parts and direct the performances, but it is also often the case that the insight is generated by having the "play" directed by someone else, or by having each participant shape the presentation according to his or her own feelings and projections about the dream. When sufficient time is available, it is also very productive to make masks of important dream figures and to enact the dream-dramas using the masks.

I once worked with a group of people who made dream masks and acted out their dreams for each other; later we exchanged masks (and the characters that went with them) and improvised dramas where the significant characters from different people's dreams began to interact with each other. It was tremendously exciting and productive and led to the creation of a very successful Sunday service at the Berkeley Fellowship of Unitarian Universalists.

When one is in the midst of group dream work, it is important to remember that one can never come to the end of the possible meanings and multiple significance of any dream. One of the consequences of this fact is that there is a tendency for group attention to one person's dream(s) to extend longer and longer. Most of our lives, we are instructed and conditioned to look for a sense of closure as the cue to move from one collective agenda item to another. This sense of closure is very difficult (ultimately impossible) to achieve in group dream work. Perhaps the single most important task of a dream group leader or facilitator is to determine when the group has done its collective best and it is time to move from one piece of dream work to another. This decision to end one piece of work and begin another is one of the most important activities of any dream group. Even when a sense of closure is achieved, it is ultimately illusory, since there is always more that could be done. It is important for group members to remain conscious of this issue and to seek for other ways of determining when the point of diminishing return has been reached and it is time to move on. Most often, the dreamer himself or herself will be able to say, "Thank you, I have enough," but even when the dreamer calls for the closure of dream work, it may still be important for everyone in the group to have one last opportunity to share any thoughts and insights that have been generated by the work.

After a person has worked on a dream—particularly if that

person has had any flashes of insight—there is a tendency for that person to become somewhat withdrawn and less attentive to group process than usual as he or she "takes it in." Sometimes people will even choose to concentrate on making notes about what has been learned, because, like the dreams themselves, the insights lifted to consciousness regarding a dream are very likely to slip back below the level of consciousness if they are not written down and fixed in the mind. Often someone will have a particularly insightful experience of dream work, and after the meeting will realize that he or she has only retained the sense of excitement and satisfaction that accompanied the insights, and that the specific insights themselves have slipped back into unconsciousness. When a person becomes less attentive after having worked on his or her own dreams (or discovered an insight into his or her own process generated by work on someone else's dream) this is to be expected and other group members should allow this to happen without hassle. Most often, it is not the group members who are disturbed by this momentary withdrawal, but the person himself or herself, who will suddenly "come to" and realize that he or she has not been paying attention and has not even registered the next dream recitation. It is as important to allow this shifting of attention to take place in oneself as it is to see and understand it in others; there is no need for apologies.

If a dreamer is "drawing a blank" and none of the questions or suggestions of group members are awakening any tingles, it is sometimes useful to have someone else read the dreamer's narrative aloud. Often, hearing one's own words in the voice and intonations of another person will serve as a trigger to insight.

It is also important to remain aware of the body. There is a tendency for dream work to attract people whose sensation function is not as highly developed as their thought, feeling and intuition. For such people, there is always an increased danger that they will ignore and fail to recognize the importance of physical life. While the dreams will invariably point to this phenomenon when it is happening, it is ironically often the case that people will sit and talk about the needs of the body while at the same time repressing the physical tension and fatigue. It is important to get up and stretch and move around periodically. It is often a good idea to take regular breaks between each piece of dream work for stretching, conscious breathing, and mild yoga.

Physical environment is also a factor of great importance. Although good dream work can be done almost anywhere and in almost any setting, the comfort and emotional tone of the setting have a great impact on the total experience. I react badly to fluorescent light for the most part, and I get quite uncomfortable if I have to sit for any length of time without back support. However, when I know I am going to be in a group where the practice is to sit on the floor without back support, I use a meditation stool. In general, private dwelling spaces are more conducive to relaxation and intimacy than institutional spaces. Often a dream group will form at a church, school, hospital, workplace, etc. and then meet subsequently in members' houses.

As the group continues, pay attention to the development of group process. Watch out for misunderstandings. If you or anyone is continually misunderstood, devote some thought to why that may be happening.

It is my experience that as a dream group continues over any substantial period of time, there almost invariably begin to occur events which seem "spooky" and even "supernatural"—dream experiences which have had odd, "impossible" resonances in waking life. Perhaps the most common of these is *déjà vu,* the sense that events taking place in the present moment have been lived before, and that there is an absolute certainty about what will transpire in the next moment. This is not an uncommon occurrence, and people who have been keeping records of their dreams are often able to go back and find the dream(s) which seemingly "presaged" the waking event.

Equally common are dream events that are apparently shared in some sort of telepathy. Actually, "telepathy" is only the simplest way of thinking about the possible reasons why two or more people should have something very much like the same dream at the same time. My experience suggests that these "telepathic" dreams tend to happen among and between people who are the focus of cathexis for one another—people who are connected by mutual emotion, or are deeply involved in dramas of development which are substantially or symbolically similar.

This is one of the reasons why it seems to me the research conducted into such dream experiences by Ullman, Kripner, Vaughn, Donohoe, Rhine, *et al.* is so impressive. Their conceptual model has been basically one of "sender" and "receiver" (a la broadcast technology) with certain people having special "skill" or "inherent ability" (a la musical talent) to "send" and "receive." Since my own experience leads me to believe that emotional associations and archetypal resonances in personality are much clearer determinants of who has and remembers telepathic dreams and who doesn't, it is even more remarkable that these scientific researchers have had such substantial success in recording extraordinary similarities between dreams and waking mental imaging, and among dreams had by people who were asleep at the same time. My experience suggests that if these researches were carried out cooperatively with people who are already in emotional relationship, then a great deal more would be learned about the phenomenon. With the advent of Stephen LaBerge's experiment in the Stanford sleep lab into the mutually verifiable phenomenology of lucid dreaming, such cooperative dream research has entered a dramatic new phase. It has been carried on outside the laboratories by groups of consenting adults for quite some time.

Let me offer just one small example of such a dream experience from among the many I have had. Some time ago my wife and I awoke together and recounted our dreams to one another and discovered that we had both had dreams involving full sized elephants with correspondingly large human hands at the ends of their forefeet. In my dream the elephant had been a woolly mammoth, while in Kath's it had been a circus elephant, but in both dreams the elephants sat back on their haunches and waved their gigantic hands at us in a gesture similar to hand gestures in a vaudeville routine. It is important to note that neither of us had been thinking about elephants, talking about elephants, reading about elephants, or looking at elephants in movies or on TV. We searched our memories with great care and could find no common experience that might have triggered such similar dreams of elephants with gigantic human hands. This is simply one example among many of seemingly telepathic cross-dreaming shared with my wife. I have noticed consistently similar phenomena shared among many people in the dream groups I have been part of over the years.

I should make it clear here that I am excluding all instances of dream similarity that might be the result of common waking stimulus, including all the exciting dreams I have had and heard recounted where dreamers agree to dream the same things and to meet and interact with each other in their dreams. These dreams are immensely interesting, but since they are the result of conscious manipulation and incubation of dream experience, they are not in and by themselves compelling evidence for the "telepathic" phenomenon, since the dramatic similarities in dream experience might be attributable to common waking stimulus and intent, rather than to actual telepathy in the dreams. However, I strongly suspect that such dream experiences may also include telepathic elements, even though it is difficult to demonstrate in any given instance.

This kind of "telepathy" by no means exhausts the kinds of "spooky" dreams that are likely to be reported and experienced in an ongoing dream group, or with ongoing informal dream work with loved ones and friends. Often people will have dream experiences which invite the interpretation of "past life recall" and "encounters with spirits." It is very common to dream the images of people who have recently died, images that suggest "heaven" and "hell," etc. These things happen all the time in dreams, and the only reason they seem unnerving and "spooky" at first is that most people do not take the time and energy to share their dreams, and thus never encounter these overlaps and synchronicities unless they are directly associated with waking life events, such as *déjà vu*. The important thing to remember, when and if such curious dream experiences come to you or members of your group, is that they happen so often that they are clearly natural and normal and not to be regarded with fear any more than any of the other mysteries of life, like gravity, or photosynthesis, human love or thought. The important thing is to remain open to as much of your *whole* experience as possible, and not to repress or ignore *any* aspect of your experience simply because it is strange and difficult to make sense of. We must overcome our fears and look clearly at these phenomena in order to develop language and structures of thought adequate to discuss and share these experiences. In so doing, we cannot help but come to know ourselves better.

The most important point to bear in mind is that *all* our experience is real. Our experiences are on different levels of consciousness and subtlety, and we are certainly more likely to make errors in interpreting and understanding the more subtle ones, but that does not make them any the less real. For this reason, it is a grave error to ignore or repress any aspect of our experience. Yet when these experiences call into question our basic worldview, or frighten us with their confusing and "spooky" implications, it is often seemingly easier to ignore them and pretend that they never occurred. This is particularly easy to do with dream experiences and other experiences of unconscious, intuitive energy appearing spontaneously at the surface of self-awareness.

There is a long global tradition of such experiences being associated with the acquisition of power and self-knowledge through yoga-meditation, alchemy, shamanism, and ritual magic. The yogis, alchemists and ritual magicians are united in asserting that to seek these "powers" for their own sake inevitably leads to inflation and to ironic self-destruction. In exploring the ever-evolving realm of dream, it is wise to keep these *caveats* in mind. If and when such *siddhis* or "powers" begin to manifest in one's experience, it is always best to greet them calmly and joyfully as indications that growth and change are taking place and that we are walking the unfolding path toward that-which-is-beyond-words.

The efforts to move more consciously in the world of dreams and to enrich one's waking life with the treasures brought back from that strange realm can be deeply rewarding. One of the most important reasons to work with dreams in a group context is to enhance the quality, creative energy and enjoyment of waking life. Working with other people, sharing dreams and exploring their possible meanings and importance in our lives, can and should be an activity that brings joy—joy made all the more real and important by being shared with others.

Summary: TWENTY-ONE BASIC HINTS FOR GROUP
DREAM WORK

1. Always remember that only the dreamer can know what a dream means. The "tingle" or "aha" or "flash" or "bell ringing" of the dreamer himself or herself is the only reliable touchstone of dream work.

2. Remember also that the "tingle test" is only a positive test. If the dreamer does not respond to any of the questions or suggestions of group members, it simply does not matter if those ideas are "correct" or not. Dreaming has an inherent tendency to self-correct and, pursued with an open heart, will always bring the important truths to the surface of consciousness.

3. For groups that meet regularly, it is a good idea to begin each meeting with a period of "touch in" where group members regularly say something brief about their internal/emotional state and what they know about the multiple reasons for their feelings.

4. It is also a good idea to have a brief period where all in the group participate together in a centering exercise to relax, cut down mental chatter, and evoke the intuition. Such exercises are also a good idea at the close of group meetings.

5. Everyone who comes to a dream group with a dream to share should have a chance to share it. Failure to share a dream at a group meeting "because there isn't enough time" or for whatever reason often results in a dramatic drying up of dream memory until the dream has been shared. One good way to proceed is to have everyone in the group share a dream and/or a list of titles of dreams, right after the centering exercise, without comment, before proceeding with work on any particular dream.

6. Share dreams in the present tense as much as possible. Refer to your written records, or read them verbatim, to make sure that nothing is forgotten. Share any expressive work you may have done in association with the dream at the same time you share the dream. (However,

the dreamer may wish to withhold any particular insights about the dream reached outside the group until
after group members have had a chance to react and
comment in order not to prematurely close consideration of the dream's possibilities.) Do not interrupt anyone sharing a dream unless you have a compelling
reason.

7. Remember always that every time we share a dream, we
   reveal more about ourselves than we consciously realize.
   It is important to be sensitive and remain aware of your
   own and others' feelings.

8. Remember that every dream has multiple meanings.
   One of the reasons why group dream work is so rewarding is that the different ideas, projections, and intuitions
   of group members are likely to touch a much wider
   range of possible meaning than can easily be reached
   working alone or with only one other person.

9. Remember that what is said about a dream always reflects the personality and symbol structures of the person making the comment as much as or more than
   anything in the dream itself. It is often useful to preface
   any comment about a dream with the idea: "if it were *my*
   dream . . . "

10. Remember also that "spooky" and seemingly "supernat-
    ural" things frequently occur in dreams (things like "te-
    lepathy," "precognition," "past life recall," encounters
    with "spirits," etc.). Don't be frightened if and when
    such things seem to happen to you or others in your
    group. These things happen so often that they are clearly
    natural, and we must learn to develop language and
    structures of thought adequate to discuss and share these
    experiences. Don't ignore or repress *any* aspect of your
    experience simply because you don't understand it.

11. Encourage yourself and others to give further creative
    expression to the ideas, images, and energies of dreams.
    Help think of ways to do this. Seek suggestions about
    what expressive exercises might be most productive in
    further constellating and releasing the best energies of
    the dream. Insight is often evoked by cooperating in the

dramatic enactment of a dream. Making and using masks of important dream characters is often interesting and productive.

12. While a dream is being shared, pay attention to imaginative, imagistic, feeling, emotional, and intuitive responses. Pay attention to it with as much of your whole being as possible.

13. After a dream has been shared, try to deal first with any questions of clarificaiton in the narrative. Feeling responses, intuitions, ideas about meaning and metaphor, suggestions for expressive work, Gestalt and Active Imagination exercises, dream drama enactments, and what-have-you should follow for as long as seems appropriate and productive.

14. Understand that you can never come to the end of the possible meanings of any dream, so get used to deciding clearly when you have done your collective best with a dream and it's time to move on.

15. After someone has shared a dream and worked on it—particularly if he or she has had any flashes of understanding and insight—that person is very likely to be more withdrawn and less attentive than usual and he or she "takes it in." Expect this and allow it to happen without hassle.

16. Be as honest and conscious with each other as possible. Remain aware of group process. Speak the truth. Treat each other with respect. (This is not a bad idea any time, but it is particularly important when dealing with dreams and the intimate feelings evoked by dreams.)

17. If the dreamer is drawing a blank, try having someone else read the dream account aloud. Often hearing one's own words with someone else's intonations is a trigger to insight.

18. Don't ignore your body. Pay attention to your needs to stretch and move around.

19. Watch out for misunderstandings. If you or anyone in the group is continually misunderstood, devote some thought to why that may be happening.

20. Many groups have had positive experiences develop

around decorating their dream journals. When time and materials are available, this is often very enjoyable to undertake as a group activity. Collage is a particularly appropriate and flexible medium for dream art and dream journal decoration. Use clear contact paper (or some other medium) to protect the collages and make the dream journal as comfortable in the hand and rugged as possible. Color photocopies also are a particularly effective and relatively inexpensive way to work with collage.

21. Enjoy yourself.

Chapter IX
GROUP WORK WITH DREAMS

We are so clumsy,

Dropping lightning bolts,

Misplacing whole species of birds,

Fumbling with mountains,

Unsure of their proper placement.

"Do you suppose this river might flow

Eventually to the sea?"

And we debate the question

Solemnly, exploring all the possibilities.

Let us lay out the subtle, spiral, spirit bodies

Upon the turning stars

To see just where they turn into earthquakes.

Uncoil!

The holes and spaces filled with darkness

Open up

Around our unfinished sentences—

We can do it!

Oooops!

Remember—most people never even see

The stars we try to use for navigation

So even our comic, cosmic failures

Look like success!

Chapter X
GATES *AND THE*
FURTHER EVOLUTION
OF COMMUNITY DREAM WORK

"Hear my words: If there is
a prophet among you, I the
Lord make myself known to
him in a vision, I speak with
him in a dream."

Numbers 12:6

There is another way of group dream work that deserves special attention—the community dream journal. I am aware of several community dream journals in the San Francisco Bay area. There may be others elsewhere in the world, since it is an idea which is likely to spring up almost anywhere there is a literate population and inexpensive means of printing. In many pre-literate societies, the community dream journal idea takes the form of an extended interest in dreams and a sharing and retelling of the most important dreams on a community-wide basis.

The oldest community dream journal I am aware of is *GATES—A Sausalito Waterfront Community Dream Journal,* published by John Van Damm. It began in 1977 and has been publishing the dreams of Sausalito houseboat community residents and non-residents who dream of the Sausalito waterfront. *GATES* is a labor of love, as all true community organizing efforts must ultimately be. The dreams for *GATES* are collected, the narratives typed and artwork photocopied, and the results printed (on mimeograph) and distributed free throughout the waterfront community in good weather and bad by John Van Damm, who lives on a beautiful remodeled landing craft anchored in the Gate #5 area.

GATES was born as a creative, non-violent response to tremendous pressures of community conflict and change. It is interesting to note that there is an almost three thousand year history of community dream work around the shores of Richardson Bay where the Sausalito houseboat community has sprung up. The Coast Miwoks were a dream-sharing people who inhabited those shores in intercommunal peace and trade with neighboring tribes until the arrival of the Spanish and later the Americans whom they resisted militarily until their eventual extinction.

We know little of their dream sharing practices beyond the reminiscences collected by ethnographers in the late nineteenth century. Apparently they paid serious attention to dreams and regularly shared dreams in their communal sod houses and temporary campsites as part of the religious ritual greeting of the new day.

To understand the reappearance of community dream work along these shores, we must also look at more recent history. When the Japanese attacked Pearl Harbor, it became clear to the Navy that more shipyards would be needed on the West Coast, particularly shipyards to build the smaller vessels (the landing craft, rocket launchers, P.T. boats, and the like) that would be needed to successfully wage the war in the Pacific. In their search for adequate waterfront spaces, they came upon the "marine scrapyard" of Donlon Arques along the north shore of Richardson Bay at the undeveloped northern end of Sausalito. The Navy occupied the land by right of their war emergency power and hastily built a shipyard to produce wooden ships under one hundred feet.

The Navy also imported shipwrights and naval yard workers to work in this new yard. The segregated housing patterns enforced by the Navy created a black ghetto just across the freeway from the houseboat community in a little bowl known now as Marin City.

When the war came to a close and the land was no longer needed, it was returned to Donlon Arques, and he fell heir to a vast amount of equipment and unused materials the Navy abandoned upon vacating. The Navy also abandoned the workers they had imported and housed in temporary Quonset huts in the Marin City basin, creating a crisis in housing and eventually forcing Marin County to create its first public housing program.

When Donlon Arques reoccupied his land, he issued an invitation to many of his artistic friends from North Beach to move and live on houseboats in his marina, paying him whatever rent they could afford. There quickly sprung up a bohemian community, from which many noted and successful artists (artists like Alan Watts, Agnes Varda, Shel Silverstein, Phyllis Diller, Phil Frank and others) have emerged. This was a charming and romantic community which still retains much of its charm, romance, and artistic fervor more than forty years later, despite the efforts which were mobilized by land development interests almost immediately to expel the "sea squatters" and make the land a source of corporate profit. It is only the tenacity of the community and the commitment of its residents to the preservation of their free lifestyles that has preserved this unique community in the face of well-financed, well-organized, and often violent efforts to drive them from their moorings.

The potential commercial value of this land (only ten minutes from downtown San Francisco by car and set in a landscape of spectacular beauty) is truly immense, and over the years it has drawn many speculators and developers, some of whom proved to be not above using violence and organized brutality to drive the community residents from their homes. The legal morass created by all these efforts has kept an army of lawyers employed for all these years.

The community has resisted, using primarily non-violent resistance and sabotage to slow the demolition, construction, and land fill. Usually the prospects of profit fade from months into years, and the investors eventually withdraw their support until the next syndicate makes an attempt to develop the land and drive the residents to move elsewhere.

In the late 1970's the struggle was renewed and the violence and brutality of the police, sheriffs, construction workers and private guard services was escalating dramatically. At this point, John Van Damm began to publish *GATES* in a subtle and conscious effort to bring the warring factions together and acknowledge their common interests and common humanity. Although it is very difficult to point to violence that did not happen (one can always point to the broken heads and bodies, but when they are not broken, it is very difficult to point to reasons) I am completely convinced, based on my experience in the community talking with many different people in many different situations, that the quiet, persistent, strange, enticing appearance of *GATES* every couple of months with its collage of emotions and waterfront landscapes has done much to help people who are deeply divided from each other, and who have an inherent tendency to dehumanize and reject each other, to recognize the common dramas that unite them and make them worthy of each other's concern and respect.

GATES has certainly not accomplished these reconciliations and mutual recognitions in isolation. Many courageous and creative people have resisted the destruction of the houseboat community and have gone to jail and suffered physical and economic injury for their efforts and convictions. But in the midst of it all, *GATES* has appeared regularly, bringing to the light of consciousness the worst nightmares and best aspirations of people on all sides of the controversy over development.

GATES has had many other interesting "side effects" as well. It has created a forum where adults and children may relate to each other as emotional equals. It has increased literacy and the interest in literacy in a community where reading and writing are sometimes rarefied skills. *GATES* has created a medium of emotional and intellectual exchange that has drawn many severely isolated people into deeper and more sustaining contact with their neighbors and the community as a whole. The demands of living and working on the water tend to draw together people who are both fiercely independent and consistently willing to come together to aid one another in times of storm, strife, and collective celebration. Even some police and the private guards have been drawn to share dreams in *GATES,* and the subsequent intensification of identification and mutual understanding is, I believe, clearly visible in the life of the community today.

The struggle is far from over. The conflicts that create the struggle—the conflicts between individuality and the values of voluntary community on the one hand and the inevitably dehumanizing drives for increased short-range economic profit and commercial/industrial development on the other—are conflicts of value and lifestyle that are deeply reflective of similar conflicts that exist around the world, conflicts born out of the deepest paradoxes of our individual personalities and the largest archetypes of collective experience. For this reason alone, the story of *GATES* and the reawakening of community-wide dream sharing in this time of trouble and uncertainty has echoes and significance that ramify far beyond the shore of Richardson Bay.

GATES is an effort to make creative, non-violent response to an inherently dehumanizing and violence-evoking situation. Each time it appears, *GATES* gently reminds its readers of the transformative power of the unconscious—it offers a regular means of touching into the unconscious, creative depths and often demonstrates the ways in which a genuinely creative thought or act can transform the situation in which it occurs, no matter how bleak or unpromising that situation may appear to be, viewed only from the perspective of conventional wisdom. *GATES* also offers its readers the opportunity to reaffirm and re-experience the bonds of community and mutual trust and intimacy that are so crucial to making life worth living. There is an affirmation of ultimate connectedness that comes from sharing dreams that has a subtle and profound effect whenever it happens.

The model of *GATES* has been used by other communities since 1977. *Paths,* the community dream journal of the Starr King School for the Ministry in Berkeley, *So Let It Be Written,* the community dream journal of the New College of California in San Francisco, and the *Rainbow Flicker Dream Journal* published in Nevada City have all been generated in creative response to *GATES* as copies have spread from person to person and hand to hand.

All of these newer community dream journals have followed the basic editorial policies of *GATES* by printing dream narratives and pieces of dream art without comment (except for self-reflective commentary when it is provided in writing by the dreamers themselves). Occasionally *GATES* and the other dream journals will print information regarding ideas for dream incubation, improving dream recall, and community events of interest to their readers. Some of the other community dream journals have adopted the policy of selling copies and subscriptions, but *GATES* continues its policy of free distribution to residents of the waterfront community. *GATES* does sell yearly mail order subscriptions for the minimal fee of $8.00 and actively solicits dream accounts from anyone who dreams of houseboat and waterfront settings. (Subscriptions should be made out to Dream Tree Press, P.O. Box #1123, Sausalito, CA 94966.)

The expanding experience of these community dream journals suggests that dream sharing on a community-wide basis can serve to enhance the quality of life and the flow of creative energy wherever it is practiced. As dream work becomes more widely understood and appreciated, other innovative forms of community dream sharing are being developed. I have attended conferences where the enthusiastic responses to small group dream work led to the setting aside of a bulletin board where the most interesting, amusing, and significant dreams of the conferees could be posted and shared with the entire temporary community. Some churches and other organizations have instituted regular columns in their newsletters and other publications where dreams are shared with everyone. In every case these efforts to extend the arena of dream sharing and awareness of the pleasure and importance of dreams and dream work appear to be leading to an increased enthusiasm in community life and an increased understanding of the common archetypal dramas we share with all other human beings.

Summary: *GATES* AND THE EVOLUTION OF COMMUNITY DREAM WORK

As *GATES—A Sausalito Waterfront Community Dream Journal* demonstrates, another most productive way to share dreams on a community-wide basis is to print the dream accounts and dream art of community members and distribute these collected dreams back to the community for all to share. Something like the same effect can also be achieved in schools, at conferences, and in short-term community gatherings by having a bulletin board set aside for the display of dreams and dream art. Instituting a dream-sharing column in a school newspaper or a church bulletin can also have a similar positive effect in inducing increased mutual understanding and recognition, as well as serving as a forum for creative self-reflection and growth, both individual and institutional.

Chapter XI
DREAM WORK IN NON-TECHNOLOGICAL CULTURES

> Respect your brother's dreams.
>
> *Native American Proverb*

In non-technological societies where people use fewer tools and are virtually without machines, dream life tends to have much more importance and prominence than it does in industrial/technological cultures. Since time immemorial, hunters, gatherers, and non-technological agriculturalists have looked to their dreams as a source of contact with transpersonal, religious energies. Dreams have been used as guides for individual and collective/communal life choices, and the celebration of dreams and dream life has served as a central focus for communal rituals and ceremonies. These communal dream sharing and dream enacting rituals bind the community together and reinforce the structures of belief upon which community life is founded. Many if not all of these belief structures can be seen to have developed from dream experiences themselves, and since these dream experiences tend to have similar, archetypal patterns, so the patterns of religious belief in non-technological cultures tend also to exhibit common elements, regardless of whether there has been any direct, "cross-fertilizing" contact among them or not.

For example, based on dream experiences common to all people, there is a recurring element of belief in "multiple souls" inhabiting the physical body while awake and often departing in dreams, some or all of which continue to have separate but related existences after death. Similarly, there tends to be an element of "animism" in the belief systems of non-technological peoples where even inanimate objects are believed to have "souls" or "spirits" which often communicate with human beings in dreams. The religious life of non-technological peoples usually consists in large measure of rituals and ceremonies designed to influence and propitiate these "spirits" and persuade them to aid human efforts to achieve their goals of more fulfilled and enjoyable lives.

Examples of these religious rituals associated with dreams in non-technological cultures are many and varied. For instance, each of the tribes of the Iroquois Federation of the Eastern woodlands, (the "Six Nations"—Mohawk, Oneida, Onondaga, Cayuga, Seneca, and Huron) had its own unique ceremonies of dream sharing and dream enactment. In Mohawk villages it was common for dreamers to make up riddles inspired by images and events in their dreams and then to give and receive gifts based on whether the riddles were guessed or not. The Seneca were the most extreme in their dream work, we are told, demanding that *every* dream be acted out in some fashion, either symbolically or actually. This aspect of Seneca social life was viewed as the single greatest stumbling block to their conversion to Christianity by the early French Jesuit missionaries.

In addition to these daily dream rituals, varying widely in specific form from tribe to tribe, there was also an important yearly celebration of dream sharing that bound all the communities of the Six Nations together in one ritual. Each year, sometime after the first snowfall, bands of young men would set out on "pilgrimage" from their local communities and travel great distances through the territories of neighboring tribes. When they reached a settlement, they would act out their dreams, wearing masks. Sometimes they would wear costumes as well as masks, and sometimes they would perform naked except for a mask. After these ritual performances they would receive hospitality in that settlement until moving on to the next.

The Jesuit missionary, Father Ragueneau, reporting to his superiors in 1649, described the underlying religious rationale for this range of dream rituals as follows: "In addition to the desires which we generally have which are free, or at least voluntary in us, we have other desires which are, as it were, inborn or concealed. These, they [the Iroquois] say, come from the depths of the soul, not by knowledge, but by means of a certain blind transporting of the soul to certain other objects. . . . Now they believe that a soul makes known these natural desires by means of dreams, which are its language. Accordingly, when the desires are accomplished, it is satisfied; but on the contrary if it not be granted when it is desired it becomes angry and . . . often revolts against the body, causing various diseases. . . . They call this *Ondinnonk*—a secret desire of the soul in a dream."

The belief of the peoples of the Iroquois Confederacy in *Ondinnonk* and its power was so great that in many tribes it was believed that one would sicken and die if his or her dreams were not acted out in some fashion in waking life. Another report from *Jesuit Relations* dated 1632 tells a story about an Indian who attempted to murder a French colonist because the Indian dreamed the murder and believed that he himself would die unless the dream murder were actually carried out. The yearly festival of traveling ritual dream theater practiced by the Six Nations was called *Onoharoia* and allowed many such *Ondinnonk* to be acted out symbolically and theatrically without injury or loss of life. Many of the so-called "false face" masks of Iroquois provenance were ritual masks used in the *Onoharoia* ceremony.

In Australia, the aborigines believed the entire fabric of the universe to be the creation of dreams. The entire structure of aboriginal society was built around the experience of dreams, and virtually all activities were regulated by the daily sharing of dreams and their ritual interpretation. Anthropologist Edward Tylor reports that once an entire tribe deserted a large area because one man dreamed of a certain owl which tribal elders interpreted as a warning from a spirit that other tribes were planning to attack them. Such stories of individual and collective action based on the interpretation of dreams abound from all peoples around the globe, and all periods of history.

Abdullah ben Zayad, a follower of Muhammed, dreamed one night of a man dressed all in green carrying a rattle. In his dream Abdullah asked the man if the rattle were for sale, saying that he wished to purchase it and use it as a call to prayer. The green-clad man replied, "Call out: 'There is no god but God, and

Muhammed is his prophet.' '' When Abdullah recounted this dream during the daily dream sharing that Muhammed had instituted among his followers, Muhammed instructed Abdullah to teach the phrase exactly as he had heard it in the dream to Bilal, whom he then installed as the first muezzin.

From China comes the story of the Shang Dynasty Emperor Wu Ting (1324–1266 B.C.) who, when his aged counselor died, offered ritual sacrifice to Shang-ti, ruler of all the gods, asking him to reveal who should take the place of the emperor's most trusted advisor. The emperor then dreamed the face of his new counselor and went about the country looking for the face he had seen in his dream. Meeting with no success, he then "caused a portrait of the man to be made exactly as it had appeared in his dream," and this portrait was circulated throughout the empire. The ancient chronicler goes on to tell us that the man whose face matched the dream portrait was eventually discovered in a far province. He was "a common workman," but so strong was the collective belief in the importance and efficacy of dreams, particularly the emperor's dreams, that the man was raised to the post of prime minister.

From Basuto country in South Africa comes this story from a missionary, Fr. Robert Keable. Fr. Keable recounts that once while on a protracted trek in the Drakensberg, he made an unscheduled stop at a small village he had never been to before. He was most surprised when a native riding a nearly spent horse entered the village calling out that he must see '' the white priest,'' and even more surprised when the man told his story. "He told me he was a Mosuto from far to the south, naming a district that I knew although I did not know the village. He said he dreamed he was to seek out this village in which I was; that in his dream he had seen the road, the village, and finally me; that he had been told that he had but six days in which to make the journey; and that he was to give me this. Thereupon he placed in my hand a golden sovereign.'' Driven by an individual and collectively reinforced belief in the import and importance of his dream, not unlike the *Ondinnonk* of the Iroquois, the man had succeeded in carrying out his dream task.

Many of the beliefs and practices of non-technological peoples related to their dreams have clear interest and potential value for contemporary dream work. In this regard, the work of Kilton Stewart reporting the dream work rituals of the *Senoi* of Malaysia deserves special mention.

Stewart's work, particularly his influential essay, "Dream Theory in Malaya" has excited much interest in the whole area of dreams, dream sharing, and their potential value in promoting mental health. His work has served as an inspiration for Dorothy Bryant's novel, *The Kin of Ata Are Waiting,* as well as numerous successful experiments in the incubation of lucid dreams, dream group practice, and the transformation of nightmares into dreams of success and good feeling.

Basically, Stewart characterizes traditional *Senoi* life as unusually egalitarian, physically pleasant, and psychologically healthy. He strongly suggests that this idyllic state of affairs is primarily attributable to the *Senoi* attitude toward their dreams, resulting in a spontaneously creative yet sociologically stable ritual life of dream interpretation and non-violent acting out of dream experiences. This ritual expression of dream energies is primarily focused on nightly communal ceremonies of singing and dancing around the central fire in the *ladang,* the communal longhouse raised on poles above the jungle floor. Stewart was first introduced to the *Senoi* in 1934 by British anthropologist Herbert Noone, who had first contacted them three years earlier. Stewart and Noone both suggest that at that time, the central feature of *Senoi* community life was the daily dream sharing which began when people first awoke in the open woven mat cubicles occupied by family groups set around the inner walls of the raised longhouse. Family members would share their dreams, and the ones deemed of most interest and importance to the community as a whole would be brought to the community dream telling that took place later in the morning around the communal hearth in the center of the *ladang.* Virtually all community activities and the great majority of individual activities were determined by the interpretations of dreams. Many of these activities centered around the exchange of gifts based on the inspiration of the previous night's dreaming.

Stewart goes into great detail describing the interpersonal communications that go to make up this sociological system, and in the course of this analysis he adduces several general and specific dream work practices which he recommends as exercises promoting mental and emotional well-being in contemporary technological societies as well.

Stewart's work is admittedly flawed from an anthropological point of view (but, then, he was not an anthropologist; his academic training was in sociology and psychology). He paints a rosy picture of traditional *Senoi* life that leaves out many of the unpleasant facts and details. For example, he fails to mention that at the time he was introduced to them, the infant mortality rate was so high that two out of three children born did not survive past the age of two, and that for this reason, among others, it was the practice among the *Senoi* not to give children individual names until after their second birthday. By presenting such a glowing portrait, Stewart's work evokes the archetype of the noble savage. His exaggerated focus of attention on the dynamics of interpersonal communication makes the *Senoi* appear very "modern" and contributes greatly to the projection of the noble savage onto his narrative. His picture of *Senoi* community life simultaneously evokes the fantasy of an unspoiled Garden of Eden in the midst of the inaccessible jungles (where human beings "got it right" the first time around), together with the longing for a future society where people act in harmonious concert with one another because they have overcome their psychological repressions and self-deceptions through the application of sophisticated, "natural" techniques of dream work. In Stewart's jungle, people are free from inhibitions and act in spontaneous, "naive" cooperation to playfully explore and express the energies of their dreams, creating a "utopian" society without sophisticated technology or oppressive social organization. This nostalgic/utopian quality of the archetype of the noble savage can be seen clearly in the expressions of this archetype in Western culture, back through Rousseau's formulation in the eighteenth century, all the way to the figure of Enkidu, the "beautiful wild man" who befriends and teaches Gilgamesh in the oldest religious epic to come down to us, first rendered into writing more than four thousand years ago. The noble savage is Adam before the fall—a human consciousness that is still so deeply connected to the natural rhythms and harmonies of the physical world that no sense of "sin" or separation is experienced.

In addition to this evocation of a powerful archetype, the specific suggestions for dream work practice that Stewart derives from his experience with the *Senoi* have shown themselves to be most practical and effective. This is a point of far greater importance and significance than their "authenticity" or the authenticity of the anthropological context which Stewart only sketches in around them. Anyone who has followed Stewart's suggestion to turn and struggle with dream adversaries, calling for assistance from friends and dream allies until the adversary is overcome, knows that this exercise can be most effective and can result in the transformation of "nightmare" situations in just the way that Stewart describes. His suggestion that one should always demand and receive a useful gift from a defeated dream enemy, as well as from dream lovers and allies, has also proven to be of immense practical use and value to many contemporary dreamers, as has his suggestion that dreamers should exchange gifts at the same time that they engage in group dream work.

In this way, Stewart's work is much like the work of Carlos Castaneda describing shamanic dream work and psychedelic practices of traditional *Yaqui* Indians in northern Mexico. Both men have described shamanic dream work practices which have been independently verified in the experience of many contemporary dreamers and dream workers. Just as many people have verified for themselves the positive results and benefits that result from *"Senoi"* dream work, so they have also discovered that Don Juan's admonition to "look at your hands" in dreams and use this act to become lucid and "set up dreaming" is a very useful and effective practice.

In this vitally important sense, the current debate over the "reliability" of the work of Stewart and Castaneda from a strict anthropological point of view is of interest and importance only to professional anthropologists. For people with broader interests the inspiration these works provide for the further development of individual and community dream work, as well as the proven efficacy of the specific techniques described, is of far more importance and significance.

Indeed, it is largely because of the "literary" quality of their work that Stewart and Castaneda have succeeded in overcoming the distancing and objectifying quality of most professional anthropological reporting. They have restored the "primitive" peoples they describe to fully human status. Stewart's *Senoi* and Castaneda's *Yaqui* shamans inhabit the same universe of emotion and dream experience that we inhabit ourselves. The shamanic skills they cultivate and the personal power and dignity they achieve in Stewart's and Castaneda's narratives are things we come to desire for ourselves—things we discover we *can* achieve for ourselves when we follow their example. The people about whom Stewart and Castaneda write are not mere curiosities of primitive culture; they are vibrant and mysterious human beings who inspire us to look more deeply into ourselves and our own dream experiences—to do the work of imagination and action that is necessary to create the world we all desire to inhabit, where the human community celebrates its subtle diversity and ultimate harmony and the promise of the noble savage that exists in each of us is fulfilled.

Summary: DREAM WORK IN NON-TECHNOLOGICAL CULTURES

Since time immemorial, people living in non-technological cultures have granted more importance to dreams and the sharing of dreams than has been the fashion in technological societies. Dream work practices of non-technological peoples around the world demonstrate certain archetypal similarities. Accounts of these dream work practices are often inspiring to contemporary dreamers and, among other things, evoke the archetype of the noble savage that has played such an important role in the development of Western culture. To the extent that these accounts inspire contemporary dreamers to more rewarding dream work, it is immaterial whether they conform to strict standards of anthropological reporting. The work of Kilton Stewart describing *Senoi* dream work practices and the work of Carlos Castaneda describing *Yaqui* traditional dream work and shamanic practices both stand out as cases in point where the value of these writings is simply not materially affected by the academic debate regarding their ethnographic reliability, since the suggestions they offer about actual dream work and meditative practice have already proved useful and effective.

Chapter XII
SOME ELEMENTS THAT ARE ALWAYS PRESENT IN DREAMS

> In sleep we dream, busily
> engaged on what occupies
> our mind, tracing nature's
> laws, and explaining them in
> our native language.
>
> *Lucretius*

It is the nature of dreams to convey multiple meanings and multiple layers of meaning in a single "narrative." There are certain elements of meaning and universal significance that appear to be basic building blocks of the dream, basic threads of metaphor that are woven into the fabric of every dream. To use the analogy of the physical body, there are the separate organs and tissues that always do their specific biological tasks no matter what the organs of consciousness are focused upon. The heart pumps, the blood circulates, the lungs breathe, the gastrointestinal system digests and excretes, whether we are happy or sad, awake or asleep, working hard or taking it easy. In this same sense, there appear to be elements of the dream which are always present, doing their respective psychological "jobs," regardless of the specific nature of the manifest content of the dream. At some moments these otherwise unconscious organs and processes may become the major focus of the dream, but they continue to function and "be present," whether the dream is directly focused on them or not. To use the analogy of weaving, there are always certain kinds of

116

threads present in any woven material—the warp and the weft. Whether the fabric is a pocket handkerchief of the lightest linen or a gigantic tapestry of the heaviest wool, warp and weft are always present. Sometimes one color or texture will dominate the overall design, sometimes another, but all dreams are woven of essentially the same kinds of threads.

The history of dream work is marked by many figures who have focused on one or more of these ever-present elements of the dream to the virtual exclusion of the rest. Indeed, it seems impossible to adequately grasp and understand the history of dream work around the planet from the earliest times unless we realize that virtually all of the theories, styles of work, religious beliefs, community dream sharing practices, etc. of various cultures and periods of history have been born out of and are focused on some aspect of the multiple, whole truth about dreams.

In my experience, everyone who has devoted serious attention to the understanding of dreams, from the most ritualistic and superstitious occultists to the most rationalistic and skeptical scientific researchers, is worth serious attention and consideration. It is in this spirit that I offer the following suggestions about elements that appear always to be present in dreams and dreaming.

At the beginning of modern Western dream work, Sigmund Freud asserted that every dream is composed of images and emotions that are related to sexuality and libidinal desire. In Freud's hands, sex and "libido" ultimately take on the quality of "life force" and become in essence religious terms (although Freud himself would probably have been appalled to hear it stated in this fashion). However, when any "natural force" is raised to the position of ultimate source of human energy and motivation, it cannot escape becoming a religious notion, no matter what intellectual reservations about formal "religion" accompany it. To a great extent Freud was a reductionist. He saw dreams primarily as "masks" of "manifest content" behind which the true, libidinal, "latent content" lay hidden. His acceptance that some dreams and dream images have multiple layers of meaning (are "over-determined" to use his technical term) demonstrates that he understood dreams to be potentially multi-leveled, serving several purposes simultaneously, even though he apparently failed to see that this is *always* the case.

Although it is possible to determine some of what a dream means when the dreamer can verify ideas about the meanings and possibilities of his or her dreams with the "thrill" of recognition, it is ultimately impossible to say with any certainty what a dream does *not* mean. When the great dream workers of history make positive statements about what they have discovered about the nature of dreams, their research is almost always convincing. However, when they assert that, having demonstrated one thing about the nature of dreams, they have somehow magically demonstrated that all *other* things about the meaning of dreams are false, they miss the mark. Unfortunately, much of the history of modern, Western dream work is characterized by arguments between and among schools and ideologies which are clearly *not* mutually exclusive. When Freud demonstrates the libidinal desire element in dreams, he by no means disproves any other basic element of dreaming. In fact, when we examine the entire body of his work, we discover that he is clearly aware of other, less scientifically verifiable, but nonetheless real, elements of the dreaming process, including telepathy, metaphors of physical health, and deep religious intuitions.

Freud also formulated his basic principles of dream work to include the notion that every dream is the fulfillment of a "wish," usually an unconscious wish. Although contemporary Freudians have tended to move away from this formulation and to reject the notion of the dream as a "wish-fulfillment," my own experience suggests that this is indeed a basic building block of the dreams and is present to some extent or another in the fabric of all dreams. Indeed, it seems to me that there is every reason to say that "unconscious wish" and "libidinous energy" are simply two slightly different ways of talking about the same thing.

Perhaps the greatest "unconscious wish" of all is the basic desire for wholeness, for reconciliation and harmonization of all interior energies and external experiences. In this sense, every dream fulfills this basic wish and comes in the service of wholeness, bringing images and energies of whatever has been repressed, ignored, denied or otherwise not yet acknowledged or recognized.

At the same time, it is also true that everything in the dream (everything—every character, every situation, every setting, every subtlety of light, every subtlety of thought and feeling in the dream—*everything*) is also a representation of aspects of the dreamer's own personality and interior life. This is the basic insight of Fritz Perls and the Gestalt School of dream work. This insight leads logically and inevitably to the major tool of dream work developed by the Gestalt School, the "dream Gestalt exercise." This usually entails the dreamer using active imagination to re-experience the dream in as vivid waking fantasy as possible, often from the point of view of some other dream character or element than the dream ego. The work Margaret did with her dream (discussed in Chapter VIII) is a good example of this sort of dream work.

This work is almost always dramatic and productive. The only pitfall I have discovered with such Gestalt work (other than my own difficulty as a facilitator in allocating group time and attention equitably, which I have already mentioned) is that I have noted on a few occasions when a dreamer does Gestalt work with an obviously archetypal or transpersonal dream figure, there is sometimes a tendency for the exercise to become overwhelming, and for the waking personality to be either inappropriately inflated (identifying the transpersonal energy jolt experienced in the Gestalt exercise as completely personal) or somewhat disoriented and depersonalized (seemingly as result of being unable to hold onto the sense of personal identity in the midst of the transpersonal energy evoked and released by the exercise). However, it is always the case that we *are* every person and everything in our dreams, whether obviously archetypal and transpersonal or otherwise, and it is always useful in the course of dream work to ask oneself, "How am I this other? In what sense is the other dream figure or situation an expression of something in myself?" By the same token, it is also always a useful question to ask others about their dreams.

At the same time that the dream always is woven from threads of libidinal/sexual life, of conscious and unconscious wish and desire, of homeostatic seeking for increasing wholeness, it is also true that every dream has a thread spun from purely physical existence, a thread representing the health and physical condition of the body of the dreamer at the moment of the dream.

It has long been understood in medical circles that dreams sometimes give indications of illness and physical distress in quite specific ways, often before the more grossly physical symptoms of these problems are visible. My experience is that this "body read-out" also forms part of the basic underlying structure of every dream, no matter what other threads of obvious and subtle meaning are also woven into it.

For instance, in most cases (but not necessarily all—only the dreamer can know with certainty whether this or any other general truth applies in any particular case), houses and architectural structures in dreams have at least one level of reference to the physical condition of the dreamer. Dreams of broken furnaces often presage and accompany bouts of gastrointestinal distress. Dreams of faulty wiring and plumbing often have a level of reference to disorders of nerves, emotions and sexual life. As Jung has pointed out, horses are often also metaphors of the body (the "steed," the "vehicle" of the living personality in the world). Thus, how horses appear and what they do in dreams is also often at one level a metaphor of the dreamer's health and bodily state.

Indeed, it is in this context of the ways in which dreams always embody as part of their overall structure some indication of the dreamer's physical health that the one exception that I can think of comes to the rule that all that matters is the dreamer's own tingles and certainties. If you are a wholistic health professional, paying attention to your patient/client's dreams as well as his or her physical bodies and behaviors, you may discover dream imagery confirming what you already suspect on the basis of other examination (or dreams suggesting a diagnosis that is later confirmed in other ways). It is not necessarily of absolute importance in such a circumstance that the client/patient "tingle" to the diagnosis in order for the healing interventions to have effect. However, it is always a good idea to have the client/patient's fullest, most wholehearted, and conscious participation in the process of healing himself or herself, and in this sense I suspect it is still always a good idea to seek the dreamer's own tingles, even when using the dream as a means of physical diagnosis.

The fact that dreams always give metaphoric images for the condition of physical health of the dreamer is the source of the "plum pudding hypothesis," so attractive to positivistic, nineteenth century Western science, that dreams are merely and only the by-products of disordered metabolisms. The error here is not in the assertion of what dreams *are*—clearly they are experiences reflecting at one level the state of the body at the moment of dreaming—but rather in the assertion that they are *nothing more.*

At this level of basic bio-physical elements present in every dream, it is clear that certain processes always accompany the experience of dreaming, and thus have their own claim to being considered as "universal elements" of dreaming. The "ocular motility" that Aserinsky and Kleitman first noted is one of these. Other such elements include alteration in galvanic skin reaction and muscle tones, particularly the tonus of the face and jaw muscles. Alterations in the levels of *serotonin* and *noradrenalin* (also known as *"norepinephrine"* in some of the medical literature) also universally accompany dreaming.

The presence of these substances, particularly the noradrenalin, in the bloodstream appears to be crucial in preventing the voluntary nervous system from responding to the events in the dream as we would to a waking event, despite the totally persuasive quality of the dream experience. While the dream is taking place, the noradrenalin apparently isolates the voluntary nervous system and tends to neutralize the nervous impulses to action generated in the brain as a result of the dream. While we are dreaming we do not speak, walk, or physically act out all the apparent actions in the dream. The noradrenalin breaks down very rapidly and is constantly replenished throughout the REM cycle. When the REM cycle comes to an end, the noradrenalin is not replenished and the body immediately returns to a state where impulses to the voluntary nerves result in physical action. It has been conclusively demonstrated that people do not walk and talk in their sleep while they are in the REM cycle. Current research suggests that sleep-walking and sleep-talking are both reflections of what happens when a particularly vivid or emotionally disturbing dream is *remembered* in sleep without awakening.

Other researchers have suggested that the universal experience of "falling" as we enter sleep, often jerking awake from the dream image of stepping off a curb or a cliff, is related to the release of noradrenalin into the blood stream at the onset of dreaming. They suggest that the sense of "falling"—proclaimed in the wide distribution of the metaphor of falling in common phrases referring to the onset of sleep, as in the English phrase "I fell asleep"—is a function of the sense of loss of control over the major voluntary muscles when the noradrenalin enters the blood, a loss of voluntary control that would inevitably lead to falling if it were to occur when we were awake. I am convinced by these arguments. What I am not convinced of is their assertion that, having connected this experience with biophysical processes, these researchers have somehow demonstrated that the experience of "falling" does not have any further, symbolic significance.

It is clear that there is an archetypal connection between the image of falling and the image of the land of the dead, the land of dreams, the realm of the unconscious being "down," below the surface, and that "falling" is one quick way of getting there. The sense of panic and sudden fear that the experience of "falling" often evokes is also symbolic in my experience of the fears of the unknown and of the repetitive dream drama of change as death and rebirth. The fact that the biophysical process which prevents us from acting out our dreams as we dream involves the release of noradrenalin into the sleeper's blood stream in no way robs his or her dreams of further meaning, and to assert that it does is the height of unscientific thinking, even when it comes with all the theater of white coats and charts and tables and lab reports to back it up.

In addition to elements related to the physical body, every dream is also constructed out of threads of immediate memory drawn from the last day or so, known technically as "day residue." Everyone who remembers dreams at all has had the experience of dreaming something and recalling upon awakening that the dream incident is related to some seemingly trivial incident occurring during the previous twenty-four to forty-eight hours. Often people feel they have "unraveled" their dreams when they recall the waking life incident woven into their dream. Although locating the waking experience is an important exercise, my experience is that it is another example of premature closure to stop with simply remembering what it was that later was re-experienced in the dream. It is important to go further and consider *why* that particular incident and not any other was incorporated into the dream. Often answers to this question will "click" into awareness around exploring the symbolic quality of the waking incident as though it were a dream. When this exercise is carried out, the incidents from waking experience are often recognized to have resonances with the dramas of interior life far beyond their seeming relative importance in the flow of exterior events.

Through this notion of symbolic resonance with waking life, day residue—perhaps the most common and commonplace element of dreams—is closely related to the element of "synchronicity"—the most seemingly unusual and unnervingly eerie of the universal elements in dreams and dreaming. I am here using the word "synchronous" in the same sense that Jung first used it, to describe the events which, though seemingly random and the product of "pure chance," are also symbolically resonant with and related to other events in waking life. That such events occur, there is no question. The controversy arises when attempts are made to ascribe meaning and significance beyond mere chance to these events. Jung termed synchronicity "an acausal connecting principle," and it is in the shape of seemingly "acausal connections" that this element appears as a shaping element in dreams. I am also extending the notion of synchronicity to include the whole range of "spooky" and seemingly "occult" occurrences in dreams (especially "telepathy" as previously discussed in Chapter VIII). My experience suggests that in addition to all the other basic elements in every dream, there is also an element of synchronicity present in every dream.

The major difficulty in dealing creatively with apparently synchronistic (telepathic and pre-cognitive) dream experiences is that their resonance with waking life events is so apparently inexplicable in causal terms. However, my strong sense, having worked with such dreams on many occasions, is that they also constellate along the same general symbolic lines as elements of day residue. It seems to me that in the vast majority, if not all of the cases, the "spooky," telepathic or pre-cognitive material has great personal symbolic value to the dreamer, in and of itself. The inevitable consequence of the eerie connections with waking events is to bring the dream vividly to mind once again. I am persuaded that this calling to mind of the dream is one of the primary psychological functions of the "paranormal" element in dreams. It is as though the waking event were foreseen and "chosen" by the unconscious forces shaping the dream in order to forcibly recall the dream to mind when the event actually takes place, because

that event is particularly appropriate, particularly symbolically resonant with some important drama of the dreamer's own life. In
my experience, it is this symbolic appropriateness that makes the
dream and the event "worth remembering," even if it is seemingly trivial and without apparent significance in waking life. Certainly this is one of the psychological reasons for the memorable
quality of many nightmares—they cling to our waking consciousness, sometimes even years later, in large measure because they
give symbolic shape to fears and uncertainties which are also very
important to us in waking life.

Unfortunately, in the case of "spooky," synchronous dreams,
the most usual response is to turn away from any symbolic understanding of the dream and the associated waking experience(s) to
concentrate on the baffling, "impossible" quality of the related
events.

I was particularly struck with the ironies of working with synchronous, seemingly pre-cognitive dreams one evening when talking with several other ministers and ministerial interns who were
doing dream work in various congregations around the San Francisco Bay area. This was soon after the assassinations of Mayor
Moscone and Supervisor Milk. Several of the dream workers recounted that members of their groups had had dreams of both
Moscone and Milk being killed well prior to the tragic events. At
the time, the work on these dreams had tended to focus on questions in the personal lives of the dreamers. Because Supervisor
Milk had been an avowed and public homosexual figure, much of
the work on the dreams in which his image appeared had focused
on homosexual impulses and homophobia. "Harvey Milk being
murdered" had been explored primarily as an image of repression, transformation, and growth of personality.

Needless to say, when we all met after the assassinations,
there was a sense of unease and dumbfoundedness as we shared
experiences of pre-cognitive dreams reported by group members
in communities isolated from one another and realized that many
people had apparently been dreaming of the murders before they
took place. As we pursued the anecdotes more closely, it became
apparent that in virtually every case the initial dream work related
to homosexual impulses had seemed to evoke tingles in the
dreamers and had seemed like productive work at the time. How-

ever, when the assassinations actually occurred, the response of the individual dreamers had generally been one of the denial of the validity of the previous work and the assertion that "it was pre-cognitive," and thus not to be considered for any other, more personally symbolic meanings. However, it was also the consensus of the dream group leaders, for whatever it is worth, that the initial dream work had indeed been authentic and productive, despite the later denials. This experience led me to wonder even more if one of the major elements involved in the constellation of seemingly "occult" experiences in dreams (and in waking life for that matter) might not be the symbolic appropriateness of the events as metaphors of interior life. An analysis, although far from systematic, of the accounts of the lives of "psychics" appears to me to offer confirmation of this notion.

In considering this question, it has also occurred to me that another functional result of such experiences is inevitably to call into serious question the "common sense" notion of the immutability of the flow of time from the past into the future. Even if such pre-cognitive events were rare (which in my experience they are not), the fact that they occur *at all* requires a drastic re-evaluation of the common sense, waking life experience of time and the passage of time. I have meditated on the idea that one of the reasons why such experiences are so common when one pays attention to dreams and shares them with others might be that the "synchronicity" is a consequence of the ultimate unity of all phenomena—another way of saying that "God is in all," indeed that "God *is* All." I am reminded of the motto Jung carved over the door of his house which translates, "Called, or uncalled, God is always present."

Certainly this intuition of ultimate oneness is multiply confirmed in other ways. Increasing intimacy with one another and the natural world as a whole appears to increase the incidence and/or awareness of these seemingly "spooky" phenomena. Perhaps this is just another way in which the truth of the ultimate identity of All and One manifests itself in our seemingly individual experience.

It is not necessary to invoke such "spooky" elements as synchronicity to demonstrate that among the universal elements of meaning and significance always present in dreams there is also an element of religious concern and search. Many schools of anthropological thought have come to the conclusion that dream experience is the source of religious ideas and beliefs of non-technological people everywhere around the world. It is the case that people universally dream of those recently dead and dream also of long-dead relatives and tribal leaders, often in connection with an experience of awe, fear, or religious numenosity. When coupled with the fact that dream experience in all cultures includes visits to "heaven," "hell," "the land of the dead," "the abode of the ancestors," etc., many anthropologists have concluded that these common, universal dream experiences are the primary source of the religious beliefs and practices of all peoples.

Much of this religious element of dreaming seems to be constellated around the perception of the inevitability of physical death and the tendency of death in dreams to be always linked with interior transformation and rebirth. The apparent continuity of personality after physical death implied by dreaming of the dead and communicating with them in the dream state is clearly one of the major foundations of the spectrum of beliefs, ranging from belief in the immortality of the soul to the belief in multiple, "subtle bodies" associated with the physical body in waking life.

It is also the case, as Jung has pointed out, that the encounter with the deeper, transpersonal and archetypal Self is at the root of all religions, and of all notions of "God," including our own. Clearly, in one sense at least, "that which cannot be spoken" is a functional definition of that which is unconscious. An alternative formulation out of the ancient Anglo-Saxon tradition is adequately translatable as "not-yet-speech ripe." Here we are clearly in the realm where psychology, poetry, and religion are one. This essential unity points again to the central importance of nurturing the creative impulse as a means of simultaneously achieving greater interior integration and wholeness together with transformation and harmonization of our external, collective life. The deep Self, the transpersonal, collective, "objective psyche," is the source from which the intuitions of the divine arise and are given ritual shape in all cultures.

Dreaming is in many ways the most primary and regular encounter waking consciousness has with the deeper self, and in this sense every dream has a religious and archetypal dimension, regardless of the obvious implications of the manifest content of any given dream. It is also the case that this element of dreaming is at times the primary component of a particular dream, and when this is the case, we have the "big" dreams that Jung and others speak of. These dreams are known and acknowledged in every culture to be of special importance and numenosity. However, this element of transpersonal, archetypal, religious meaning exists in the very fabric of even the most ordinary and seemingly mundane dream.

Indeed, this is clearly the case with waking life as well, when we pause to consider it. Someone once asked Walt Whitman if he believed in miracles, and he is reported to have spread his hands in a gesture encompassing the whole scene and said, "I know of nothing else." Occasionally we experience moments of great joy and insight in waking life where the miraculous and deeply meaningful quality of our experience is more consciously clear to us. Such moments are extraordinary and to be deeply cherished, but we live in the same universe that we know to be so miraculous in those moments, even when we are harassed and distracted by the difficulties and fears and frustrations of "normal life." It is obviously this reality to which the Zennists refer when they say that "enlightenment" is never something which is "won" or "achieved," it is something that is *recognized,* something that exists always in its own right, no matter how much apparent effort must be exerted in meditative discipline to prepare the mind to encounter it consciously.

However, even though such transpersonally significant elements are always present in the fabric of every dream, no matter how seemingly mundane and personal the memory may appear to be, more often the elements that are easily visible are more clearly personal and related to the unique circumstances of the dreamer. Among these more "personal" threads is an element representing power and dominance relationships in waking life. Alfred Adler emphasized this universal aspect of dreaming, and his own way tended to reduce all dream symbolisms to "masks" of the "urge to power and competence." Clearly, at one level, this is simply a different formulation of the same truth that Freud gave shape to with the notions of "libido" and "wish." There are, of course, distinctions to be drawn between and among these definitions, and the consequences of such definitions for the practical strategies of dream work, but their similarities and mutual resonances are ultimately far more important.

A related formulation is the ancient wisdom that "a dream is a picture of a feeling." Clearly, in addition to reflecting the physical condition of the dreamer, the dream also renders not only feelings, but also sensations, thoughts, intuitions and emotions into metaphoric images and experiences. Associated with this quality of metaphoric rendering of feeling there is always a thread of childhood and adolescent experience. This thread is often in turn connected with the general question: "When in my life did I first become aware of feeling the way I feel now at this moment?"

Constellated with these elements there also always appears to be a thread of future speculation, usually associated with the question: "What might be likely to happen if I did thus and such?" Most often the inter-relationship among these various elements is quite complex from the perspective of waking consciousness. However, the symbolic method of association serves as the unitary, "simple" vehicle for all these apparent complexities. Dream work can serve as a clarifying focus on those complexities perceived among the many on the road to wholeness—to conscious perception as One.

Put in yet another way (and thus constituting another universal thread of dream significance), every dream is constructed out of the apparent opposition between polarities (light and dark, good and evil, life and death, possible and impossible, etc.). Careful consideration reveals that the same may be said of waking reality. Contemporary physics makes essentially the same assertion—every atom of the known universe appears to contain within it an absolute and dynamic balance of positive and negative electromagnetic forces.

Our reality, awake and asleep, is constructed out of our perceptions of polar "opposite" phenomena. In the dream we are deceived (unless we dream lucidly) into believing that our experience is real, that is to say, *physical* experiences of the same order as the physical experiences of waking life. However, when we awaken, we perceive the distinction between dream and waking with new eyes, and we know that everything in the dream was, at one level at least, a physically interior experience had while the body was in sleep—an awareness that defines lucidity in the dream state. (For more on lucidity, see Chapter XV.)

In this way, every time we awaken and remember a dream, we are made aware of the ways in which we deceive ourselves with our limited and partial consciousness of the whole, true nature of our experience. Usually we do not apply this same perception to our waking lives, but it is equally true, as the dreams themselves reveal when we make the decision to remember and consider their possible significance. When we do this, amidst the many, we begin to perceive the pattern of the One. Einstein formulated his perception of essential unity into the principle of modern physics: $E = mc^2$. This means that matter and energy can be converted into one another. The capability of atomic fission and a greater understanding of the atomic fusion processes in the hearts of the stars are one consequence of this formulation. Another consequence is that there is now further physical evidence that ALL *really* IS ONE. Nothing really exists permanently except the one essence that matter and energy both are. Because we can begin to make physical manipulations based on Einstein's revolution in theoretical thought, we know that the formulation (like Newton's before him) is a way of giving shape to a single truth.

We know that we are at least physical beings, so at least to that extent Einstein's formulations describe our own physical bodies as well. When we enter the realm of the "psychological" (the "intangible" realm of psyche, spirit, religion, and the transformation of both individual and collective consciousness) we discover that the same principle applies: ALL IS ONE. We are so deeply and subtly intertwined with one another and with the biosphere, and by implication with all that is, that we cannot truly say where "I" stop and "they" begin in any ultimately certain way. Such distinctions only *seem* clear in dreams until we wake up, and they only seem clear in waking life until we remember and begin to understand our dreams.

Consider for a moment in this regard the ancient Chinese symbol of the *Tao*. The circle of One Whole is divided into the black and white polarities of individually conscious experience.

Despite this division, however, the white "tadpole" always has a black "eye" and the black "tadpole" always has a white "eye." In this way the ancient Chinese formulate Einstein's dictum. William Blake formulated it by stating that "opposites are never true contraries." Everything and everyone is made of the same essence of energy/matter, even and especially the things we imagine are "opposites." For this reason alone (among the many) it is demonstrably clear that we are all subtly, inextricably, and absolutely inter-related with and interpenetrated by everyone and everything else. This is particularly and ironically true of those things we think of as "opposite" and "mutually exclusive."

If you begin to graphically develop this basic symbol of the Yin and the Yang, you create the mandala forms and "meanders"

known in all the traditions of religious art. At this level, the metaphoric significance of all these forms is one—the ultimate connection of one (individual experience) with ALL ("God"), despite the seeming conflicts between light and darkness at any given moment.

In this sense, the recent photographic views of the earth from

space stand clearly in a very ancient and continuingly vital tradition of religious art, demonstrating as they do the same swirling, vortical, interpenetrating relationship among the "opposites" of hot and cold, wet and dry, light and darkness, etc.

In the midst of the vortex of experience and the apparent conflict and irreconcilability of "opposites," the perception of the coincidence of opposites has a quality of ultimate mystery and importance. It forms an awareness of "solidity" and "timelessness" that grows out of and is ultimately indistinguishable from the perceptions of the play of opposites itself.

Here it is useful to think of the ancient shamanic/religious belief that *everything* is alive. Clearly we are alive, and since we are of the same essence as all things, it is reasonable to suppose that *all* is alive, and that the seeming distinction between "animate" and "inanimate" is actually a distinction between obvious and subtle.

In this connection, the ancient shamanic belief in "rebirth from the bones" reflects essentially the same religious perception. When the physical form decays after death, the bones stand out as the most permanent and enduring element. It is from the permanent—the physical universe and the collective/objective psyche—that the impermanent is born, and to which it returns. The impermanent—the sense of individual identity and awareness—is reborn again and again from the permanent, metaphorically revealed in the ancient belief in reverence for the bones because they are the source of rebirth.

"_____"—that which cannot be spoken, "God," the essence of energy/matter appears to play hide and seek with Him/Her/Them/Itself in us, in every moment, awake and asleep. The conscious attention to dreams can make this game of hide and seek more meaningful, enjoyable, and creatively productive. We have no choice but to play the game. The only choice available to us is the degree of conscious self-awareness with which we play it. It is "the only game in town." The point of this game of hide and seek appears to be itself—a metaphor of play, a spontaneously motivated activity of the universe, of essential energy/matter.

Another way of thinking about the simultaneously multiple meanings of dreams is to compare them with the rules to the game. At any one moment of play, any one rule or group of rules may apply, but *all* the rules are still the rules and define the context of play at every moment, whether any particular rule is immediately applicable at any given moment or not.

The basic rhythmic pattern of the divine game of hide and seek in human consciousness is the conversion of unconscious energy into self-aware experience in the dynamic and ultimately impermanent permutations of matter and the physical world. The basic polarities that comprise our experience are consciousness and unconsciousness. We know that that which is unconscious at any given moment is still part of it all, even if we are not paying conscious attention to it in any given instant. Consciousness, even at its best, is partial and intermittent. Unconsciousness, if only because by definition it includes everything else, is not.

In the dynamic interplay between conscious and unconscious that shapes the experience of dreams as well as waking life, there is always an implication, a possibility, an intimation of wholeness. This intimation of wholeness, this evocation of that which is missing, means that there is always an element present in dreams of "compensation," of balancing and constructively criticizing the prematurely closed, partial perceptions of waking life and behavior. Among the other elements he discussed, Jung emphasized this element of "compensation." In this important sense, every dream brings energies and images of "that which is missing" and necessary for increasing wholeness and integration of attitude and action in waking life. Thus the images and energies of the dream "compensate" for the imbalances of waking life and strive to establish and maintain individual and collective health homeostatically. Even the worst nightmare has, as a large part of its reason for being, the correction of some imbalance in attitude or behavior.

Like the other universal threads of dreaming, this one is inextricably intertwined with all the others. Another way of adjusting the focus on the one thing that dream and waking are is to say that all dreams have a thread of meaning involved with waking life emotional relationships, or the lack of them. The compensatory aspect of dreams is most often clearly visible in association with issues of emotional relationship.

This balancing, compensatory element is often associated in turn with another universal element of dreaming—the element of anniversary. The ability of the unconscious to maintain awareness of the cyclic return of anniversary dates of significant emotional events along with the appearance in dreams of elements of memory apparently long forgotten, or never even consciously noted, suggests strongly that in fact *nothing* is *ever* forgotten. Here we can begin to see the symbolic reference to the verifiable common reality of such "occult" notions as the "Akashic Record" and "The Book of All Knowledge." The practices of religion and ritual magic associated with "reading" these "universal records" have reference on multiple levels to increasingly conscious exploration of both the personal and the collective unconscious.

The Tarot deck is clearly one concrete example of this archetypal tradition of "The Book of All Knowledge." There is a story that the Tarot deck was born in the imaginations of the last librarians of the great library at Alexandria as they watched the collected wisdom of the world disappear in flames during the Moslem invasion in 646 A.D. As they saw the library burn, they are said to have turned to one another and agreed that they must never allow the collected wisdom of the ages to be so easily lost again. They set about creating a set of images embodying the wisdom that had been lost in the fire—the archetypal patterns of the knowledge of the collective unconscious. They fabricated these images and invented popular entertainments and games of skill and chance using these images so that the uninitiated common people would love the deck and take it with them everywhere, dispersing it over the face of the earth so that it could never be lost in such a fashion again.

Whether or not such stories actually reflect the historical origins of the Tarot and/or the regular deck of playing cards, they are clearly evocative of the archetypal nature of the images, particularly the figure of the Major Arcana. In many ways, the relationship of the Major and Minor Arcana is reminiscent of the relationship of dreams to waking life. The images are powerful and "magic," but they are often ignored and deleted from the "game" because their relative value is much more difficult to determine. They are, as author Charles Williams called them, the "Greater Trumps."

This same essential relationship characterizes the tension between the exoteric and esoteric threads in virtually every religious tradition. It can be seen in the relationship between the Book of Revelation and the rest of the New Testament and in the relationship of the Kaballah to the Torah and Midrash. In this sense, the curse at the close of the Book of Revelation, "I warn every one who hears the words of the prophecy of this book: if any one adds to them, God will add to him the plagues described in this book, and if any one takes away from the words of the book of this prophecy, God will take away his share in the tree of life and in the holy city, which are described in the book" (Rev 22:18–19), is simply a description of the consequences that can be expected from denying the unconscious and repressing the life of dreams and the unconscious, intuitive experience.

In another important sense, the Book of Revelation, the Tarot, the Kaballah, *et al.* are carefully crafted fields upon which to project one's own interior energies, embodying images of archetypal significance in the same way that our dreams do, and for the same reasons. As in dreams and the paranormal waking life events related to dreams, it is the principle of symbolic resonance that offers the major key to understanding their multiple levels and layers of significance.

Because one purpose of dreams is always to promote increasing wholeness there is always a thread of constructive self-criticism in every dream. In one sense, this self-criticism is so intertwined with the compensatory element as to be indistinguishable from it, but in another sense it is a distinct element in that "self-criticism" is more often focused on specific decisions and actions in waking life, while the "compensatory element" tends to be more generalized and to highlight developmental energies over time, rather than specific moments.

However, it should now be clear that all these universal elements of dreams and dreaming are at a fundamental level all reflective of each other. It is ultimately a matter of taste and aesthetics what element, if any, you choose to become the center, the "atom" to which all the others may be reduced. In this sense, all human conflicts may be understood as disagreements in taste and aesthetics, i.e., what one perceives to be "ugly" as opposed to "beautiful." At this level, dream work is an aesthetic occupation, hopefully extending the conscious appreciation of the beautiful until, as the Navajos say, "Everywhere I walk, I walk in beauty."

It is impossible to "walk in beauty" *everywhere* unless there is beauty within as well as without—unless we have learned to love our enemies. When this affirmation and search for beauty is carried out in the realm of dreams as well as the realm of waking life, transformations of personality and character and access to creative energies are the result. Such is the stuff of miracles, and, like Walt Whitman, I perceive nothing else.

Another universal element of dreaming derived from their inherent effort to promote wholeness is that every dream also contains a thread of creative inspiration and problem solving. Many of the dreams already mentioned show this element with great clarity, and even a particularly "psychological" dream, like

Margaret's dream of leaving the dance, reveals a level at which the entire shape of the dream experience is designed to "solve a problem" creatively. It is always a good idea to look for possibilities of creative solutions to life's problems in dreams.

However, it is important to note that examining one's dreams for creative possibilities for waking action is a very different thing from "looking to one's dreams for answers about how to live one's life." People who turn over the decision-making function of their lives to their dreams regularly fail to understand the subtlety, complexity, and multi-leveled significance of the dreams they are using for specific guidance. Most often, the result of this premature closure and abdication of conscious responsibility is that the "dream answers" turn out to be wrong, and the quality of life is not enhanced by the decisions made "because it is what the dreams said to do." Only on the rarest of occasions in my experience do the dreams speak directly and unambiguously about waking life decisions, and even when they do, there are also always other levels of resonance and significance in addition to the "clear message."

Let me offer an example out of my own life. I once had the experience while traveling alone of falling in love with a woman other than my wife. In the midst of that experience I had two very clear and unambiguous dreams on successive nights. The first came in the form of spoken admonition: "Be satisfied with the ring." The following night I received an equally clear message, "Remember the innocent who are not seen," together with the knowledge that there was a deep level of reference to my daughter, then aged seven. In both cases the dreams (for once) gave clear instructions: remember my most basic commitments and find satisfaction in adhering to them. Both dreams were most clear and unambiguous at the level of waking choice-making, but both dreams also had, and continue to have, resonances beyond the immediate decisions involving relationship. At another level, the "ring" is not only the "wedding ring"—it is the "ring" of human community and friendship in which I found myself at that time. My daughter is not the only "innocent who is not seen." My choice to remain within the monogamous commitment of my relationship with my wife had to be based upon conscious choice, not

on "instructions from dreams." The information in the dreams reminded me of the larger view of my life which in the passions of
the moment I might have overlooked or otherwise undervalued.

Yet another way of understanding the universal language and
import of dreams is to say that every dream embodies an element
of "return to the womb" and "return to the crucible for melting
and recasting." To the extent that every image in our dreams represents aspects of our own interior energies, every time we dream
we are watching the "melting down" and distillation of our personalities into constituent parts. All the interactions in our dreams
are, at this level, metaphors of the changing metabolic, energy-dy-
namic relationships between various elements of our total unconscious being. When these dream interactions reflect and help
create genuine changes in those energy dynamics, the waking ego
personality which is reintegrated and reconstituted from those
parts upon waking is also transformed. In this sense each sleep period is indeed a "little death," each awakening a "rebirth into
new life."

Recent research has also demonstrated that, in addition to all
the other universal elements present in every dream, there is also
an element of basic structure associated with the conversion of
short-term memories into the basic categories of long-term memory, using the element of cathexis (emotional/mental focus) as
the organizing principle. Indeed, this is another way of saying the
same thing, of describing the same phenomenon that all the basic
elements describe. The reduction of dreaming to an "information
processing model" is no more in error than any other reductionist
assertion about dreaming. Dreams certainly do reflect and model
information theory, but this is only one way of understanding
their multiple-layered significance.

In my experience, the dreams of a single night are always related to one another thematically. Some researchers have even
gone so far as to assert that the dreams of a single sleeping period
are related to one another in a formal, structural fashion, not unlike the elements of Aristotle's "Laws of Tragedy." My own experience suggests that this may be overstating the case. However,
even when the exploration of the dreams of a single night fails to
reveal a thematic thread running throughout the dreams, my sus-

picion is that it is a result of the failure to detect the meanings that are there, rather than an indication that the dreams are actually unrelated.

To close this excursion into the universal elements present in dreams, it is also the case that every dream contains within it an element of humor. This is not to say that all dreams are experienced as "funny"—clearly they are not. However, even the most gripping and "unfunny" nightmare always has the ironic, humorous twist of being "only a dream" when we awaken. Theories of humor abound, but all of them have somewhere close to the center of their formulation the idea of "paradox" and "anomalous juxtaposition." All dreams are constructed out of the juxtaposition of images and elements which from the "objective" perspective of waking consciousness are unrelated. The dream casts these seemingly anomalous elements into intimate relationship, and thus embodies the basic element of humor, even when the immediate subjective experience of the dreamer is far from humorous. However, as work is undertaken with nightmares and other such upsetting dream phenomena, my experience is that the inherent element of humor becomes more and more easily visible over time. It is often possible to review the nightmares of the past from the perspective of increased consciousness in the present and to see clearly the humorous side of these intense adventures. This is particularly poignant when we become aware of the evolution and development of dream characters and situations over time. Like the transformative literary characters of Italo Calvino and John Hersey, we see that the frightening monsters of yesterday become the friends and allies of today. We see in retrospect that even when they first appeared in their "wrathful forms," they had clues and cues as to their true possibilities—clues and cues which we overlooked at the time, but which become more dramatically and amusingly clear as we live with them. Most of the recognition of this humorous element accompanies our alteration in feeling that can only be described as learning to "love one's enemies."

There is no theoretical end to this list of universal elements always present to some degree or another in all dreams. The selection of elements presented in this chapter, although not arbitrary, is still partial, and this must be emphasized. Sometimes one group of elements will predominate in a dream, sometimes another. Whatever the case, it is always useful and productive to ask whether or not one or more of these elements is a major determinant of the dream experience. When looking for universal thematic elements in myth and dream, it is always important to remember that there is no such thing as a myth or a dream with only one meaning. Even on those rare occasions when a dream speaks unequivocally and recommends a particular course of action, it is always constructed in multiple layers of subtlety that resonate beyond the obvious, manifest content of the dream.

Summary: SOME ELEMENTS THAT ARE ALWAYS PRESENT IN DREAMS

It is the nature of dreams to convey multiple meanings and layers of meaning with a single "narrative." To use the metaphor of weaving, there are always certain kinds of threads woven into the fabric of every dream. Sometimes one color or texture will dominate the overall design, sometimes another, but all dreams are woven of essentially the same warps and cross-threads, no matter what the particular pattern. The history of dream work is made more comprehensible when we realize that different schools and styles of dream work emphasize different universal aspects of dreaming, and are not mutually exclusive (no matter what claims to exclusive truth any school may make). In this spirit, here is a partial list of some of the universal threads of meaning and significance that seem to be woven into the process of dreaming itself.

1. Every dream comes in the service of wholeness and the effort to harmonize interior and exterior life.
2. Every dream contains an element of "libidinous," sexual desire. Sigmund Freud emphasized this element in his work.

3. Every dream contains an element of unconscious wish-fulfillment. This is also a basically Freudian notion, although many contemporary Freudians have disavowed this principle.

4. Every dream depicts elements of the dreamer's personality, interior life, and vital energies in its imagery. This is the basic insight of the Gestalt School of dream work. At one end the people and things and situations in your dreams all represent aspects of yourself, but they also often represent waking life people, things, and events *at the same time.*

5. Every dream contains an element of reflection of the physical health and condition of the body at the moment of the dream. For a long time, this "plum pudding hypothesis" dominated scientific thought, and experiment and dreams were considered to be merely a function of disordered metabolism.

6. Contemporary research demonstrates that certain biophysical and biochemical behaviors accompany the act of dreaming. Among these are increased ocular motility, particular fluctuations in muscle tonus, and dramatic fluctuations of the levels of *serotonin* and *noradrenalin* (aka *norepinephrine*) in the blood. This latter amine appears to be associated with the isolation and immobilization of the voluntary nervous system, so that we do not act out all our dreams physically as we dream them. Sleep-walking and sleep-talking have been demonstrated to take place only outside of the REM periods, and thus appear to be associated with memory rather than immediate dream experience.

7. Every dream has an element drawn from the memories of the preceding day or so, known technically as "day residue." The important question to ask regarding day residue is not so much *what* particular event is being recalled, but rather *why that* particular event instead of some other has been woven into the experience of the dream.

8. Additionally, there is always an element of the dream's

construction associated with the "information processing" of memory—the conversion of short-term memories into the categories of long-term memory associated
by emotional/symbolic content, rather than by objective
form or relative importance in waking life.

9. Every dream has an element representing power and
dominance relationships in waking life. Alfred Adler
emphasized this aspect of dream work.

10. Every dream has an element of childhood and adolescent reminiscence, often associated with the question,
"When in my life did I first feel the way I am feeling
now?"

11. At the same time, every dream has an element of speculation about the future, often associated with the question: "What might happen if I did thus-and-so?"

12. Every dream renders feelings and emotions into metaphoric images. Thoughts, sensations, and intuitions are
also rendered in dreams in metaphoric/symbolic forms.

13. Every dream takes the shape it does because that is the
best "fit" that can be achieved, given the multiple meanings carried by the dream. The basic organizing principle of these multiple layers of significance and
information is symbolic resonance.

14. Every dream has an element of archetypal drama. Even
when dreams are terribly personal and seemingly mundane, there is always some way in which the universality
of all human experience is hinted at.

15. Every dream has an element of "anniversary" or "com-
memoration" of significant waking life and dream
events.

16. Every dream contains an element of constructive self-
criticism.

17. Also, every dream contains an element of creative inspiration and problem solving.

18. Every dream has an element of religious concern and intuition about the inevitability of death. Religious beliefs
from around the world can be seen reflected in common
dream experiences (such as "leaving the body," dream-

ing of someone who has recently died, dreaming of "heaven," "hell," "past lives," etc.).

19. Every dream has a balancing or compensatory element relative to waking consciousness. Even the worst nightmare or recurring dream has, as a major part of its purpose or reason for being in the form it is, the correction of some imbalance in waking attitude or behavior.

20. Every dream is constructed out of the seeming opposition between polarities (light and dark, good and evil, life and death, possible and impossible, etc.). There is also always a complementary element which hints at the ultimate unity of these seeming opposites in a single, all-embracing reality.

21. Every dream contains an element of "synchronicity" (*déjà vu*, telepathy, pre-cognition, and the like).

22. Every dream has an element of "return to the womb" and "return to the crucible for melting and recasting." Each dream is a step in the evolution and development of personality and character, and every awakening is a rebirth into a potentially new life.

23. The dreams of a single night are almost always related to each other thematically. The failure to detect a theme or thread of meaning in the dreams of a single night is probably a result of our inability to unravel the multiple levels of meaning rather than an indication that the dreams are actually unrelated.

24. Every dream reflects a concern for waking life emotional relationships or the lack of them.

25. Every dream contains an element of humor. Obviously this does not mean that all dreams are experienced as funny—clearly they are not—but even the worst nightmare has as an ironic and humorous twist being "only a dream" when we wake up. In addition, the radical synthesis and juxtaposition of incongruous elements that always takes place in dreams is the fundamental basis of humor.

There is no theoretical end to this list. Some elements will predominate and obscure others at various times, but my experience is that these elements are always present to some degree or another in all dreams. It is always worthwhile to ask if one of these elements is a major determinant of the dream experience, and how it may interweave with other universal dream themes.

Chapter XIII
SEX IN DREAMS

> Basically, he [Freud] wanted
> to teach—or so, at least, it
> seemed to me—that,
> regarded from within,
> sexuality included spirituality
> and had an intrinsic meaning.
>
> C. G. Jung

Freud originally proposed that the dream is a kind of mask, manufactured every night by the "guardians of sleep" to prevent the spontaneous sexual urges and feelings, which well up when the faculties of conscious self-awareness are relaxed and diminished in sleep, from awakening the dreamer with their unacceptable imagery and intensity. Contemporary medical research has confirmed the deep association between genital sexuality and dreaming by demonstrating that penile erection and clitoral swelling occur regularly during REM sleep. However, if Freud's formulation were wholly correct, then it would be reasonable to expect that this universal "censoring" and "protecting" function would all but eliminate explicitly erotic imagery from remembered dreams, and that when and if explicitly sexual imagery were to somehow evade these controls and appear "unmasked" in dreams, then this occurrence would tend to awaken the dreamer immediately. This is simply not the case. Virtually everyone has sexually explicit dreams from time to time, and far more often than not, these dreams do not precipitate immediate or agitated awakenings.

On the other hand, it is true that "Freudian" dream work, focusing on the possible sexual meanings of common dream experiences, such as climbing and descending stairs, encountering long,
sharp, penetrating objects, encountering concave, hollow, encircling objects, plunging into bodies of water, etc., often elicits
strong tingles and aha's of confirmation from people who spontaneously dream such images and are not consciously aware of their
sexual connotations. Clearly, Freud was exploring one strong element among the many multiple elements that are always present
to one degree or another in every dream. Every dream is composed of "masked" sexual imagery and energy in much the fashion that Freud described. However, Freud's exhaustive
demonstration of this fact in no way addresses the question of
what other elements are also eternally present woven into the fabric of every dream.

Part of the legacy of Freud, even among non-Freudian dream
workers, has been a tendency to view overtly erotic elements in
dreams as "self-evident" and thus to shy away from further symbolic analysis of sexual metaphors, concentrating instead on exploration of whatever waking life issues of sexual and emotional
relationship are brought up by the dreams. This is always a productive way to proceed, but it is not the only way. When, in addition to pursuing sexual/relational tensions in the dreamer's
personal life, the dream work also includes further exploration of
the symbolic quality of the sexual images themselves, other, deeper layers of meaning and significance are almost always revealed.
The explicitly sexual images in dreams are as symbolic and multi-
leveled as all the other images in dreams.

The tendency to perceive physical sexuality as an "irreduc-
ible" element of human life is in keeping with the general cultural
idolization of "science" and the belief that anything that cannot
be "objectively observed" and measured is somehow less "real"
than things that can. This attitude amounts to an archetype of psychological repression itself, and as such is largely responsible for
the exploitive and oppressive quality of so many contemporary
sexual mores, just as it is also close to the center of other aspects
of our contemporary technological crisis.

However, just as dreams of death often have an archetypal association with the growth of personality, my experience is that

dreams containing explicitly sexual and erotic imagery and experience also have an archetypal tendency to be associated with issues of religious, philosophical, and spiritual concern. Most often, overtly erotic imagery contains a level of reference to the desire for direct experience of spiritual reality, the desire to understand directly what's *really* going on beyond the obvious appearances of life, the desire to commune more directly with the energy of the divine. This archetypal resonance between sexuality and spiritual search is also clearly visible in the poetic testimony of the world's avowed and acknowledged mystics. Over and over again the mystical writers of all religious traditions couch their descriptions of their transcendent experience in sexual terms, giving shape to their encounter with the divine as a metaphoric encounter with the "Lover." St. Teresa, Rumi, Julian of Norwich, the anonymous author of *Secret of the Golden Flower,* Kabir, the Nahuatl religious poets of Aztec culture, Mechtild of Magdeburg, the anonymous authors of the *Kama Sutra*—the list of men and women who have employed erotic metaphors to express their deepest religious and spiritual intuitions and experiences is virtually endless.

One reason for this archetypal association between sexuality and spiritual life is that adult sexual encounter always involves a simultaneous stimulation of multiple levels of self-awareness, ranging from the purely physical to the mental and emotional. Even oppressive and exploitive sexual encounters have the effect of simultaneously stimulating these centers of experience in a negative way, while loving, communicative sexual encounter often awakens depths of awareness previously unimaginable. For this reason alone, there is an obvious archetypal resonance between sexual experience and the experience of more direct communion with the energies of the divine, which also characteristically involves a discovery of previously unimagined depths of awareness and harmonization of all levels of perception, from the obviously physical to the ineffably emotional and intuitive. At the same time, sexual encounter is the course from which each of us springs, and in this sense as well there is a deep archetypal resonance between sexuality and the most profound human religious and philosophical questions and concerns.

Contemporary medical developments, such as artificial insemination, amniocentesis and the ability to predict sex and potential birth defects, *in vitro* fertilization of human eggs, and the invention of increasingly sophisticated life support systems potentially capable of bringing a human embryo to "birth" without gestation in a woman's womb have all created ethical and moral dilemmas which have no solutions—unless the "unmeasurable" elements of human emotion and love are clearly understood to be as real and as important as the machines that make these medical procedures possible.

Human beings come into existence as a consequence of sexual encounters between individual men and women, no matter how many complex medical procedures may also intervene. Arguments over the use and ethical implications of these procedures often lose sight of the emotionally charged sexual nature of human reproduction. Human reproduction is ultimately sexual and emotional, even when this fact is ignored and "sublimated" into mechanical medical procedures. Perhaps Freud's greatest contribution to the successful continuation of human life on the planet may be his uncompromising demonstration that whatever else we may be, we are sexual beings first—both biologically and psychologically. No matter how far removed our conscious motivations and intents may be from sexual encounter, some aspect of the energy we call upon to think and act is sexual in nature, no matter what else it may also be at the same time.

In my experience in working with explicitly sexual and overtly erotic dreams, I have detected a pattern in which dreams with frightening, oppressive, and otherwise unpleasant sexual feelings and images are often associated on one level with repressed, unresolved, or inadequately resolved religious and philosophical problems. Conversely, my experience with explicitly sexual dreams where the experience is happy, pleasurable, or rapturous is that there tends to be an association between these dreams and the greater recognition and resolution of philosophical and spiritual concerns. Indeed, when the sexual element of the dream appears explicitly, as opposed to being in a "masked" state, it is often an indication that increased consciousness and self-awareness has been brought to the waking life relational tensions, and that the philosophical and religious implications of waking life relational choices are beginning to emerge.

The fact that sexuality and spiritual life are deeply intertwined has been recognized universally. It is at the root of the many prohibitions against spontaneous sexual expression imposed by the world religions on the one hand, and of the seemingly opposite but actually complementary strains in Eastern and Western religious and occult tradition which celebrate the cultivation of sexual encounter as a form of worship, meditation, and spiritual discipline on the other.

In the evolution of human consciousness, the conscious control and suppression of spontaneous, "animal" sexuality is a central event. The myths of the world are filled with stories suggesting this archetypal act of individual self-awareness where the sexual instincts come into conflict with developing ego consciousness and an ambiguous struggle ensues. Among these myths, the story of the birth of Athena and Hephaestos' unrequited passion for her is most interesting and revealing.

Zeus, like his father Chronos and his grandfather Uranos before him, began to fear once he had seized power that his children might grow to overthrow him, just as he had overthrown his father. Again like his father and grandfather, Zeus chose to devour his children the moment they were born, rather than let them grow into whatever they might become. He himself had escaped this fate and grown into maturity only because his mother Gaea had foiled her drunken husband and substituted a stone for her baby son when Chronos came to eat him. Perhaps because of this, Zeus was not fooled by similar attempts on the part of his wife/mother to save her children from his all-devouring desire for eternal, unchallenged supremacy.

At last, however, he developed a terrible pain in his head that could not be assuaged by the power and healing magic of all the gods. Zeus lay in agony on his ceremonial couch, and he finally summoned Hephaestos, the shaman/god of fire, tool craft, and metal work, to split his head open and release him from his torture. At first Hephaestos refused his lord's command, but when he was able to extract prior forgiveness and absolution from Zeus for any and all consequences of the terrible act, he struck Zeus' throbbing forehead with an axe, splitting it open.

Out stepped Athena, "fully armed" we are told, and "shining." Athena was Zeus' child who had continued to grow and develop in his brain even after he devoured her. It was her continued growth inside his skull that had been the cause of Zeus' headache, and once she was released, Zeus was immediately restored to health and vigor.

Hephaestos, however, was so struck by Athena's splendor and beauty when she emerged that he immediately fell in love with her and tried to press his affections on her on the spot. Athena did not return his positive regard, and she repulsed his advances immediately and effectively.

The phenomenon of "love at first sight" as experienced by Hephaestos is not an unknown phenomenon in contemporary life, and is always associated at a deep level with the projection of previously unsuspected unconscious material and energies out onto the "loved one." Thus, at this mythological moment we have a picture of the two simultaneous aspects of repression and projection—in Zeus' "headache" we can discern the interior consequences of repression, and in Hephaestos' "love at first sight" we can see the tremendous emotional power of the complementary projection.

Hephaestos never wavered from his passionate desire for Athena, we are told. Even when Zeus gave him Aphrodite, the goddess of love and sexual passion, for his wife, he still sought after Athena. Indeed, all the stories of Aphrodite's unfaithfulness to Hephaestos take place against the backdrop of Hephaestos' continued unrequited love for Athena, his "unattainable ideal."

Several stories relate how Hephaestos pursued Athena, fabricating all manner of clever mechanical devices as gifts for her—robots, and other "labor saving devices"—all to flatter her and demonstrate to her his cleverness and worthiness to be her husband. Athena spurned them all, and at one point Hephaestos decided to follow her on one of her solitary rambles along the snow-covered lower slopes of Mount Olympus and rape her so that she would be forced to accept him as her husband. When he attacked her, Athena feigned submission, but at the last moment, when Hephaestos was about to impregnate her, she threw him contemptuously aside into the snow. As the sperm spurted from Hephaestos' penis, it fell on the snow and congealed into the shapes of statuary—lifeless but passionately evocative images of Hephaestos' frustrated desire. These figures became the famous "Sculpture Garden of Hephaestos" which Phidias and other classical and later sculptors claimed to have visited in their dreams to receive the inspiration for their greatest work.

In this myth at one important level we can see a representation of the psychological mechanism of "sublimation" of raw sexual energy into creative work which was so important to Freud as an explanation of the creative process. At another level, the Sculpture Garden of Hephaestos and the story of Athena's emergence from her father's head also represent the moment of archetypal struggle and development when sexual desires and instincts come under the increasing control of conscious self-awareness and will.

It is interesting to compare this story with a similar story from the Hindu tradition—the story of the birth of Dawn. It is a similar moment—Brahma sits absorbed in yogic trance. All that is is himself, and as he becomes increasingly aware of his infinite depths, he manifests the forms and existences of the other gods. He is the "Father of All," but even he does not know what he will manifest out of his unconscious depths as he meditates. So he is greatly surprised when suddenly he manifests "Dawn," the first goddess, and the morning light simultaneously. The poems tell us that she is also "shining" and "beautiful" beyond all previous imagining, and Brahma immediately conceives a similar passion for her. He reminds himself, however, of the prohibition against sexual union between fathers and daughters. In other versions, it is Shiva who reminds him with a mocking rebuke. Once reminded, Brahma exerts his will and controls his desire, but the effort is so great that it causes beads of sweat to break out all over his body. These beads of sweat roll down his body and transform into all the "demons of desire." They march off his body shouting and chanting, "Fear! Rage! Lust! War! Greed! Murder! Suicide!" In other versions, it is human beings who are born of Brahma's sweat of repressed desire.

These desire demons fill the myths of Hinduism and Buddhism, and when Gautama sits beneath the Bo tree in his final heroic effort to penetrate the true nature of reality, it is these demons whom Mara summons up to attack the Buddha and prevent him from attaining full enlightenment. When Buddha calmly dismisses Mara's demon army as a mere illusion, unworthy of attention in the midst of his meditation, he redeems Brahma's "original sin" in an echo of Jesus' redemption of Adam and Eve and all their children under somewhat similar circumstances of concerted attack.

The story of the manifestation of Eve from part of Adam's interior and her subsequent association with the source of evil and discord places the Genesis story into the same archetypal scene. All three stories (and many more besides) testify to the central place that the development of conscious influence and control over instinctive, spontaneous "animal" sexuality has in the development of human consciousness. These stories also hint at the possibilities inherent in increasing consciousness of sexual energies for the meditative reconnection of human consciousness with our deepest archetypal roots. The story of Hephaestos and Athena is particularly poignant in connection with the contemporary scene since it pictures the deep schism between Wisdom (personified by Athena) and Technology (personified by Hephaestos). Wisdom does not love Technology, and unless these two archetypal energies in ourselves can be reconciled, we will surely destroy ourselves in particularly nasty and horrible ways.

This story also points to the submerged truth that all the horrors we have created for ourselves with our clever technology and our incomplete wisdom are, at one deep level, frustrated attempts to give love-gifts. In another ironic but by no means accidental coincidence of seeming opposites, the frustrated sexual energies that unconsciously motivate so much of our self-destructive behavior are themselves among the very energies which are necessary for a satisfactory resolution of our current predicament. If sexual energies are only acknowledged and explored with increasing consciousness into the areas of transcendent religious, spiritual and philosophical concern where they inevitably lead, then erotic desire itself can become a meditative means to increasing wholeness, deepened spiritual experience, and vital human reconciliation.

Summary: SEX IN DREAMS

My experience is that explicitly sexual and erotic imagery and dream material is as multi-leveled and symbolic as any other dream experience. Most often, when overtly sexual dream images are explored beyond their more obvious references to waking sexual and emotional tensions, they reveal levels of significance associated with deep philosophical, religious, and spiritual concerns. Dreams with pleasant, enjoyable and rapturous sexual images are often associated with solving spiritual and moral problems, while dreams with frightening and repugnant sexuality are often associated with the repression of spiritual and ethical concerns and the inadequate resolution of religious and philosophical problems.

The conscious domination and control of spontaneous, "animal" sexual urges appears to be a primary metaphor of the development of human consciousness and individual self-awareness. The desire to foster this conscious domination is obviously at the root both of the prohibitions against spontaneous sexual expression imposed by so many of the world religions on the one hand, and of the complementary traditions which celebrate sexual encounter as a spiritual discipline on the other. These seeming contradictory approaches both affirm the deep association between sexuality and spirituality and the importance of gaining increasing consciousness amidst the flows of sexual energy. A more conscious and less repressed attitude toward outselves as sexual beings is absolutely necessary for our collective survival.

Chapter XIV
ENCOUNTERING
THE ARCHETYPES
IN DREAMS AND WAKING LIFE

> History is a nightmare from
> which we are trying to
> awake.
>
> *James Joyce*

When we examine dreams with an eye to their meaning and structure, we discover that dreams speak a universal language of metaphor and symbol. This universal language of dreams also reveals itself to be the symbolic language of mythology and religious practice and belief. The correspondences among the spontaneous dreams of individual people from various cultures, the myths and religious practices of various cultures, together with the perception that human life embodies recognizable developmental stages, led the Swiss psychiatrist and historian of culture, Carl Gustav Jung, to formulate the idea of the "collective unconscious." Jung himself admitted later in his life that the choice of the term "collective unconscious," although descriptively accurate, has been the source of some confusion and misunderstanding. Jung suggested that he might better have proposed the term "objective psyche" to describe this realm of basic patterns of human experience and self-awareness. Jung was led to his formulation by a number of experiences suggesting that the human unconscious has a tendency to spontaneously manifest certain categories of symbolic drama and imagery in association with certain developmental stages of the growth of individual personality on the one hand, and certain stages of collective, cultural, historical development on the other. These patterns he called "archetypes." The collective unconscious, or objective psyche, is composed of these archetypes of primary human experience. These categories or archetypes are shared among all peoples, at all stages of individual and collective development in essentially the same fashion.

It was this notion of the association of particular archetypal imagery and ritual practices associated with collective developmental stages that allowed Jung's ideas to be seized upon by the racist intellectuals in the Nazi and Fascist movements in the 1930's. Despite the fact that the use of Jung's ideas as an ideological justification of conquest and oppression represents a severe distortion of his work, there was a period (between 1934 and 1938) when Jung's own utterances, particularly his editorials in the *Zentrablatt für Psychotherapie,* regarding the Nazi movement in Germany and the issues of "racial unconscious," are, at best, ambiguous. In the words of one of Jung's most clear-minded and candid biographers, Laurens Van der Post, ". . . [this ambiguity] is only too understandable if one remembers that in the infant years of Nazi upsurge in Germany [Jung] himself was still under the spell of how much his own encounter with the collective unconscious had enriched him and inclined him to assess any activation of it in others positively rather than negatively. But within two years he had changed his mind. His warnings against events in Germany became more frequent, urgent, and unqualified, ending in such outright condemnation that when the war broke out his books were banned in Germany and he himself placed in the Nazi blacklist for liquidation at the first opportunity."

The question of the positive and negative potential results of the increased activation of collective archetypal energies (the energies that fuel all forms of collective change, from war and destruction to peaceful evolution and collective reconciliation) is equally poignant and important today. The fact that Jung himself made initial errors in the assessment of the importance and direction of popular political and social movements of his day should make us all the more wary of making similar errors of moral judgment out of our own prematurely closed views.

Whatever one's attitudes toward particular popular movements at any given moment, the fact that such movements reflect basic archetypal dramas is inescapable. The archetypes create the basic framework for both individual and collective life. In this sense, everyone has "a religion." Paul Tillich's definition of religion as "ultimate commitment" describes the same reality from a slightly different point of view. Even the suicidal nihilist has an ultimate commitment to negation, and thus can be said to have a "religion of denial."

To use the analogy of the body once again, there are obviously basic patterns of archetypes of biological form. Everyone has the same basic biological apparatus—skin, muscles, bones, heart, lungs, brain, blood, etc. These may be thought of as "archetypes" of biological form. On the one hand, every person alive is a unique physical specimen, while on the other it is simultaneously true that all human beings manifest the same basic physical form. So it is with the psyche as well. Each of us embodies the archetypes of the objective psyche or collective conscious in our own unique and personal fashion, while still repeating the same basic pattern shared by all human beings.

Understanding the archetypes and how they are inter-related with one another is a complex and subtle task without apparent end. The archetypes are reflected both as interior, "personal" categories of experience, and simultaneously as external, collective patterns of history and culture. In fact, when we encounter any symbolic pattern or drama which spontaneously recurs both in the dreams and fantasies of individuals, and in the shape of collective, historical experience as well, we have discovered a formulation of an archetype. It is this quality of carrying essentially the same symbolic, dramatic energies on both the personal and collective scales that characterizes and defines the archetypes.

Any serious work with dreams will inevitably lead to an encounter with archetypal energies in one form or another. For this reason, I would like to offer a brief introduction to some of the archetypes most often encountered in the earlier stages of dream work. Like the list of universal elements present in the structure of dreams and dreaming in the previous chapter, this list is also partial. Definitions of the archetypes themselves may be formulated from various perspectives, emphasizing different elements of their inherently complex, multiple and subtle levels of meaning and significance. The figures of the Tarot deck and the poetic images of the *I Ching* are two alternate examples of systematic formulation of the archetypes.

In reading through this introduction to the archetypes, it is important to bear in mind that they always interpenetrate and inter-relate with one another in multiple ways. Like the organs of the body, they form a living whole. Also like the organs of the body, any effort to isolate and distinguish one from the rest in any absolute and final way destroys the living dynamics and leaves only a corpse. However, just as one can point to the heart and say that it does different things and serves different purposes than the liver, one can also delineate major functions for the archetypes, remembering always that life and living require them all working in balance and harmony with one another. Dreaming is a natural and spontaneous process which serves to maintain that evolving, dynamic balance. Conscious work with dreams can facilitate, enhance and intensify that natural, homeostatic process of growth and development.

To begin this brief excursion into the realm of the archetypes, let us look first at the archetype Jung named the "Persona." This is the archetype of psychological life most closely analogous to the skin—it is the part that shows, the visible "outside" of the whole dynamic system. In certain ways, the Persona is also analogous to Freud's formulation of the "ego" and the "super-ego," although Jung's development of the Persona lays greater stress on the unconscious and universal roots of this phenomenon, rather than upon its particular shape in any given society. The name "Persona" is drawn from the word the ancient Greeks used for the masks they employed in ritual religious theater. These masks served the dual purpose of exaggerating and formalizing the facial features of each character, making them individually identifiable, even from the back of the amphitheater, while also serving as megaphones, directing and projecting the actors' voices so that they could be clearly heard in their outdoor setting.

The archetypal Persona serves these same basic functions; it creates the consistently identifiable, formal face we wear, both individually and collectively. Just as everyone has a skin, everyone has a persona, no matter what any given Persona may look like.

The Persona is most easily recognizable in the specific decisions we make about how we wish to be perceived—in our choice of clothes, hair styles, figures of speech, public identifications with various groups, etc. Much of modern psychology has focused on the Persona and has made observable public behavior the primary universe of psychological discourse. In its most exaggerated form, this kind of Persona psychology is a little like imagining that the human body is composed of nothing but skin tissue, and prescribing skin lotion for everything from eczema to heart disease and broken bones. Where the Persona is directly involved, such "skin care" psychology will be effective, but where it is applied to matters more directly concerned with other archetypes below the "surface" of observed behavior, it will have a tendency to go astray and become counterproductive.

In relation to this metaphor of ego-as-skin, it is interesting to note that in the early development of the mammalian embryo, the brain begins as apparently undifferentiated skin tissue which implodes into the area of what is to become the head, forming a "bubble" of cells which then develops into the brain.

The tendency of Western psychology at the beginning of this century to focus on a prematurely closed fashion on issues related to the Persona was one of the cultural trends against which Jung struggled most consistently. For this reason, many archetypal scholars and therapists have tended to view the Persona somewhat negatively, particularly in contrast with energies from "deeper" within the collective unconscious. However, it is important to realize, amidst this "bad press" that the Persona has tended to receive, that the Persona is the archetype of interface between self and other, and is thus the basic archetype of all human society and culture. Without the Persona in its multiple manifestations in each of us, human society would be impossible, just as physical life would be impossible without the skin to protect the rest of the body from fluctuations in the environment and intrusions of dangerous external elements. In this vitally important sense, the collective resistance to alterations in traditional Persona forms can be seen as a basically healthy and life-preserving impulse, even though the rigid adherence to outmoded Persona forms and ideals is at the root of many of the most difficult and dangerous dramas of collective life.

It is in the act of contact between and among individual expressions of the archetype of Persona that human society is created and maintained. Even if a person rebels against the notion of "social convention" completely and decides to go forth naked, foregoing language and society altogether, all he or she does is to constellate a Persona of feral wildness, and thus gives that particular form and expression to the archetype. Even the seemingly bizarre personae of schizophrenic and autistic people give expression to the archetype in the same fashion as the personae projected by "normal" people in society. Indeed, in my experience there is always a poignant and ironic relationship between the accepted, collective forms given to the Persona, and the grotesque parodies of these forms manifested by psychotics.

We can see the ways in which this archetype expresses the same essential quality on a continuum from personal to collective. The Persona can be seen to be constellated into all the "public faces" of nation states, religions, and social institutions. Traditions of religious vestment, flags, official uniforms, anthems, legal codes, styles of public architecture, received interpretations of religious, national, and ethnic history, etc. all give specific shape to the archetypal Persona on a collective level, in exactly the same fashion as our individual choices of language, dress and hair style. The only meaningful distinction is one of scale, not of symbolic form.

One of the great archetypal problems of both individual psychology and historical/collective life is our tendency to believe that the expressions of the Persona constitute the whole of reality, and to deny and repress all other unconscious, irrational energies.

One way of better understanding our tragic, collective history of war and oppression is to recognize that where "God" is closely identified with the Persona, as in great measure it has been in the figure Yahweh/Jehovah/Allah, then it is inevitable that the repression of other archetypal elements will manifest itself in the violent oppression of those upon whom those repressed elements are projected in the historical scene. To the extent that the "God" of the Jewish/Christian/Islamic tradition is exclusively male, authoritative, and beyond question, and "eternal" (i.e., beyond change—despite the other equally real elements of archetypal human psychology which are repressed from this conception of the divine), to this same extent "God" is a metaphor of Persona masquerading as the totality of the psyche. The consequences of this archetypal error are known, tragic, and continuing.

The Middle Eastern tradition of monotheism has a tendency to promote premature closure by promoting the idea that there is only one truth for everyone, and anything which does not immediately appear to be formulated in the way the One Truth is formulated in your own particular religious franchise must be wrong, and hence *evil*. The dramas of repression and projection are mobilized in the name of absolute religious truth and the horrors of war, crusade, pogrom, and jihad are unleashed with a "clear conscience." These monotheisms, despite the genuine truths they proclaim, constantly exert a subtle influence to select only one view or myth as true, and to reject all others as false, in violation of the multiple, subtle, many-things-all-true-at-once quality of immediate, pre-conscious experience.

Another consequence of the prematurely closed monotheism of the Middle Eastern tradition has been the development of the scientific method in the West. The idea of "one truth" has more recently taken the form of the "one truth" of science and the increasing ability to manipulate and alter the natural environment through the application of the scientific method of analysis to the development of technology. It is ironic but far from accidental that this same manipulation of the physical world has also become the obvious source of our most pressing and catastrophic collective problems. The problem is not "science," but the prematurely closed, "monotheistic" notion that science is the only way to view reality.

The psychological truth of the ancient "polytheistic" religions is that we do indeed encounter the collective unconscious in the form of multiple archetypes; history and dream alike speak to us with many, conflicting voices. Indeed, I find it virtually impossible to imagine how human consciousness could have evolved without at least an initial perception of "many gods." If the divine were only perceived as One from the very beginning, then the basic separation between the perceiver and that which is perceived—the basic distinction upon which human consciousness and self-awareness rest—would be impossible. Unless the divine, transpersonal, beyond-the-grasp-of-words, unconscious energy is initially perceived in multiple and even competing forms, the experience of dynamic tension between competing demands, between the tug of "opposites" from which conscious choice and self-awareness emanate, could never come into existence.

There is good reason to suppose that one of the "secrets of the initiates" in ancient, seemingly polytheistic mystery cults was that indeed, behind the illusion of "the gods," All Is One. In our own epoch, it is clearly one of the "secrets of the initiates" into the modern esoteric knowledge of psychology that although All Is One, the immediate experience of unconscious energies welling up spontaneously into waking life is one of multiple forces and energies—partial and seemingly separate elements of interior life not always in harmonious concert with each other. In this coincidence of seeming opposites lie the roots of the spiritual debate over "free will" versus "determinism." If God is truly One, how can free will exist? If there is free will, how can God be One and all-powerful? Part of the solution to this apparent paradox is to expand the concept of "God" beyond the limits of the archetype of Persona.

When we manifest the Persona in the world, we are forced to exaggerate some elements of our spontaneous being and to edit out others. Each time we make choices about what to say and do in order to facilitate the orderly and peaceful progress of our lives, we fail to give conscious expression to the more disorderly and potentially disruptive impulses that spring spontaneously from within. Thus each one of us gives shape to the archetypal energy most directly counterpoised to the Persona—the archetype that Jung named the Shadow. Just as our physical bodies cast shadows in sunlight, so our psychological personae create a Shadow— a dark outline in the same shape as the Persona where the light of consciousness does not fall, as a result of our habitual repression. In this sense, the Shadow is the archetype of the threshold between conscious self-awareness and the unconscious. The Shadow is composed at this level of all that we have repressed and denied, both individually and collectively. In another, deeper sense, the Shadow is composed of *everything* that is unconscious in us—the entire content of our unrecognized interior life. For this reason,

there is a tendency for the Shadow to be archetypally "dark,"
symbolizing the darkness where the light of consciousness has not
yet fallen.

The association between darkness and that which is unconscious is universal and is in itself an archetype. One way that this
archetypal association manifests itself in dreams is that there is a
tendency for the quality of light in dreams to be metaphoric of the
quality of waking consciousness that has already been brought to
the main theme of the dream. Thus when dreams are brightly lit
and well illuminated, I tend to look first for issues and consider-
ations that have already been well formulated and thought about
in waking life. Conversely, if precisely the same action takes place
in dream that is badly illuminated where the dreamer has difficulty seeing things clearly, I tend to search first for problems and developments that are still relatively unrecognized by the dreamer
in waking life. I have even had the experience of realizing that the
memory of a past, "poorly lit" dream has changed and become
"brighter" as a result of work bringing significant elements of the
dream's meaning "to light."

The Shadow most often appears initially to us in one dream
as ugly, evil, and frightening. Closer examination reveals that in
the midst of that darkness is the very thing that has been lacking
and is most required for further healthy development. The
"dark" figure of the Shadow always bears the great gift. In order
to receive the great gift, the fear and repugnance first awakened
by the "dark" aspect of the Shadow must be overcome. The
dreams of Elias Howe and of "Margaret" both clearly illustrate
this archetypal drama.

To turn for a moment to the collective, transpersonal manifestation of the Shadow, we can see this archetype clearly constellated in the concrete forms of religious architecture around the
planet. There is a marked tendency for all religious sanctuaries
and places of worship to be guarded by grotesque and horrific images: there are the gargoyles of Christian architectural tradition,
the skull markers of shamanic practice, the wind demons in front
of Shinto temples, the gigantic grinning serpents that guard the
temples in Indian and Central American tradition, the dragon
door-guards of Chinese temple architecture—the list is very long.
In each case, the seemingly horrific figure serves two purposes.

First, it serves to discourage and frighten off anyone who is not an initiate into that particular religious tradition (in part by giving warning of the non-human status of non-initiates). Simultaneously, it serves to educate those who are permitted to enter the sacred precincts that such images are only "playful"—that they mark the entrance to the sacred space where communion with the divine takes place, and are not at all to be feared. Thus at a level often well below consciousness, the demonic door-guards built into the facades of places of religious worship all over the world "preach" the same message: "Fear not." They give concrete representation to the symbolic/psychological/spiritual truth that conscious access to the transpersonal realm of the archetypes is only gained after encountering and transforming the fear of the Shadow.

Once the fear of the Shadow has been overcome and the personal shadow is accepted as an inner reality, the dreamer often encounters other constellations of archetypal figures and dramas. Jung once commented with regard to the work of Freud that in formulating the Oedipal Complex and identifying its mythological dimension, he was defining an archetype, but only one among many. The fact that Freud found it possible to see the archetype of the Oedipal drama as the one basic model to which all other formulations of interior life could be reduced is in part a result of the fact that the archetypes do possess the quality of metamorphosis into one another. Once again, it is finally an "aesthetic" choice where one decides to stand in order to view the vortex of relativity that is human experience, where one decides to assert the absolute ground, even though ever-increasing experience suggests that ultimately there is no ground—only the processes of energy turning into matter and back into energy again.

Acceptance of the Shadow is not something that can be done once and completed. Every step of growth and development, every dream death and subsequent rebirth, leads to a reconstellation of the energies and archetypal figures of interior life. The Shadow takes on a new shape and requires the basic moral act of honest self-relflection all over again.

The Persona and the Shadow are often among the first archetypal figures to be encountered at the beginning of dream work. Dreams of hair style, clothing, and public occasion are often related to issues of the Persona. The common dream of being naked or impartially or improperly dressed at a public occasion is often related at one level to the fear of "exposure"—the fear of self-revelation as the mask of the Persona is lifted. When dreams are shared openly, the more complete and true self beyond the formulations of the Persona becomes visible. Whether or not the nakedness in such dreams is cause for anxiety and concern on the part of the dreamer is often, at one level at least, an indication of how the dreamer feels about the revelation of the self behind and beyond the Persona.

The Shadow is most easily recognizable in dreams in the figures who are the most threatening and repulsive. In waking life, the projection of the Shadow can be recognized most easily in the shape of those whom we most dislike and fear. As long as we continue to perceive these Shadow energies in ourselves only in projected form, we will never be able to deal with them adequately. This sense of inadequate response drives us to ever greater and more ironic efforts to control external realities. This vain effort to control "others" makes us more and more out of control of ourselves. As the mechanism of repression and projection drains off more and more energy from our interior dynamics, we feel increasingly frantic, trapped, and at the mercy of circumstances beyond our control. The drama of repression and projection creates the horrors and ironies of our individual and collective lives.

The same drama of repression and projection of the Shadow can be seen on a larger, historical scale; it is ironic but not accidental that the Nazis believed that the Jews were attempting to take over the world through a combination of military and conspiratorial means because they believed themselves to be the exclusive "chosen of God." This projection allowed the Nazis to feel justified in attempting to take over the world through a combination of military and conspiratorial means because they perceived themselves to be the "chosen of God"—the racial group with the best and strongest physical and cultural characteristics. It is ironic but not accidental that medieval Christianity was prepared to sacrifice men, women and children to the sword in the name of the "Prince of Peace," and to torture and murder "heretics" and "witches" in the name of God's love. The litany of tragic ironies born of repression and projection of the Shadow is almost endless. In every case, from the most personal and idiosyncratic to the most collective and historical, the archetypal nature of the drama remains the same. The Shadow is denied and repressed as internal reality and is projected so that it is observed as an exclusively external reality. The strength of the driven, psychotic response to the hallucinatory perception of the Shadow as wholly other is in direct proportion to the size of the self-deceptive repression. We seldom project the Shadow upon people who are themselves wholly without the traits we are projecting, but the intensity of the fear/repugnance/dislike is a barometer of the strength of the repressed energies within, not a response to the traits as they actually exist in the other. In the process of repression, we deny our own humanity—we deny the humanity of the Shadow element in ourselves. Thus it becomes easy to deny the humanity of others, and to treat them as objects as we project our shadow energies on them.

The projection of the Shadow is clearly at work in the midst of the horrors of war, racism, sexism, agism, and the technological destruction of the biosphere. At the collective level, the repressed collective Shadow of white-male-technological culture is repressed and projected out onto the non-white, non-male, non-technological world as a "justification" of exploitation and oppression. In the collective, it is clear that the very elements which are projected by racists, sexists, and technocrats (the spontaneity, emotionality, physicality, relatedness to nature, etc.) are themselves the very elements that are required for the positive transformation of our authoritarian, suicidal technological society. Once again, this is the historical height of irony, but it is far from anomalous or accidental. To save ourselves, we must acknowledge the Shadow as an interior reality, individually and collectively. In fact, it appears that we can save ourselves collectively only as we heal ourselves personally. The two efforts are merely different aspects of the same archetypal process. In this vitally important sense, the nature of the archetypal human predicament is not fundamentally altered by technology—we are still faced with the fundamental choices of self-knowledge or repression, life or death, utopia or oblivion. The Christian admonition to love our enemies and the older pagan admonition to know ourselves are at this level simply different ways of describing the same process of archetypal development.

The Shadow is not the only archetype to be repressed and projected, however. The phenomenon of "love at first sight," as well as less dramatic and more commonplace forms of mutual attraction and emotion, is always based to a great extent on the repression and projection of the sexual complement. Jung called the archetype of sexual complement in men and women the "Anima" and "Animus" respectively. Each figure represents and constellates our deepest knowledge and intuitions about the opposite sex. The Anima is the archetypal woman in the psyche of every man, and the Animus is the archetypal man in the psyche of every woman.

The earliest personal shape is given to these archetypes by the contrasexual parents or parental substitutes. In this fashion, the Animus and Anima are also deeply related to the archetypal parents—the Great Mother and the All Father. The particular shape we give to these archetypal dramas of Man/Woman, Mother/Father, Self/Other in our individual experience determines the particular shapes of our individual relationships.

These archetypes and archetypal dramas have collective, historical/mythological forms as well. Each society also resolves the tensions and dynamics of Animus and Anima in its own unique fashion, while at the same time repeating endlessly the same themes and forms. The collective oppression of women since the collapse of the great pre-historic matriarchies at the close of pre-literate times reflects the collective state of the repression of the archetypal Anima in men. In historical, patriarchal times, the Anima and the Great Mother have been repressed and fragmented into dichotomous images, such as the "virgin" and the "whore." The forcible fragmentation of expressions of archetypal femininity into seemingly polar, mutually exclusive figures is a function of this repression. The repression and denial of humanity to the Anima is the archetypal drama of sexism, just as repression and denial of the humanity of the Shadow is the archetypal drama of war and racism.

In the Catholic tradition, the figure of Mary unites the fragmented images of Anima and Great Mother in a single form, and here again we see an example of the tendency of the archetypes to metamorphose into one another in rhythmically repetitive, shape-changing dance. In Margaret's dream of leaving the dance, the

Animus and the Shadow merge to create the figure of the "black rapist/murderer." At the same time, in the ambiguous figure of the black man, we also have an embodiment of another archetype—the Trickster.

The Trickster, like all the archetypes, is at once a mythological figure and an element of our own interior psychological make-up. The Trickster is another archetype standing at the boundaries between consciousness and the unconscious. The Trickster can be either male or female and manifests in a figure representing both the self-deception and creative possibility of consciousness itself. Most often, the Trickster is lowly and despised in the hierarchy of social power and importance but at the same time, all over the world, the advances of consciousness and human civilization are considered to be the gifts and creations of the Trickster.

In Margaret's active imagination/Gestalt work exercise with her dream, the Trickster is revealed in the figure of the black man as he transforms himself in her active imagination from a murderer into a protector and gift-giver. He is Shadow, Animus, and Trickster in one. In the same fashion, the Shadow and the Trickster constellate together into the figures of the "cannibals" in Elias Howe's dream. The Trickster is the "messenger of the gods" who chooses to take many different playful forms. The Trickster simultaneously embodies both the creative possibilities and the habitual stupidities of human consciousness.

The new consciousness, the new way of thinking and feeling and being that is always the Trickster's tricky gift, is itself embodied in another archetypal figure, the Divine Child. The Divine Child is almost always born amidst trouble and has seemingly miraculous powers of speech and locomotion at birth, and even in the womb before birth. The Divine Child most often survives to bring about a total change and transformation of the world. Perhaps the most familiar example of the archetype of Divine Child in Western culture is the infant Jesus.

However, the figure of the infant Jesus is clearly related to the other divine children, born amidst trouble, of divine parentage, possessed of miraculous powers, who later alter the shape of human society entirely. The birth stories of Hermes, Hercules, Dionysus, Tammuz, Teliessin, Moses, Buddha, Muhammad, *et al.* reflect the same archetypal pattern and can be seen as slightly different embodiments of the same archetype. In John Wyndham's novel, *The Midwitch Cuckoos,* the children born after the mysterious visitation from space are contemporary examples of the mythic drama of the Divine Child, the drama of the birth of new consciousness. In Wyndham's novel, the "changelings" are all murdered by the leaders of nation-states out of fear of the children's telepathic interconnections. In this story, we have a reflection on how the drama turns out when Herod's armies are successful in murdering the infant whose birth was foretold. Even with this unusual twist of plot, we can see that the same basic archetypal/mythological drama of the Birth of the Divine Child is being enacted.

Most often, the Divine Child survives the efforts of the old, doomed order to destroy him or her. In the mythological narratives, as well as the dreams of individuals, animals often play a critical role in the preservation of the Divine Child into adulthood. The Animals constitute another archetype usually encountered near the beginning of dream work. The Animals are always present, no matter what stage of individual and collective development has been reached. Jung has suggested that the archetype of the Animals is at one level a symbolic shape of instinctual "animal" drives. This is a particularly persuasive suggestion when we consider the evolution of religious iconography from the earliest archeological remains. The earliest figures of the Great Mother and the earliest representations of shaman figures on the cave walls of the last Ice Age (circa 15000 B.C.) always are found in close association with representations of animals. In the case of the shaman figures, the animal and human forms are blended into one. Looking at these figures, the idea of men dressed in the skins of animals for ritual purposes is inescapable. Another, more subtle, but nonetheless inescapable idea that arises when contemplating these ancient images of shamans is of animal consciousness turning into human consciousness, and human consciousness turning back into animal awareness again in shamanic/religious trance. The speculation is all the more convincing when we discover that this is in fact the trance practice of shamans in historical and contemporary non-technological cultures the world over. The shaman becomes the animal in trance and has the animal's experience.

At this level of archetypal significance the animal-headed deities of Egypt and elsewhere can be understood as representations of the evolution of human consciousness into increasingly more developed and individuated states. In myth and dream, when the animals come to offer aid or rise to hinder and threaten, at one level we are looking at metaphoric representations of the energies of instinct and wordless, unconscious, natural drives in our lives. Within this general archetypal pattern, specific animal forms often have specific reference to particular instincts. As has already been mentioned, there is an archetypal resonance between the image of the horse and the physical condition of the dreamer at the moment of dreaming about horses. The dream images of dogs and cats have a tendency to constellate masculine and feminine instinctual sexual energies. The cat has been an archetypal symbol of feminine sexuality since even before the institutionalized worship of Bastet was organized in ancient Egypt more than three thousand years ago. At the level of instinctual life, history and archetype reflect one another.

In myth and dream, Anima turns into Cat, and Animus turns into Dog, hinting at their secret unity in the One that is All. Clearly, sex is not the only instinctual drive embodied in the archetype of the Animals. Jung has suggested that the relative evolutionary development of the archetypal Animal in any given instance is often a reflection of the evolutionary stage of development of the instinctual energy in the dynamic makeup of interior life. Thus dragons represent an ancient instinctual lineage. The archetype is now currently constellating into the notion of the "reptilian brain" currently in fashion among some brain researchers.

The Animals, like the Shadow, represent that which is not conscious. This connection often results in figures which end up of both Shadow and Animal. We see the two archetypes merging in figures like Cerberus, the horrifying guard dog at the threshold of the underworld. Animal and Anima merge into the figure Al Buroq, the human headed sphinx/horse that carries Muhammad on his dream tour of the cosmos of Allah. It is interesting to note that such hybrid human/animal combinations as the sphinx and Al Buroq appear spontaneously in the dreams of people who have no conscious knowledge of these mythological figures. Like the Manticore in Robertson Davies' novel of the same name, these animal/human hybrids most often represent an uncompleted process of development and transformation, much as if one were to look into an insect chrysalis before the metamorphosis from crawling-form to flying-form was complete. Once again, the archetypal drama is one and the same at both the individual psychological scale and collective/historical scale. The dimensions of combined animal/human form represent transitional phases of developing consciousness.

An Animal archetype that deserves special mention here is the Spirit Bird. This archetype can be recognized in the shapes of mythological birds around the world who serve as messengers from the realm of God, or the gods, the realm of human consciousness. Again, the most immediately familiar example of this archetype comes from the traditions of Christian iconography. The "Dove" form of the Holy Spirit is clearly related to all the other bird forms who bring the divine message from the upper realms to the surface of the earth where human beings dwell in their limited, time-bound existence. Raven, Thunderbird, the Phoenix, Zeus' Eagle, Vishnu's Garuda—all are exemplars of this archetypal figure. The ancient religious practice of divining from the flight of birds is another example of the ways in which this archetype manifests itself in our collective experience. In the East, and in Native American mythology and religious belief, this archetype has a tendency to manifest in the shape of water fowl—ducks, geese, swans, loons, herons, *et al.* In this form, the Spirit Bird carries the divine message not only down from the sky to the "middle earth" realm of human habitation, but up from the watery depths as well.

The archetypes manifest themselves in collective experience through the metaphors of ritual religious practice. The archeological evidence of pre-historic religious practice clearly shows that the first intuition of divinity in human consciousness took a feminine rather than a masculine form. For at least twenty thousand years, between the time of the last major Ice Age and the invention of writing around 1500 B.C., the primary conception of divine form was the Great Mother. The ritual practice of her worship became increasingly elaborate and complex, reflecting the increasing elaboration and complexity of human social forms after the establishment of settled communities and the introduction of agriculture. By the time of the great, patriarchal, Indo-European migration/invasion, the worship of the Great Mother was clearly established in the highly developed, agricultural/urban civilizations of Europe, Asia, and the Near East. The Great Mother was worshiped under many names in different localities, but the ritual formulation of the archetype was fundamentally the same.

The Great Mother required no masculine aid in conceiving children. The entire physical universe was conceived of as her body, and all living things as her children. She gave birth to all and nourished all, but at the same time she condemned all to inevitable death. The Great Mother devoured all her children in death, promising rebirth and reincarnation to those who followed her law and celebrated her seasonal rituals. When the Indo-Europeans burst forth from the Trans-Caucasian region of what is now the Soviet Union, they brought with them a different vision of the divine. With the imposition of their military and political hegemony, the Indo-Europeans deposed the Great Mother and replaced her with the All-Father, a corresponding formulation of divinity in masculine form. The patriarchal, masculinist cast of the majority of historical world religions today is the result of this pre-historic politico-religious struggle.

In historical times, the mythology and religious practices of the matriarchal, Great Mother religion were collectively repressed into the shapes of "folklore" and "old wives' tales." Several scholars have argued quite convincingly that the metaphors of "witchcraft" and "fairy folk" represent a repressed but nonetheless relatively continuous tradition of persistent worship of the Great Mother. In Greek mythology, the myths of Demeter and Persephone and Eros and Psyche retain their mythological/religious status, and also point clearly to the similarities of archetype shared by the folk and fairy stories which represent the continuation of the religious tradition of the Great Mother even into modern times.

The systematic repression of the religion of the Great Mother has in no way diminished the unconscious power of the archetype of the Great Mother in the contemporary psyche. The persistent importance of this archetype can be seen in the phrases "Mother Nature" and "Mother Earth." The fear of death which plays such a large role in the repressions of modern society is deeply and inextricably intertwined with the collective repression of the archetypal Great Mother. The matriarchal non-technological concept of the sacredness of the earth—the belief that the earth is the living body of the Goddess and must be treated with awe and reverence—stands in stark contrast to the masculinist, patriarchal notion that the earth is merely a "stupid" and inanimate mass of natural resources to be exploited in the most brutally "efficient" fashion. These contrasting attitudes and the collective actions that stem from them show the extent to which the repression of the archetypal Great Mother as a formulation of the divine exists at the center of the ecological crisis.

In comparison to the Great Mother, the All-Father is a relatively new and "young" archetypal figure. Several scholars have undertaken symbolic analysis of the evolution of this archetypal figure from its first appearance as the male consort of the Great Mother. In its earliest form, the archetype of the divine-as-masculine appeared as the so-called "Lord of the Animals" associated with the ritual practices of the seasonally dying and resurrecting son/consort of the Great Mother. These dying/resurrecting gods developed eventually into figures of the omnipotent All-Father, who has no more need of feminine help in creating life than the Great Mother needed masculine assistance to create an offspring.

It has been argued quite persuasively by many scholars that male ignorance of the role of copulation in impregnation lies close to the center of the social and religious structures of the worship of the Great Mother. Branislaw Malinowski's work among the Trobriand Islanders prior to World War II revealed a contemporary society in which men were ignorant of their role in procreation, believing that women incarnated the souls of deceased ancestors through private rituals, or only in the company of other women. Malinowski did not interview Trobriand women on this question, and he merely assumed that women were also ignorant of paternity.

Research into the initiation and cult practices of women in the ancient Mediterranean matriarchies strongly suggests, however, that a part of the "secret knowledge" was a rendition of "facts of life," together with a most potent and binding oath not to reveal this knowledge to men. It is recorded by the early Greeks that any man found within a certain distance of the Great Mother's cult and initiation center at Elusis was summarily executed. Robert Graves, among others, has suggested that in addition to military superiority derived from riding on horseback, instead of using horses merely as draught animals, the Indo-Europeans conquered the great matriarchal societies because they brought with them the knowledge that women could not conceive children unassisted. It has been suggested that the figure of the "centaur" in Greek mythology springs from the first amazing sight of a man riding a horse, appearing as a single creature. This identification of the centaurs with the horse-riding Indo-European invaders is even more persuasive when we recall that all the sons of kings and aristocrats were required to spend their late adolescence under the tutelage of centaurs to learn the art of war.

The archetypal figures of the Great Mother and All-Father may appear in the dreams of individuals, but the closely related archetypal figures of the Wise Old Woman and Wise Old Man appear with much greater frequency. Jung called these figures "Mana-Personalities," suggesting that like the Animus and Anima, they are sexually differentiated faces of a single archetypal energy. These figures are the embodiment of the oldest and wisest and most loving possibilities in ourselves. The figures of the Old Man and the Old Woman in my dream of killing Clint Eastwood (recounted in Chapter VIII) are clearly representative examples of this archetype. The dream records of several great poets and religious leaders reveal exemplars of Great Mother and All-Father, as well as many other archetypal figures. These figures also appear in the dreams of profoundly disturbed people. In these instances, there is often the most poignant and ironic evocation of the Persona as well.

In association with these figures, the archetypal figure of the Willing Sacrifice also often makes its appearance. (This figure is also discussed briefly in Chapter IX.) Conn Edda's horse is at one level a close relative of Deer Brother in Native American religious practice. It was the widespread belief in many Native American cultures that hunted animals could only be killed and eaten if they agreed. Every day for perhaps more than a million years, shamanic prayers and trances were practiced to convince the Deer Brother to allow himself to be killed and eaten again. In a reflection of the ecological good-sense that flows from more conscious acknowledgment of the Great Mother, the Native American hunters would never kill does and fawns unless buck deer were absolutely impossible to find, and even then would resort to killing a female or immature deer only to avoid starvation. When such a kill was made, the ritual expiation that necessarily followed was unusually intense.

The archetype of Willing Sacrifice is at the center of Christian religious intuition. It is often difficult for Christians to grasp that this archetype does not begin or end with the figure of Jesus. Christian mythos embodies ancient, archetypal themes found around the world from the earliest periods. Many traditions depict the tree-cross-gallows upon which the Willing Sacrifice is offered. Odin (Wotan) sacrifices himself upon the World Tree for seven full days in order to gain the knowledge that he is himself and god, literally the "All-Father," at one and the same time. To the extent that the Great Mother embodies the entire physical world, she too is an original expression of the Willing Sacrifice—giving her body to the lives of her children, and then sacrificing herself to herself, devouring them in death.

This ancient lineage of Great Mother-as-Willing Sacrifice is given graphic form in India in the worship of Kali. Ritual images of Kali often show her having severed her own head, holding it by the hair away from the body so it can drink the fountain of blood that spouts from the severed neck. Westerners often find such Hindu images "barbaric" and "horrifying," while at the same time seeing the equally barbaric image of Suffering Christ Upon the Cross as the height of sublimity. To Eastern eyes the graphic realism of crucifix images makes them appear much more "crude" and "barbaric" and "horrifying" than the dream-like image of the goddess and her living severed head. Here again, we see the ironic ways that repression and projection alter our crucially important aesthetic judgment. Christians who have difficulty in acknowledging the fact Christianity stands among the religions of the world in embodying the archetype of Willing Sacrifice, not above them, also seem to have difficulty in perceiving the manifestations of the archetypes in the metaphors of contemporary scientific research. Einstein's demonstration that matter and energy are merely manifestations of a single essential process also gives shape to intuitions of the divine. The complete inability of contemporary research to distinguish in any absolute way between waves and particles, the grudging scientific acceptance that there is no "objective reality" separate from the human perception of it—all of these contemporary "conclusions" in a process where there are clearly no conclusions, no limits to truth beyond the arbitraries of language—point to and echo the ancient myths where "God" dismembers and willingly sacrifices Her/Him/Them/It-self in order to create the universe experienced by human consciousness.

For the Hindus, the Willing Sacrifice is carried out in the midst of dreaming. That the waking world is but "God's dream" is a metaphor of simultaneous sacrifice and dismemberment into partial fragments, while at the same time remaining absolutely whole, calm, and ultimately one unmoved. Waking life itself is perceived as the dream where the divine One is in All the Many that we are, and in each in particular. In this sense, the Hindu concept of human life and history as a "divine dream" is a source of the Universalist movement in world religion. There is no "eternal damnation" because everything and everyone, even the greatest "sins" and "sinners," ultimately come from God and thus are returned to God and reconciled utterly and completely in the One when the dreaming demiurge awakens. In Hindu and Buddhist religion and psychology, all human experience takes on the quality of infinite mathematical regression—every "state of consciousness," other than the total extinction of the self in the Self through meditative discipline, is merely a dream within a dream, within a dream . . .

The archetype of Willing Sacrifice passes through the images from animal to human and beyond into the shapes of the cosmos itself. The Mandala is another archetypal image evoking the totality of All in the perception of One. The Mandala form always combines the circle with the angular figure. It is interesting to note that although "proto-Mandala" and spiral forms appear in the legacy of images handed down in the archeology of pre-history, the Mandala as combination of circle and angular form does not appear until the agricultural revolution and the abandonment of a completely nomadic way of life. This has led Joseph Campbell to suggest that one archetype of the Mandala is the archetype of dif-

ferentiated, urban civilization itself. It is clear that the Mandala is
also clearly associated with the invention of the potter's wheel,
which also appears in the earliest discovered remains of settled,
agricultural communities yet discovered. These earliest agricultural communities appear in the plains of what is now Turkey and
are dated to roughly 7000 B.C.

Mandala forms are found around the planet, in all cultures,
associated always with religious contemplation, meditation, trance
and prayer. The Mandala always has a defined center, and is most
often divided into four quadrants. In this way, the figure of the
square and the figure of the circle are brought together to create a
new image embodying and harmonizing them both. The rose-
windows of the Christian tradition, the sanskrit mandalas of Hindu, Buddhist, Jain, Taoist, and Shinto practice, the Esquimo
"pocket prayer discs," the Native American medicine wheels and
dream shields, the stone circles of prehistoric European provenance, *et al.* are all examples of the Mandala archetype.

Jung even goes so far as to suggest that the metaphor of the
Flying Saucer is a species of Mandala image. In his *Flying Saucers—
A Modern Myth of Things Seen in the Sky,* he describes the archetypal, centering quality of the Mandala and calls it an "individuation
symbol." The ritual practices involving contemplating the Mandala around the world all involve identifying consciousness with the
central point and individuating the four functions and the energies of interior life so that they are conscious and in harmonious
balance—mirroring the harmony and balance and "centeredness"
of the Mandala form. The Mandala, being an archetype, reflects
not only the interior process of centering and contemplation of
the divine center and source, but also the outer "Mandala" of organized society and culture. The Mandala arises with urban life,
and the design of the sacred and later "ideal" city is archetypically
depicted in Mandala form. The divine ruler stands at the center of
the properly ordered state—the central intermediary between the
realm of human waking existence and the realm of the gods or
God. Jung goes on to provide a volume of examples of this collec-
tive/historical manifestation of the Mandala, demonstrating its
deep association with the idea of divine harmony and order reflected in the well-ordered structuring of collective human life.

Having established the archetypal nature and function of the Mandala in its collective/historical forms, Jung goes on to point out that Mandalas also appear spontaneously in the dreams and fantasies of individual clients in analysis, serving essentially the same "ordering" and "centering" function when they appear. Based on this analysis, Jung suggests that the "flying saucer" appears, at one level at least, to be a Mandala that is not seen directly, face-on, but rather one which is perceived in the air, in the middle distance, seen at an angle, almost always in association with the most cosmic and far-reaching possibilities of change and communication with "superior beings." Again he musters many persuasive examples from both the individual and collective realms to demonstrate that the "flying saucer" variety of Mandala is deeply associated with periods of cataclysmic social and individual change. The image of the flying saucer/Mandala has an archetypal tendency to appear at moments when the "old order" (both within and without) has begun to crumble, and the "new order" that is to replace it has not yet revealed itself, but exists *in potentia*. The flying saucer imagery is thus a metaphoric representation of that sense of impending cataclysm combined with the intuition that the possibility of creating a completely new, "divine" social and personal order and harmony exists in the midst of the frightening perception of increasing chaos. In this sense, the "flying saucer" often comes immediately before the birth of the Divine Child (as it does in the John Wyndham novel) and in many other popular myths of "things seen in the sky."

In the West, the Compass Rose is one of the most important and significant exemplars of the Mandala archetype. The Compass Rose points to the four directions and orients the map reader, placing him/her in the center of the great circle of his or her own cosmos as defined by the encircling horizon. The Compass Rose orients and orders the universe. The map reader is quartered by the four directions, at the center of the cross they form. In this way, the "secular" act of map reading with the aid of the Compass Rose symbolically reflects and reduplicates the same act of centering the proper placement in the cosmos associated with overtly religious meditation on the Mandala form. These examples also show the nature of the Rose as the Mandala-flower of the West, just as the Lotus is the natural Mandala-flower of the East, each symbolizing the inherent, "divine" order and beauty of the spontaneous natural world.

In the rose and the lotus, humankind has perceived the inherent, natural Mandala-form of radial symmetry. In this sense, the Mandala is an archetypal form generated by unconscious nature well prior to the evolution of human consciousness. Even older than the lotus and the rose, and more profoundly woven into the very fabric of the universe, is the archetypal form of the Spiral. The Spiral manifests spontaneously on every scale of perception—from the shape of galaxies to the shape of the DNA helix. Human consciousness perceives and understands consciously that the Spiral form is the inevitable result of rhythmic, repeating, cyclic processes manifesting in the inexorable forward flow of time. There is good reason to believe this perception of archetypal/divine order and meaning inhering in the very fabric and nature of the universe and spontaneously experiencing itself in archetypal Spiral form that led the earliest prehistoric human ancestors to venerate the Spiral form of seashells, most particularly the fossil forms of ammonite shells when they discovered them in stone, far from any sea. The Spiral appears spontaneously in dreams in association with this notion of rhythmic, cyclic patterns of growth and development of the psyche. It appears often as spiral stairs, spiral paths up mountains, or down into chasms. It even is echoed in the spiraling flight of birds, planes, "flying saucers," etc. in dreams.

Closely associated with the archetype of the Spiral is the archetypal image of the Perilous Journey. Throughout the world at all periods of history, human life is metaphorically depicted as a perilous journey. The shape and spiritual geography of the journey is often in spiral form (such as Dante's descent into Hell or the hero's penetration of the labyrinth). The journey invariably takes on the quality of a quest—a covenant with some greater power or ideal to search until the "treasure," the thing of lasting value, has been found or recovered. When we dream of being on a journey, at some level there is almost always an archetypal resonance of the image with our "life's journey." Often the journey dreams depict the specific dangers and distractions we are encountering on our path at this particular moment in our waking lives. Such dreams often have as one of their central meanings the evocation of a larger perspective on our lives than we may be consciously maintaining.

The Perilous Journey often takes us down into the darkness, down into "hell," or down into the "land of the dead." All of these locations are at one level archetypal representations of the unconscious as a whole. The visually dark quality of these descents is most often an archetypal representation of the lack of conscious awareness we have regarding the energies residing in our unknown depths. In mythology, the heroes and heroines who undertake this journey, the "journey of individuation," are often warned that they will "never return." At one level this is simply a representation of the social and cultural forces which always mobilize to prevent change, but at another level these warnings are also statements of truth—when the journey of increasing self-awareness is undertaken, the person who first begins the descent into the depths indeed never does return. The one who returns is someone who has died and been reborn into a new form. This mythological transformation will occur many times over the course of a lifetime of journeying.

In the realm of myth and dream, as in physics, energy cannot be destroyed, only transformed from one state into another. Each dream death is the necessary prelude to the rebirth of the transformed self. Individually and collectively, change always brings us face to face with our fears of death. The "death" of the old to make way for the new is a psychological and spiritual death we fearfully equate with physical death. Acting out of this fear of change-perceived-as-death, we create a kind of "living death" where both personality and society are held in some rigid, "eternal," unchanging image. When we are in the grip of this fear of death, we project death outward onto others in a desperate attempt to avoid our own repressed internal agonies of frustrated growth. We go to obsessive lengths, like Dracula and Herod, to preserve our "undying" state.

In this sense, Herod and Christ are opposite sides of the same coin. Herod, when faced with the knowledge that the Divine Child has been born and that not only are his days as monarch coming to an end but the "eternal" order which he represents is passing away, attempts to kill the spark of new possibility. He becomes an archetypal vampire and drinks the blood of others in a clear metaphor of the process of repression and projection. Christ, on the other hand, when faced with the inevitability of his own death, preaches faith in rebirth and acceptance of death as the necessary prelude to resurrection in divine union with the All-Father. At one crucially important level, this is an archetypal metaphor of the psychological process of death and rebirth that is at the center of the process of individuation.

The vampire's illusion of "immortality" is only purchased at the cost of obsessive, repressive behavior. In the midst of the drama of repression and projection the ego cannot "reflect," cannot look inward. This is metaphorically depicted in vampire folklore as the inability to cast any reflections in mirrors. The vampire can survive in this state only by metaphorically drinking the blood of others, which all too often takes on the waking life form of warfare and organized bloodshed. As the vampire stories so vividly depict, this is indeed a state of "living death" where all change is resisted and "immortality" is synonymous with mummification. I suspect this is a major reason for the perennial popularity of the crudest of vampire stories. Somewhere below the level of consciousness we recognize the drama as true, as accurately reflective of the horrors we visit upon ourselves when we confuse change with death and try to create a completely stable, "changeless" reality which inevitably turns into a sort of "living death."

This archetypal vampire drama also reflects itself in the life of the intellect. An intellectual equivalent of the vampire's illusion of immortality is the system of thought and world view which is total, complete, and beyond the need of further questioning or revision. It is only through the holes and spaces and at the edges of what we know that what we do not yet know and understand can enter our consciousness. If we pretend that there are no holes or spaces or confused growing edges in our lives and systems of thought and belief, then we are creating for ourselves an illusion of "certainty" and "changeless immortality."

The dispelling of such illusions is always initially frightening and painful. But when we let go and accept the death of the old in ourselves and in our culture (often experiencing it as death in dreams), this act releases the energy previously wasted in maintaining the self-deception of repression and projection, and brings about "rebirth" and "life everlasting"—an archetypal message imbedded in each of the world religions and expressed in the symbolic social and cultural vernacular of every people.

Again, the conscious acceptance of the Shadow in ourselves must always accompany each new step on the path of individuation. A waking life meditation that I have found particularly useful in this regard comes from Ram Dass. He suggests the mantra (similar to the "ejaculatory prayer" of the Christian tradition) "I am that too," to be consciously recited every time we are particularly moved by some event in the outer world. This means saying "I am that too" to oneself no matter what the feelings evoked by the situation may be. In situations where horror and repugnance are evoked by the outer experience, the understanding that "I am that too" is simultaneously a meditation upon loving one's enemies and accepting to consciousness the Shadow within at one and the same moment. Extraordinary states of awareness and insight can be achieved by remembering to recite this mantra in dreams as well as waking life. The tremendous energy released by meditative efforts of this sort comes in large measure from the rechanneling of psychic energy away from repetitive unconscious preservation into conscious choice. It is only when we are calmly conscious that "I am that too" that we are able to tap and make creative use of our deepest energies.

Summary: ENCOUNTERING THE ARCHETYPES IN DREAMS, MYTH, AND HISTORY

When we examine dreams with an eye to their meaning and structure, we discover that dreams speak a universal language of metaphor and symbol. Basic patterns of human instinct and development are revealed in the dreams of each person, and these same patterns are also reflected in the myths, religious beliefs, social practices, and cultural circumstances of all people around the world. Carl Jung, the Swiss psychiatrist and historian of culture, called these basic patterns "archetypes."

Just as there are basic patterns, or archetypes, of biological form, so there are also basic structural patterns to the human psyche. Each person is an absolutely unique physical specimen, while at the same time embodying the same basic physical structure shared by all human beings. So it is with the psyche. Each one of us embodies the archetypes of the objective psyche, or "collective unconscious," in our unique and personal fashion, while still repeating the same basic pattern shared by all human beings.

Understanding the archetypes and how they inter-relate is a complex and subtle task without apparent end. The archetypes are reflected both as personal, interior categories of experience, and as collective patterns of history and culture.

Very briefly, some of the major archetypes often encountered at the beginning of dream work are:

the *Persona* (the part that shows, the "mask"—analogous to the skin—made up of our choices about how we wish to be perceived, individually and collectively);

the *Shadow* (the part that is denied and repressed, the dark, scary, "immoral," unpredictable, and unconscious/unknown part of ourselves);

Light & Darkness (archetypes of consciousness and unconsciousness—the quality of light in dreams is most often a metaphor of the extent to which the main theme of the dream either is or is not already known and acknowledged in waking life);

the *Animus & Anima* (the man inside a woman, and the woman inside a man respectively, figures representing our deepest intuitions and feelings about the opposite sex);

the *Trickster* (a figure representing human consciousness itself—simultaneously knowing and foolish, overblown, yet the source of all the gifts culture);

the *Divine Child* (a figure representing new consciousness and self-awareness—born amidst trouble, yet most often surviving with its miraculous powers and the aid of . . .);

the *Animals* (figures often representing instincts and natural drives—elements of life that are vital but not yet consciously differentiated, creatures and servants of . . .);

the *Great Mother* (Mother Nature, Mother Earth, cyclic time, the divine perceived in feminine form, the feminine principle[s]—multiplying, dividing, nurturing, bringing forth all life, and simultaneously condemning all to inevitable death);

the *All-Father* (the thunderer, the law giver, linear time, the divine perceived in masculine form, the masculine principle[s]—abstracting, constructing, judging, and calculating with objectifying will);

the *Spirit Bird* (a figure representing and embodying communication with the divine—unites the realm of the sky with the plane of the earth);

the *Wise Old People* (the figures representing the oldest and wisest and most loving possibilities of our being—figures sometimes referred to as "mana-personalities");

the *Willing Sacrifice* (a figure representing and embodying the increasing consciousness of interior and exterior oneness—the One dividing itself into the Many, and the many in the act of dying to rejoin the One);

the *Mandala* (an image uniting the circle and the angular figure exhibiting radial symmetry and a defined center—an image of harmony, beauty, balance, order, often used as a visual aid in meditation and worship);

the *Spiral* (image of evolution—the spontaneous archetype of cyclic, repeating rhythmic processes occurring amidst the forward flow of time—visible at all scales and levels from the shape of galaxies to the DNA helix);

the *Perilous Journey* (image of life and being alive, often a sea journey, a descent into the earth, or into a labyrinth, the journey to the land of the dead, the search for treasure, wisdom, immortality);

Death & Rebirth (in the realm of dream and myth, as in physics, energy cannot be destroyed, only transformed. Each dream death is a liberation of psychic energy from specific form and is linked inevitably with a new birth).

There is also no theoretical end to this list. The archetypes inter-relate and metamorphose into one another in complex and subtle ways, and like the organs of the body, they form a living whole. Any effort to separate one from another in any absolute and final way destroys the living dynamics and leaves only a corpse. However, just as one can point to the heart and say that it does different things than the liver, so one can delineate major functions and purposes for each of the archetypes, remembering that life and living require them all working in balance and harmony. Dreams serve to maintain the evolving, dynamic balance.

Brief Thoughts on the Archetype of the Shadow

As Jung pointed out, the Shadow in its unique, personal manifestation in each of us always holds, as a hostage of the negative and generally repressive way we view it in ourselves, the very energy, or idea, or way of thinking, feeling and being which has been missing from our consciousness, and which is absolutely necessary for our further growth and development. Thus, at the collective level, the very elements which are collectively repressed in our white, male-dominated, technological culture (the spontaneity, sexuality, emotionality, relatedness to nature, etc.) are also the very same elements which are projected out onto the non-white, non-male, non-technological world in "justification" of exploitation and oppression, while at the same time they are also the very elements that are required for the positive transformation of our racist, sexist, agist, suicidal technological society. This is ironic, but it is not accidental.

At the level of the individual, it is the failure to consciously admit our own Shadow energies that becomes the mechanism whereby the fears and hatreds and stupidities that fuel the collective dramas of oppression and eco-cide become mobilized and projected. However, when we admit to ourselves that we are evil as well as good and allow ourselves to stay imaginatively aware of our own Shadow energies, then we are freed from the ironic, self-defeating, compulsive dramas, and the energy previously wasted in repetitive, unconscious, neurotic behavior is released and made available for conscious, choiceful, creative use.

Acknowledgment of the Shadow as a personal reality is the most difficult thing any of us ever has to do in our lives, and we must do it over and over again, each time we grow and change. It brings us face to face with our fears of death, because in order for the personality or the society to evolve and mature, the old self must die and make way for the new. This is a psychological and spiritual death we fearfully equate with physical death. Acting out of this fear of change-perceived-as-death, we create a kind of "living death" where the personality and the culture are both held in some rigid, unchanging image. We go to obsessive lengths, like Dracula and Herod, to preserve our "undying" state.

However, when we let go and accept the death of the old (often experiencing it as death in dreams), this act releases the energy previously wasted in maintaining the self-deception of repression and projection, and brings about "rebirth" and "life everlasting"—a message embedded in the metaphors of each of the world religions and expressed in the social and cultural vernacular of every people. The Shadow is most easily visible in the shape of those whom we most dislike and fear, awake and asleep. These are the people we perceive as our "enemies." In this sense, the Christian admonition to love our enemies is simply a statement of psychological fact—unless we can love our enemies, we will never become whole inside ourselves. It is only when we are actively aware, in the words of Ram Dass, that "I am that too" that we are able to grow and change and make creative use of our deepest energies.

Chapter XV
THE GIFTS OF HERMES
AND THE TRANSFORMATION
OF CULTURE

I saw a woman sleeping. In her sleep she dreamt Life stood before her, and held in each hand a gift—in the one Love, and in the other Freedom. And she said to the woman, "Choose."

And the woman waited long: and she said, "Freedom!"

And Life said, "Thou hast well chosen. If thou hadst said, 'Love,' I would have given thee what thou didst ask for; and I would have gone from thee, and returned to thee no more. Now the day will come when I shall return. In that day I shall bear both gifts in one hand."

I heard the woman laugh in her sleep.

Olive Schreiner

We have a model of the social structure of the nomadic Indo-European bands that conquered the great pre-historic agrarian matriarchies in their religious poetry. All these epic/religious poems, from Gilgamesh to the Hindu Vedas, from the works of Homer and Hesiod to the Irish "cattle raid" epics, were previously parts of oral traditions of ritually memorized and sung poetry of even greater antiquity than their first rendering into the earliest scripts. From these accounts it is clear that the Indo-Europeans had a way of life distinctly similar to the Hun, Goth and Vandal invaders of Europe during the fourth century, and to the Mongol invaders under Temujin (Genghis Khan) who came again in the thirteenth century.

These successive waves of invaders each in turn worshiped their own rough collection of martial war gods associated with lightning and the storm. Although the time span separating the Indo-Europeans from Genghis Khan is more than two thousand years, the archetypal structure of the religions of nomadic, male-dominated, horse riding, cattle stealing peoples is essentially the same. Many scholars have speculated that this "barbarous" form of religious intuition and ritual life is an extrapolation from the basic metaphor of herd life among the wild cattle, horses, reindeer, bison, and the other animals hunted and domesticated by nomadic herders. In nature the herd is dominated by the strongest adult male who is eventually overthrown and replaced by a younger and more virile adult male. This archetypal base metaphor of the natural order and religious hierarchy of the universe is in stark contrast to the archetypal base metaphor of the agricultural, settled, urban, matriarchal societies which the Indo-Europeans overcame. The base metaphor of those societies was the celestial and seasonal round of agricultural life—the earth as Great Mother, bearing, nurturing, and then devouring all her children in endless rhythmic succession, and promising rebirth and reincarnation to those who submitted to her unchanging laws.

Not only did the Indo-Europeans develop the techniques and military skills of riding horses and bring with them the religious celebration of masculinity and paternity, they also arrived at a moment when the basic existential/religious foundation of the matriarchies appears to have been crumbling. This thought is inescapable when you examine the remnants of the body of ancient myths and poems that survive from the time of the invention of writing.

This is exactly what Georgio de Santillana, the former Historian of Science at MIT, and his colleague, Hertha von Dechend, did in their monumental book, *Hamlet's Mill—An Essay on Myth in the Frame of Time.* The story of how the book came to be written is in its own way as interesting as the book itself. De Santillana had come to the conclusion out of a lifelong exploration into the history of science and the roots of the scientific method that all the poems from that crucial period at the close of the pre-historic era reflected in their metaphors perceptions of celestial phenomena. Primary among these celestial events described in the earliest written accounts is the phenomenon known as the "procession of the equinoxes." Von Dechend had come independently to precisely the same conclusion from her lifelong study of anthropology, ancient languages, and literature. When they met in 1959, the astonishingly different routes by which they had come to the same conclusion electrified them both. Unlike Darwin and Wallace to whom the same eerie thing had happened a century earlier, de Santillana and von Dechend were able to share their discoveries and collaborate on the presentation of a unified theory. The history of contemporary intellectual life could not but be changed if Darwin and Wallace had collaborated instead of seeing their discoveries and theories as in competition. A contemporary, unified theory of evolution must use Wallace's clearer understanding that natural selection has as much to do with collective and cooperative social patterns within a species as it does with the adaptation of the physical biological form of the individual organism.

What de Santillana and von Dechend collaborate to demonstrate in their exhaustive and scholarly fashion is that embedded in the ancient mythology and poetry is a single story of the heavens being thrown off their axis and chaos and misery being the result. They demonstrate this, along with a variety of other specific celestial and calendrical references. The prototype myth upon which they focus is the myth of Amlethus, the mythological progenitor of the Hamlet of Scandinavian lore and Shakespeare's play.

In this variant of the story, the Mill of the Gods is given over to Amlethus for safe-keeping. It turns endlessly without ever slowing down, grinding out immortality and happiness for the creatures of the earth. However, Amlethus' relatives become enraged because Amlethus does not raise them above others to whom he is not related, as they had expected him to do when he became the Chosen Guardian of the Mill. They ask him to raise them up and give them a special place, but he refuses, saying that he must guard the Mill of the Gods and distribute its products equally among all. His relatives then plot his overthrow, telling each other that Amlethus has betrayed the ties of blood and thus is not a fit keeper of the Mill (in yet another ancient and clear example of the metaphor of repression and projection).

Amlethus is attacked by his relatives while he guards the Mill where the gods placed it on the shore of the ocean. In the ensuing struggle, the Mill is knocked off its axis and tumbled into the sea. Since it is the Mill of the Gods it does not cease to turn even after it has been overthrown. Now, however, instead of producing happiness and immortality as it once did, it grinds out salt tears and the salt of the sea.

In this story and the many like it that they discover in ancient cultures from around the globe, they see a single metaphoric story—the story of the mill of the gods which is overthrown with consequent catastrophe for humankind. They associate this metaphor with the procession of the equinoxes, a celestial phenomenon whose progress is very, very slow, but whose inexorable effects become observably clear over a period of about two thousand years.

Because the earth's own axis of rotation is not exactly perpendicular to the plane of the earth's rotation around the sun, the sun shines more concentratedly on one hemisphere than the other in a successive rhythm which we experience as the passing of the seasons. Human beings have marked this seasonal course by observing the background of stars against which the sun appears to rise and set, depending on the season of the year. The precise days on which the sun makes its apparent shift of direction in its seasonal drift have always been the days of religious ceremony, as well as the fixed points for calendrical and divinational calculations. On the morning and evening of those "pivotal" days, the sun rises and sets against the same background of stars as it did the year before and will the year afterward.

However, there is in fact an infinitesimally small shift in the relation of the orb of the sun and the background of stars every year because the earth is also rotating very slowly around the pivot of its own rotational axis and the plane of the ecliptic, rather like a top starting to wobble as it runs down. The earth, however, takes about twenty-four thousand years to complete just one full revolution of this "wobble." This means that every two thousand years or so, the effect of one-twelfth of this revolution becomes visible in comparison with the celestial background two thousand years earlier on the same date—the sun will rise against the background of the constellation next to one against which it rose two thousand years ago. This effect is not clear to the naked eye until more than one hundred generations have passed. Since the time of Christ, the sun has risen on the day of the Vernal Equinox against the background of the constellation Pisces, and hence the time intervening is sometimes known as the "Piscean Age." The "Age of Aquarius" refers to the period (roughly after the year 2000 A.D.) when the sun will be observed to rise against the background of Aquarius on that day.

In a non-literate, oral culture where the preservation of tradition depends upon the accuracy with which ritual poetry is passed from generation to generation, a poem that defines the background of stars against which the sun will rise or set on the days of the equinoxes and solstices will have for a long period the quality of divine oracle—predicting the will of the gods with perfect precision. However, over the course of one hundred generations or more, it will become clear to the keepers of this sacred poetic tradition that the events in the sky no longer correspond with precision to the predictions of sacred verses. The entire tradition of religious and social organization and belief which has drawn its inspiration and confirmation from the endlessly orderly round of the seasons celebrated in the sacred songs will begin to crumble, if only because those of the elite religious and political leaders who understand the tradition most fully begin to lose faith in it themselves. In many ways, we are experiencing a similar crisis of faith in the contemporary world as the bright promise of science and technology, the primary "religion" of the West today, increasingly reveals itself to be incapable of offering adequate principles for living, and, even more, becomes increasingly clearly visible as the source from which our most dangerous and seemingly insoluble problems seem to stem. In fact, the problems of technology are only the same problems of human consciousness itself, raised to "earth-shattering" proportions, but it is science and technology which have increased the scale of disaster so dramatically.

In our own increasing discomfort, unease, and anguish we have an echo of the crisis which was apparently faced by our matriarchal ancestors at the dawn of history. The human sacrifices, the asceticisms, the religious passions had all been expended in the name of a religious tradition which was proving itself to be false and incomplete, just as our own "religion" of science and technology appears to be increasingly false and incomplete.

It may well be that the matriarchies fell before the invaders as much because of a failure of their religious vision and oral tradition as because of Indo-European military superiority and celebration of the knowledge of paternity. In the words of Cavafy, "the barbarians" may have been for them "a kind of solution."

The Indo-Europeans themselves were clearly nomadic bandits, with a culture and a religion celebrating drunkenness, battle-fever, cattle theft, rape, pillage, and warrior's honor. These are the occupations of their chief gods, and like old bulls of the herd, these gods are doomed to be overthrown and replaced by their sons in rituals of bloody combat. Their alliances are matters of immediate opportunity, and they fight and kill each other more often than they band together to fight others.

The nomadic bandit style of life for these folk was to ride and raid over the near horizon for as long as the good weather held and then to camp out and terrorize the local population for a season, riding on again with the coming of spring and summer. This is a way of life metaphorically not too unlike our own, depending as it does on a limitless horizon on the one hand, and the promise of unlimited resources to be exploited and tossed aside on the other. This is a way of life that must change when the shore of an ocean is reached, or when the natural resources are exhausted. At that point, one must either settle into permanent communities on the shore, or turn and retrace one's steps through the burned and pillaged land filled with new generations of embittered enemies. The Huns and the Mongols chose to retain their nomadic way and retrace their steps; the Indo-Europeans, Goths, and Vandals chose to settle and change their way of life.

In order to successfully accomplish this transition from no-madic banditry to settled urban life with an agricultural base, the Indo-Europeans had to radically transform their religious practice, their economic forms, and their social structures. The central fig-ure of this radical transformation is Hermes. Hermes is the figure who transforms cattle theft, war, and vendetta into commerce, law, and government. In addition, he becomes the patron of com-munication, progress, art, and science. Not unrelatedly, he also is honored as the Bringer of Dreams and the Guide of the soul to the Land of the Dead.

His *mythos* is most instructive. His lineage is traceable back into the pre-historic worship of the Great Goddess where he first appears as an archetype of masculinity in the form of the "Lord of the Animals." When sheep, goats and cattle are domesticated in the Pelasgian period, his role transforms into "Guardian of the Animals." In this guise, he is clearly a progenitor of the image of Christ as Good Shepherd, particularly those representations where he carries the sheep across his shoulders—a pose and arche-typal stance identical with the Pelasgian Hermes.

Despite this clear and ancient lineage, Hermes is also said to have been born of the nymph Maia by Zeus. It is interesting to note that the month of May was first named for Maia, who is also know as "wise one," "grandmother," and "midwife." Her festi-val was the Festival of the Flowers, usually held on May 1. This ritual still survives in the Catholic practice of dedicating May 1 to Mary in her guise as "Mistress of Spring" and "Queen of the Flowers." Here we see clear evidence that Maia embodies the same aspects of the Great Mother archetype which are later em-bodied in the figure of Mary, just as Maia's son Hermes embodies an earlier manifestation of archetypal energy later embodied by Mary's son, Jesus.

In these versions of his myth, Hermes is clearly an exemplar of both the Divine Child and the Trickster. Hermes is able to speak, plan mischief, and carry it out the moment he is born. The day of his birth he steals several of Apollo's divine cattle, slaugh-ters them and eats them. Apollo returns from his ritual task of regulating the passage of the sun through the heavens only to discover that someone has had the audacity to steal his cattle. (It should be remembered that cattle theft was a way of life for the Indo-Europeans. The ancient poems show clearly that they stole cattle from their neighbors whenever they believed they could get away with it, even if the season before they had all been allies in battle. In stealing Apollo's cattle, Hermes is unusual only because of his extreme youth.)

Apollo seeks everywhere for clues to the lost cattle. Like Demeter seeking for her lost daughter Persephone under similar circumstances, Apollo has little luck finding out what has happened until the birds tell him that the cattle were stolen by the infant Hermes. At first Apollo refuses to believe that one so young could have accomplished such a raid, but when he goes to the cave where Maia is recovering from the labor of childbirth, he discovers the child amidst the dismembered carcasses of the cattle, blood-smeared and bloated and playing with the entrails. Apollo is enraged and seizes the child, carrying him up to Olympus to face the wrath and judgment of Zeus.

On the journey up the mountain, Hermes continues to play with the remains of the cattle. He takes a skull and strings pieces of intestine between the horns. When he completes his grisly construction, it emits odd tones and harmonies. Apollo notices this strange contraption and grabs it away from the infant to inspect it more closely. Hermes innocently says that Apollo may keep the skull and points out how the strings of intestine may be plucked to produce musical tones and sequences. This is, in fact, the first lyre, which Hermes has invented while they traveled up the mountain. When they arrive before Zeus' throne of judgment, Apollo makes his accusations and demands that Hermes be forced to pay with his life for the theft of the sacred cattle of the sun.

At this point, Hermes speaks up in his own defense, pointing out that Apollo has already accepted a present made from the very remains of the cattle he claims were stolen. Hermes suggests that since Apollo accepted the lyre, there is no theft involved, only commerce—acceptable payment for goods received. Zeus is greatly amused and throws the case out of court. Apollo is annoyed, but says that the lyre is his now, and he will be the patron of music and song, not Hermes.

In this story we can clearly see a mythological justification for the abandonment of thievery in favor of more orderly economic modes of commerce and contractual agreement. We can also clearly see the archetypal roles of both the Trickster and the Divine Child played out in the narrative. The Divine Child survives the efforts of the most powerful forces of the old established order to destroy him and succeeds in establishing an entirely new order. As Trickster, he simultaneously delivers "come-uppance" to the figures most filled with hubris, while simultaneously serving as the carrier of the creative impulse, the bearer of the new idea that has never been conceived before. Both the ironic "come-uppance" and the creative invention of the lyre are brought about through pointing out fundamental relatedness among elements that were previously considered to be unrelated. Because of his lowly and despised status as "infant," and because of his audacity in challenging even the powerful god Apollo and his voracity in devouring the cattle once they are stolen, Hermes exhibits elements of the Shadow as well. To the extent that Hermes was a constellation of the masculine principle in Pelasgian society prior to the Indo-European invasion, he also embodies aspects of the Animus of the culture of the Great Mother.

The ritual practice of the worship of Hermes carries these archetypal themes and resonances of his myth into social reality. There were no temples to Hermes as there were to other gods and goddeses. Instead, "herms," phallic raised posts or stones dedicated to him, were raised throughout the countryside, particularly at crossroads and other places on the roads and trails where ambush by bandits was likely. Hermes' role as protector of travelers grows directly out of his transforming, civilizing character. In order for thievery to be transformed into commerce, travelers, merchants, and particularly royal messengers had to be free to move about in relative safety. The royal messenger in particular had to be protected from the tendency amongst barbarians to kill the bearer of bad news. To enforce his guardianship of travelers, Hermes also becomes the "Psychopomp"—the Guide of souls to their rest in the Land of the Dead. A violation of the code of Hermes meant that one's soul might wander endlessly after death without the guidance of Hermes. Here again we see clear indications of some of the ways that the figure of Hermes presages the figure of Christ in later Western tradition.

Since in ancient mythology the "Land of the Dead" and what we think of as the "unconscious" are one and the same, it is not surprising that Hermes also becomes the Bringer of Dreams, the Messenger of the Gods in sleep. The creative impulse springs from the unconscious in the many forms of the Trickster. In many ways, the dream itself is the basic model for the Trickster archetype; it appears fanciful, crazy, meaningless, and yet it reveals startling insight and truth. It convinces us of its reality while we are in the midst of the experience, and then reveals itself to be only a dream upon awakening.

To the extent that the worship of Hermes provided the religious and social framework for the transformation of pre-historic, matriarchal society into the patriarchal culture we have today, it demonstrates that such radical transformations and reformations of society are possible and suggests archetypal structures within which such developments can take place. The archetypes themselves are virtually unchanged since that time, and if we are to succeed in transforming our own planetary society, we must call upon the same energies of the unconscious and the creative impulse that are embodied in the myth of Hermes.

Summary: THE GIFTS OF HERMES

The period of the invention of writing and the overthrow of the matriarchal urban/agricultural civilizations of pre-history by the nomadic Indo-Europeans (circa 1800–1400 B.C.) is an epoch of tremendous global cultural and political change, much like our own. The archetypal patterns established in that period are the patterns we are still elaborating upon, even as we perceive these patterns to be increasingly inadequate and in need of radical reformation. There is compelling evidence to suggest that the failure to predict the procession of the equinoxes contributed to the downfall of the great pre-historic matriarchies.

The nomadic, patriarchal Indo-Europeans are primarily responsible for the masculinist formulation of society and religion we experience today. However, at the outset, the nature of Indo-European society was too barbaric and disorganized to support settled life, being much like the social organization of the Mongol "hordes" in recorded history. The Mongols conquered all, but melted away and left no substantial imprint on the culture of Europe because they did not reorganize their religion or their society to handle the task of administering conquered populations. They did not accept agriculture as a way of life, and they continued their nomadic way of life, ebbing back into Central Asia after their extraordinary military/migratory explosion.

The Indo-Europeans, however, did make the transition from nomadism to settled life, primarily through the invention of new social and religious forms. In the establishment of the Greco-Roman branch of Indo-European culture to which Europe and America owe so much, the figure of Hermes stands at the center of this social and religious transformation. Hermes is clearly a Divine Child, a Trickster, and a Shadow. It is no accident that he is the patron of commerce, communication, and travelers, particularly official messengers of the state. It is also no accident that he is also the guide of the souls of the dead to their final existence in the Land of the Dead, as well as the Bringer of Dreams.

In his guise as Divine Child/Trickster, Hermes creates the mythological/psychological/religious ground for the transformation of disorganized barbarian society, based on raiding and cattle thievery, into civilized commerce and government. His rude phallic shrines stand at crossroads to remind all would-be bandits and cattle thieves that travelers, particularly commercial travelers and government messengers, are under the special protection of Hermes.

As the figure from whom medicine and the arts of civilization are descended, Hermes also represents the imagination and the creative impulse. The Gifts of Hermes are the gifts of genuinely creative life and action. These gifts are always delivered in a surprising and ironic fashion. The genuinely creative act is always surprising because it has not been imagined before. This aspect of the archetype of the Trickster makes it difficult to confine and define. The Trickster always brings the creative impulse in the form of demonstrating that things held separate by conventional wisdom are in fact deeply connected. In this way, the Trickster simultaneously delivers ironic "comeuppance" to figures bloated with hubris and an inappropriate vision of their own power and importance in the conventional scheme of things, while at the same time being the source of the creative idea that transforms the entire situation.

In this way, the myth of Hermes describes the transformation of both individual personality and character, and the reformation of society and culture at one and the same moment. The radical transformations of religion and culture that took place two thousand years ago echo the radical transformation of religion and culture that we are in the midst of today. If we are to succeed in transforming ourselves and preserving the planet's ability to support mammalian life, we must again seek the Gifts of Hermes actively and consciously. Dream work is one of the primary means of doing this. Remembering and working with dreams prepares us to receive the Gifts of Hermes.

Chapter XVI
LUCID DREAMING
AND DREAM YOGA

> The soul in sleep gives proof
> of its divine nature.
>
> *Cicero*

When in the midst of the experience of a dream we realize that we are dreaming—that the seemingly active and compelling things that are happening are taking place while we are physically asleep and quiescent—then that dream is said to be "lucid" or to contain "lucidity." Lucidity in dreams is a linguistic paradox, but it is also a relatively common dream occurrence—which is to say that almost everyone will spontaneously realize, "Hey! This is a dream!" or "I'm dreaming!" from time to time. People who become interested in the experience of lucid dreaming, for whatever reason, are often able to increase the occurrence of such dreams dramatically through various sorts of "incubation" exercises.

The possibilities of the lucid dream state are truly extraordinary. When we recognize in the midst of the dream that we are dreaming, one of the awarenesses that surfaces in consciousness is that all we behold is a mirror in which our own interior being is reflected in metaphoric form. We realize consciously in the dream that it is aspects of our own being that we are seeing and dealing with. In this sense, the act of repression is withdrawn, becomes conscious, and ceases to be repression. The identity of "me, the dreamer" is known and understood to be co-equal with all that is experienced in the seemingly "external" reality in the dream. Often people will use the experience of lucidity in the course of an unpleasant dream to wake themselves up. However, the decision can also be made to continue the experience of the dream while retaining the lucid "double perspective"—that the experience is in fact a dream, even though it continues to provide impressions that are at least as vivid and compelling as those of waking life.

Interest in this "altered state of consciousness" has been growing in the West since the 1920's when "objective observers" first began to investigate and report on their lucid dream experiences. However, the tradition of organized attention to the incubation of lucid dreams in the East has been steady and unbroken for perhaps twenty-five hundred years. The subjective experience of lucid dreaming is so symbolically resonant with ancient Asian religious conceptions of how God creates the universe that the cultivation of lucid dreaming has been a religious and meditative discipline since before Patanjali first wrote down the oral poems of instruction in yoga meditation around 800 B.C.

Interestingly, certain historians of witchcraft and ritual magic in the West have suggested that the rituals described in the grimoirs and elsewhere were not intended to be waking life activities, but rather as rituals to be performed in lucid dreams. These scholars believe that the threshold of initiation that separated "true" witches and magicians from "self-deluded" ones was the understanding that the rituals of magic were to be performed in waking life primarily as incubation exercises for actions in lucid dreams or in deep trance states.

In the East, the cultivation of lucid dreaming has always been woven as an esoteric element into the religious practices of Hinduism, Buddhism, Taoism, and the other various religious traditions that trace their roots back to these great sources. The Tibetan Buddhists (almost all of whom are in exile since the annexation of Tibet by China and the unsuccessful rebellion against Chinese rule in 1959, after which the Dalai Lama himself went into exile) have carried this tradition of lucid dream incubation to a state of great elaboration. The Tibetan strain of Buddhist thought declares that the experience of the dream is one and the same as the experience of the "soul" after death. The Tibetans believe in successive reincarnation, and for them the "soul" is more often referred to as the "entity"—the continuity of personality and "karma" over successive lifetimes. It is this part of the total psychic being which experiences dreams while alive, and this part which goes right on dreaming after death.

For the Tibetan Buddhists, each time we sleep we experience the condition of the soul in our dreams. If we were to die in our sleep, we would simply continue the dreams we were having. The Tibetans believe that these dreams of the dead transform into dreams of light, bliss, and satisfaction, and then slowly transform into dreams of increasing horror. Each of these stages of bliss-to-horror is called a "Bardo World" and is described in some detail in their "Book of the Dead." In the midst of the increasingly horrible nightmare of the soul after death, the entity is driven either to reincarnate anew in the womb of a woman, or to dissolve totally into the Self that is All, never to reincarnate again.

Thus, for the Tibetans the ability to remain lucid and self-conscious in the dream state is a matter of the utmost religious importance and significance. Their belief is that in the great majority of cases people who have not meditated or developed themselves with some spiritual discipline die and are driven to reincarnate again out of terror, in a vain attempt to escape from the increasingly horrific dream-scape of the soul after death. Certain scholars of the Western occult tradition have suggested that this same metaphor also appears in the images of "Ragnorok" and the descent into the Underworld. Some have even gone so far as to suggest that the "decay" of the soul's dream after death is related to the physical decay of the corpse, and that that is why such emphasis was placed on embalming and funerary preparation in Egypt and subsequent Mediterranean and European cultures. The archetypal resonance of these ideas is certainly cross-cultural. Varieties of this belief can be found throughout this world.

The Tibetans in particular believe that through cultivating dream lucidity while alive, the entity can then perceive the Bardo Worlds for what they are. "O nobly-born," the Tibetan Book of the Dead admonishes, "whatever fearful and terrifying visions thou mayst see, recognize them to be thine own thought forms." In doing this, the entity repeats Buddha's act of enlightenment under the Bo Tree. Just as the Buddha dismissed the attacking demons of Mara, the God of Death and Destruction, as mere illusions, unworthy of breaking his yogic concentration for, so the soul in the Bardo World dismisses the illusions of increasing horror as mere illusions—mere projections of unconscious energies into the illusions of dream.

Having achieved this recognition and insight into the nature of life after death, such an enlightened soul can pass into total and complete union with the divine. With such self-awareness, the discarnate soul can also choose to reincarnate and re-enter the world of human existence consciously as a "boddhisattva"—a being devoted to the enlightenment of all others and the consequent alleviation of all illusions of pain and misery. Certain doctrinal disputes separate one school of Buddhist thought from another at this point, among others. Some sects take the "Boddhisattva's Oath" to "return until every sentient being is enlightened," others "to return until even the grass is enlightened," while still others swear to reincarnate with increasing clarity of consciousness and intent "until even the stones are enlightened."

The Tibetan Buddhist exercises for the acquisition of lucidity are many and varied. (Sources for many of these exercises appear in the Resource Guide at the back of the book.) Almost all of them involve manipulating the environment of the dream in specific ways once lucidity has been achieved, and meditating on these activities while awake. In such a manner, over the course of a lifetime, the Tibetans believe that the will and resolve are strengthened and the entity is prepared to reunite with God or reincarnate with equal consciousness.

The Hindu yogic tradition of dream work holds essentially the same theological position, but has developed the techniques of lucid dream incubation to focus on achieving the same "undifferentiated consciousness" in the dream state as in the states of waking meditation, and has tended to reject the Tibetan emphasis on manipulation of the dream experience in favor of "merging with the light." From the Hindu point of view, the manipulation of the dream experience is a species of "Siddha"—a power that comes naturally with psycho-spiritual development, and not something to be sought for its own sake, lest the entity be deluded and distracted from the one goal of union with the divine.

Ancient Egyptian funerary practice appears to involve a similar belief in a sort of intermediary "Bardo" place where the judgment of the soul is carried out before being assigned to its appropriate reincarnation or after-life. In Egyptian belief, the soul of the deceased is multiple, with different constituent parts destined for different experiences. The main element of the "soul," roughly identified with the "self" or the "personality" in waking life, could become immortal, but only if it succeeded in identifying itself completely with Osiris. If this complete identity could be achieved (and it seemed more likely if prayers were said by large numbers of people focusing on it, and if the written texts describing how it was to be done were buried with the corpse in the wrappings and emblazoned on the walls of the tombs), then the soul-one-with-Osiris would participate in the timeless and ever-repeating resurrection of Osiris into eternal life with the aid of his sisters Isis and Nephthys.

All of these beliefs and practices from Tibet to Egypt suggest formulations of the archetypes of the collective unconscious. To the extent that the archetypes are continuous and "immortal"—beyond the life and death of any individual organism—they are parts of ourselves that clearly live on after we are gone. There seems to be a single thread in these traditions suggesting that one way to alleviate the fears and uncertainties about the meaning of life and the inevitable prospect of death is to meditate on the archetypes and identify one's being with them while alive. The various images of the supposed life of the soul after death in all the world religions are constructed from similar archetypal constellations. Thus, at one level all the world's religions make essentially the same psychological claim with regard to archetypal elements of being that are timeless and beyond the grip of death.

Religious ideologies differ greatly about the number and character of the "souls" that separate and depart the body at death and in dream. One extreme was expressed by Mark Twain, who suggested that every dream figure, every literary character invented or imagined, every thought entertained and every feeling felt had "a life of its own." Twain speculated that all these separate parts of the individual psyche were released to go their various ways whenever a person died. In all of these intuitions and speculations about the possibilities of life after death, the basic archetypal connection between death and sleep and between the life of the discarnate soul and the experience of dreaming stands out clearly.

The achievement of lucidity in dreams brings a new element to our consideration of these problems in the West. For example, what would be required to incubate lucid dreams which were simultaneously telepathic? Dream workers like James Donohoe have already begun to explore these areas. In the East, there have been myths and stories for centuries about certain groups of enlightened spiritual masters meeting at regular intervals in lucid, telepathic dreams to shape the course of history more to their liking.

There are certain people who are reluctant to attempt to become lucid in their dreams, for fear that the intrusion of an element of waking consciousness usually absent from dreams might tend to "poison the well"—to dominate and control the dream experience so that the spontaneous unconscious will have an even harder time bringing the "natural" healing, compensatory, balancing energies into the experience of the dream. It is certainly possible to be preoccupied with comparative trivialities in lucid dreams, but the unconscious element of our being from which the dreams spring is so much older, wiser, stronger, more creative, loving, and reconciling than we even imagine that it seems to me that even aggressive triviality on the part of a lucid dreamer (or even a group of telepathic lucid dreamers) can easily be absorbed. To imagine that the dreaming unconscious could be totally overwhelmed and controlled by even the most practiced and disciplined lucidity seems to me to be simple hubris at worst, and at best a failure of perception and imagination.

Many religious, psychological, and philosophical authors have suggested that we are entering a new era of human evolution where human consciousness must participate actively in its own transformation, no longer relying on the archetypal forces of unconscious life alone to shape the evolution of species. As a myth, as a formulation of archetypal image and energy, these suggestions reflect the undeniable fact that human technological manipulation of the environment is shaping the evolutionary possibilities of all species and rapidly bringing about the extinction of many in our competing efforts to achieve economic and political domination over one another. In this sense, this notion is simply stating the obvious. (However, it should be remembered, as Conan Doyle says: "It requires an unusual mind to undertake an analysis of the obvious.") At another level, however, the notion that we must begin to participate consciously in the evolutionary development of the human species has profound implications for the increasing interest in lucid dreaming.

What can be "done" and "achieved" in the lucid dream state is limited only by imagination and belief-structure. For a period of time I became very excited about flying in my dreams. I would attempt to incubate lucid dreaming with the focus of attention that I would fly. Eventually I had a dream in which I was cheerfully flying and altering both my dream body and the landscape over which I flew, when I encountered a group of "older, wiser magicians" whose disparaging thoughts I telepathically overheard. "There he goes," they said to one another with a tone of resignation and disappointment, "flying again." I was taken aback in the midst of the lucid dream and realized that I was indeed becoming distracted from more serious and important matters by my exclusive focus upon the act of flying. This experience suggests strongly to me that the naturally self-correcting and self-criticizing quality of dreams pervades the dreams of even lucid dreamers. The dream accounts of the Tibetan adepts and enlightened yogis evoke the same impression—the dream is able to introduce the element which has been prematurely closed out, even if the premature closure has the weight of religious tradition and a lifetime of devoted meditation.

In this sense, William Blake's dictum is reliable and trustworthy: "Let the fool persist in his folly and he will become wise." Persist in folly, and sooner or later you *will* become wise. This is as true in waking life as it is in dreams. There is a self-correcting quality in the relations between consciousness and the unconscious. Truth will indeed make us free, and it will return again and again in the effort to liberate us from our prematurely closed notions, whether we recognize it initially or not.

The various techniques for incubating lucid dreams are many and varied. All of them have in common the clarification of the intention to be lucid. Indeed, it seems to me that the techniques for achieving lucidity are all comparatively easy compared with the question of *what to do* when lucidity is achieved. My own incubation practice is currently to focus my attention during the day on the tasks before me as fully and wholeheartedly as possible. In the moments where my attention is not directed to the tasks of waking life, I imagine how I would have reacted differently in my dreams if I had been lucid at the time of having them. I have also extended this active imagination, Buddhist fashion, into thinking how I would behave differently if I knew that the events of waking life were also a dream. When I prepare for sleep, my last act before going to sleep is to prepare my journal to receive the notes of the night's dreaming. I write the following morning's date and day of the week. Then I focus myself on the question of *why* I am bothering to remember my dreams at all—what *is* the point of this exercise *really*? Then I write a line which captures the answer to this question in the most evocative and economical fashion in that moment just before sleep. Occasionally the answer will focus around finding out more about a particular life dilemma, or inviting the creative impulse to give me an idea or a way of looking at something that I have not yet imagined. Most often, however, the answer is more general and diffuse. Recently I have taken to silently resonating (others might call it "prayer" or "meditation") while I write the ancient Sanskrit "Aum" (ॐ) across the line after the date and day.

Let me share three lucid dreams to suggest how this incubation process and the dreams that have come in response to it have evolved over the years.

Some years ago I dreamed: I am sitting at an old-fashioned writing desk, writing with an old-fashioned steel pen that has to be continually dipped into an inkwell. I am enjoying my writing when suddenly a little figure made entirely of flame comes dancing into my line of vision from my left. This little "flame person" dances across the blank page I am just about to write on. The figure leaves little whirling scorch marks on the page as he/she dances along from left to right. These scorch marks look like purposeful writing, even though I cannot decipher them. I am utterly charmed by the little fire sprite, but the thought comes to me, "You'd better not stamp down too hard in this writing-dance or you'll set the whole page on fire!"

At this moment, the little figure does a leaping pirouette up and out into the room in front of me. As the little flaming figure leaps off the desk, he/she begins to expand and grow, until in less than a moment I am confronted with a huge figure made of flame perhaps eight feet tall, standing with legs wide spread in front of me. I am literally struck in the face with the blast of the heat from the flames. Out of this bonfire-person, the mocking voice comes telepathically: "You don't have to worry about that. I am not a paper burning demon. I'm a *flesh* burning demon!"

I am terrified at this sudden turn of events, but in the midst of my terror I realize, "Wait a minute! I'm having a conversation with a talking bonfire. I must be dreaming!" I am immensely excited and pleased to be lucid. The fire demon laughs mockingly, and I realize that this is the metaphor my dream is offering me and I had better deal with it. Since I know that I am dreaming, I know that no physical harm or pain will come to me no matter what I do. I wonder briefly what this figure in my dream signifies, but I am still too focused on my startled frame of mind and my fear to center on this question and demand an answer from the dream. I decide that I must somehow overcome my fear. I decide that the best way to do this is to attack the fire demon a la the *Senoi*. I lunge forward, but my arms pass through the flames as they would in waking life, and the demon laughs even more mockingly.

I suddenly remember that down the street from my dream apartment there is a building with a large bell hanging in the doorway. Perhaps I can use this bell like a gigantic candle snuffer and deal with the fire demon that way. I think myself in front of the building in an instant. The bell all but blocks the doorway to an inexpensively constructed building like a school gym or a public recreation center. There are many people standing around outside drinking coffee and chatting. [Later, I recognized with an undeniable "tingle" that at one level this building was an image of my perception of the Unitarian Church.] I mutter excuses and apologies as I rush through the crowd of coffee drinkers and wrench the large bell from its mounting.

I return to my apartment in one flying bound, carrying the bell by the rim and holding it up over my right shoulder. The demon has grown even larger during my brief absence, and I can barely contain it as I push the bell down over it. The bell immediately begins to heat up and starts to glow from the heat of the demon trapped inside. The bell glows red hot, and then white hot.

For an instant I lose lucidity and panic, thinking that my hands will be "burned off" if I continue to hold the bell in place over the demon. I recover my lucidity and remind myself that I am dreaming and will come to no harm. I remind myself that I must somehow overcome this fire demon, and that holding the bell down over it seems like the best way to do it at the moment. The bell gradually cools, returning to red hot, and then back to dull, bell-metal color. I am apprehensive. Is it a trick? I decide that I must lift up the bell and see what's going on.

I lift the bell and see that there is a perfect circle of blackness scorched in ground. I realize that I am now outside, that the setting dissolved and reformed around me while I was struggling with my fear and holding the bell in place. I look inside the bell to make sure the fire demon is not lurking inside. At that moment my attention is drawn to the scorched circle on the ground. A tiny pure white wisp of smoke rises from the very center of the circle, and at the same moment the bell begins to vibrate. The vibrations intensify and I can feel them passing out of the bell into my hands and up my arms into my whole body. The sound is a deep, sustained tone with many subtle harmonics. The vibrations fill me with a sense of energy and well-being that is intense and profound. The feelings are so strong that I burst awake with them, unable to continue the experience of the lucid dream any longer . . .

The fact that I was able to recognize that I was dreaming allowed me to act more courageously and creatively than I have in other similar dreams, where I usually flee in terror or merely wake up. In working with the dream, I realized that at one level it is about writing and the way that sexual energy is sublimated into acts of creative expression, particularly writing. I also realized that at one level it was a good humored pun on St. Paul's famous dictum, "it is better to marry than to burn." At that level, the bell is a wedding bell. At another level, the dream addresses the major problem of my life at that time, which was how to pursue my creative life without abandoning my responsibilities as a husband and father or betraying my call to ministry. This dream continues to reveal resonant subtleties every time I example it and turn it over in my memory.

The second lucid dream I would like to share comes from a period of my life some years later:

I am in a dim, urban apartment with low ceilings. There are several people around, mostly male, and mostly younger than myself, although I am vaguely aware of being only in my mid-twenties myself. I am clean shaven. Suddenly I am greeted affably by one of the people—Al the printer. He comes up to me and calls me loudly by name and claps me on the shoulder. His gesture seems both friendly and hostile to me all at once, and I am confused. I am flooded with memories of working with Al when I was editor of my campus paper. I think to myself how the relationship was always friendly and yet always filled with tensions— how I would imagine an older brother and younger brother might relate. I remember how we used to argue about whether he would print my editorials against the Vietnam War, and how I used to threaten to go to another printer if he refused, which he never did.

Al goes over and sits down on a couch and produces a silver coin out of his pocket. I think of it as a "quarter," even though it is larger than a silver dollar. I notice with shock that Al's right hand is scarred and crippled, as though it had been plunged into the molten lead reservoir of a linotype machine. Al sees my shock and laughs harshly. He rolls the coin across his knuckles, back and forth like a stage magician, as though to demonstrate to me that, scarred though his hand may be, he can still "manipulate" very well. Then he gets up abruptly and leaves the room. As he leaves, I notice a pile of "quarters" on the floor next to the couch where he had just been sitting. I call out to him to draw his attention to the money, thinking that he must have dropped it while perfecting the coin trick earlier. Either he does not hear me or he chooses to ignore me. I think to myself that he may be consciously choosing to leave the coins as a gift of "small change" for our somewhat scruffy commune. I decide to take a handful of the coins for myself. I squat down and pick up as many as I can fit into my left hand jeans pocket.

Later, I am sitting with a small crowd of people in a room like a chapel or a small theater with banked seating. I see many friends there. I particularly notice Rob and other Unitarian Universalist minister friends. Everyone is silent. I have the impression that it is the moment of quiet, expectant, meditative hush before the service or performance begins. I remember Emerson saying that it was the part of the service that he liked best, and I smile to myself about such a "Puerish" thing to say—to prefer the moment of mobilized expectation and potential to the moment of commitment and action. The silence lengthens and I realize with surprise that I know everyone present, even though I am sure that many of them do not know each other, since they are all people I know from different periods in my life living in widely separated places. I am baffled by this and decide that I must somehow be "central" to the ceremony of performance about to take place. My interest, excitement and curiosity is growing, as is my frustration at waiting. I finally start to whisper and wave "hello" to various people, trying not to disrupt the quiet too much. People smile, nod and wave back. I turn around to see if there are any more people I know sitting in the rows behind me. I am shocked and surprised to see that the seats are filled, but that I do not recognize a single face, even though I make eye contact with one or two people who seem hauntingly familiar. A woman with dark hair going gray and a heavily tanned face gets up suddenly and says loudly, "This is not for me!" She walks swiftly out the doors at the back.

I am very hurt and surprised by her vehemence. I realize that everyone is waiting for me to begin the service. I decide that I will give the very best sermon/show I am capable of. [Just at this point when I was first recording this dream in my journal, I realized with a flash that at one level the "people sitting behind me" were a metaphor of "people whom I had not yet met in waking life," just as the "people sitting in front of me" were a representation of "everyone I had ever known."]

The moment I make the decision to speak and perform the service myself, I am no longer in my seat in the auditorium. I am standing facing a door, dressed in a light blue robe with gold trim. I know the door opens into the auditorium. I am about to make my entrance. Someone opens the door for me and I step forward, expecting to walk briskly down the steeply sloping aisle to the stage/pulpit area below. However, I step out onto a tiny balcony with oak railings overlooking the auditorium from the back of the room. I am frustrated and surprised by having my way blocked in this fashion. People begin to turn in their seats and crane their necks to look back up at me. Clearly I cannot address the crowd from the balcony in this fashion, but neither do I wish to "back out" the door and look for another entrance. I am desperate with embarrassment and frustration. I decide to rip the oak railings away and jump down and make my way to the front. I tear the railing away and break it in half so that I have a piece of railing in each hand. As I do this, I realize: "*Oak* railing! I'm breaking inches-thick oak railing with my bare hands. This must be a dream!"

I am filled with excitement. I am dreaming lucidly. I decide again that I am going to give the best performance of religious theater I am capable of. I step forward and walk/float down the steep aisle toward the central stage area. I take the two pieces of oak railing and twist them together so that they wrap around each other like the snakes on Hermes' caduceus and the molecules of the DNA helix. I decide that I will use the archetype of the double spiral as my "text." As I float down the amphitheater, I hold the pieces aloft as a concrete example of the archetype of spiral, evolutionary development.

As I do this, I realize that I am in telepathic contact with each person in the audience/congregation and that my "sermon" has already begun. I am also aware that in the book I was reading before sleep (*World of Wonders,* by Robertson Davies) there is the suggestion that the "strong man act" is always the one to have outside the tent to tantalize the people into paying and coming inside. I think to myself wryly that I am operating out of a very ancient tradition of theater and religious ceremony.

I think/preach that all things are One—all reality is a great dream, and that the dream can be joyful and beautiful if you understand the timeless, archetypal realities that create the structures of our own lives and the world simultaneously. Interior, personal life and the external world are seemingly two different things, which are in fact one thing—the same, beyond the illusion of separateness. This is the archetypal idea/state-of-being I focus on in the midst of my knowledge that I am dreaming. I profess this truth, embodying it myself, before my many selves, in the midst of the dream.

As I hold up the oaken helix, it metamorphoses in my hands

into a large, self-luminous sphere within which the genetic material can be seen repeating the shape of the oaken pieces. I am surprised and filled with joy at this transformation. The thought
comes to me that this spontaneous image comes from the greater
unconscious that is creating the whole dream. It was not consciously called forth by me in this moment, but at the same time it
is in perfect resonance and harmony with the "text" I am preach-
ing. The shiny spherical image is a kind of confirmation from the
dream itself that my lucidity is not merely a manipulation of the
dream experience by ego, but rather an activity in harmony with
my deeper being.

　　This thought becomes part of the sermon/show as I think it.
I realize that because I have been speaking telepathically, the
scene is still hushed and silent. "It would be nice to have music,"
I think to myself. At that moment I can suddenly see out of the
back of my head. I see that a young, blond woman is sitting at a
keyboard instrument. She is also dressed in a blue robe with yel-
low-gold trim. I take my hands away from the glowing egg/
cell/sphere and it rises slowly into the air in the center of the
room. The young woman begins to play beautiful music, and I realize again with surprise and joy that the music is new. The instrument she is playing is also extraordinary—it sounds like a
combination of harpsichord and piano. It is the perfect instrument
for music, which has the delicacy and clarity of Bach's harpsichord
music, while at the same time having a swelling, sonorous, rich
emotional color like Beethoven's piano music. Again I thank the
dream for this extraordinary gift of beauty, knowing I am dreaming.

　　The genetic material in the middle of the glowing, floating
zygote ball begins to quiver and divide. We all rise and take each
other's hands in concentric circles up the amphitheater and begin
to sing and dance with the music. The glowing sphere/cell continues to divide, creating a pulsing, three-dimensional mandala, or
series of mandalas. I think/preach that this is how the living universe becomes joyfully conscious of itself—repeating this same,
basic, always unique, but infinitely repeating pattern of structure.

　　I am intensely excited, calm, and happy. I realize that I am
waking up. I want very much to remain with and in the dream,
but the thought comes to me clearly that I have a choice: I can stay

with the experience of the lucid dream, but if I do, the next lucid episode will obliterate the memory of this one, until eventually I will lose whatever it is that allows me to remain lucid. At this point I will slip into a regular, non-lucid dream, and thence into deep, dreamless sleep. If I do this I will eventually awaken and remember nothing. The other alternative is to awaken now and make notes, in which case I will not experience the next lucid episode. I am deeply torn, but decide that I will be happier to have an account of this dream in waking life than to have another continuing experience of lucidity which I will then forget.

I awaken and begin to scribble notes with my light pen, beginning with the hush before the service and recognizing the many different people from my past. Then, having made these notes, I suddenly remember the earlier sequence with Al the printer. It was another surprise—an unexpected gift, somehow confirming the rightness of the decision to awaken and affirm the importance of conscious awareness of dreams in waking life.

I have worked with this dream extensively in the years since I first had it. I know that at one level it constellated at a time in my life when I was debating the question of whether I should seek ordination or pursue what I perceived to be my alternative ministry of dream work without official ties to any denomination. The major "block" to making that choice cleanly was the drama of desiring and simultaneously rejecting the mantle of authority that ordination inevitably brings. Like the earlier lucid dream, it also constellated elements related to sexuality and the creative process. What had to be transformed in order to make the decision about ordination was the drama of authority, symbolized in part by the stance of "addressing the crowd from the balcony," a la popes and dictators. The religious and philosophical elements woven into the dream are relatively clear. The archetypal energy of the images continues to resonate in my life.

The third lucid dream I wish to recount is much more recent, had during the period of preparing this manuscript for the publisher. In it I am at home, writing, in a scene indistinguishable from waking life. My daughter has brought a friend home with her after school and I can occasionally hear them playing in the sunny backyard. Someone comes to the door. I rise to see who it is.

It is a family of three—a woman in her late thirties, her patently schizophrenic son, "Eric," and the man she is currently in relationship with (not Eric's father). The man is of indeterminate age with blond hair turning gray, a deeply tanned face, and sunglasses that hide his eyes. He does not speak. The woman introduces herself, and it is quickly clear to me that she is almost as crazy as her son. She tells me that she wants to leave her son in my care. She attempts to persuade me to do this by flattering me outrageously with references to my reputation as a therapist. She tells me that she is sure her son can be healed and returned to sanity through my care and attention. She talks continuously and vacillates between unblinking eye-contact and no eye-contact at all.

I do not wish to invite these folks into the house, so I step out into the front yard with them to talk. I tell her that I do not want to take her son, but that I know a place in Berkeley, a residential treatment program that specializes in treating profoundly disturbed young people. I tell her that it seems to me that her son Eric might do well in placement there. While we are talking, I notice vaguely that there are cut stumps of much larger trees than in fact grow in the yard in waking life. I think to myself, "It must be the future," but I am also aware that my daughter is her current age, so it can't be the future. This conundrum slips from consciousness as a little girl with a dirty face appears and sits silently on one of the stumps. "Is she part of this family too?" I wonder. Then I realize that it is more likely that she is my daughter's playmate whom I heard but did not actually see when they came home from school. I ask her, "Where's Tristy?" and she shrugs silently and looks away. My take on her gesture is that yes indeed she is my daughter's playmate, but they have had a falling-out while playing, and she is dawdling on her way home. I realize that I should go and check with my daughter and make sure she is all right, but I do not want to do this until the family has departed.

I tell the woman that she must leave now, that I have other things that I need to do. I escort her and her companion up the steps to the street. "Where is Eric?" I wonder. Suddenly, I am covered with some brown substance that smells bad. I look up and see that Eric has climbed a tree and thrown this substance down on us. I'm sure it's excrement. "Hey!" I call out. "Your son just shit all over us!" She does not turn around but says without emo-

tion, "Oh, it's not shit." I look down and see that she is correct—
in fact, it's commercial potting soil that Eric has scooped from the
bag inside the front porch. He apparently grabbed the stuff,
climbed the tree, and then waited until we passed beneath him on
the stairs to throw it down on us. I think to myself that this bespeaks a certain level of consciousness and ability to plan actions
and carry them out with focused and sustained attention. Some
such consciousness is necessary for therapeutic interventions into
the delusions of schizophrenia to have effect, and he has it. It rein-
forces my suspicion that he would probably do well at the place in
Berkeley. I look back at the two adults. I am sad. I do not believe
that they are going to take him over there.

I awaken. The dream has a disturbing quality. I make notes
with the light pen and lie back down and return to sleep.

I am utterly amazed to be right back in the dream. I have
read about people making the transition from waking consciousness directly to lucid dream without any diminution of self-awareness in a matter of seconds, but I have never before had the
experience myself. I am stunned. I think feverishly—if these elements of my own interior life had not had some healing purpose,
they would not have come in this dream and asked for healing. I
must heal them myself—but how? Who is this mysterious man?
What's going on here? While I am thinking this, I see Eric climbing the stairs to the street to accompany his mother and her companion. They are opening the doors of their car. I have the sense
that it is all moving too fast for me to think, so I try to step out
of the flow of time and see with shaman's eyes. I "freeze the
frame" by encasing Eric with a golden light. I realize that we must
all be encased in golden light for the "time-slowing" to work, so I
enclose myself, the man and the woman in corresponding fields of
golden light. I remember my concern about my daughter—where
is she? I extend my vision and see her playing beside the fountain
in the backyard. I also see the dirty-faced girl, still sitting in the
front yard. I encase both of them in golden radiance. As I do this,
I am startled by straight beams of golden light which suddenly
manifest themselves among us all, so that each one of us is connected to each of the five others with a separate "ray." I think to
myself that these "connectors" are like the lines in a molecular
model.

I turn my attention back to Eric. Now I can see the "spirit form" of his mental illness—it is a horrible, horrifying thing clinging to his right side. It looks like a colostomy bag filled with excrement, only the brown substance is alive, writhing and twisting inside the "bag" like an insect inside a cocoon. I am shaken and disgusted by the sight of it. Eric himself is apparently totally unaware of the spirit form clinging to him. The thought enters my mind that this thing is the remnant of a twin who did not develop past the embryonic phase. I must do something about it, but I can't think what. I look at the woman and realize that I can also see the spirit form of her craziness—it is a brown crab-like creature inside her chest cavity, crouched with its jointed legs wrapped around her heart. I look at the man. At first I cannot see a spirit form associated with him. Then I realize that I must "look differently." I do so and see that he does have a "spirit form" to his craziness, but it is a machine rather than a living thing. I see that around his waist he "wears" a machine that is composed of chainsaws at different angles. I recognize suddenly that this is an interdependent system of craziness in this family, and that the man enters into it because when the craziness is on the woman in a sexual form, she is an incredible sex partner. The man releases his sexual insanity with her at those times, and for the rest of the time just hangs around grimly relating as little as possible. I realize that I am he. I feel the machine around my own waist. I realize that I cut "wood" with it with a masturbatory gesture of the hips. The wood is cut simultaneously by blades at different angles and the logs separate into cut pieces that are "quartered" and fall in a mandala form. I remind myself again that all of these people are parts of myself. I now understand I must "heal everyone at once." If I fail to do this, the unhealed crazinesses remaining will reconstruct their necessary complements all over again in other people. The only thing to do is get it all done at once. Then there is hope for sanity.

I realize that I must remove these spirit forms from the bodies of the people in the dream. I do this, making sure that no tendrils or fragments remain attached to the dream bodies. The crab-creature is particularly tenacious and keeps wrapping its legs around the heart again as soon as I pry it loose. I realize that this too "must be done all at once." At last I succeed in prying all the

legs loose at one time and pluck the creature out of her chest cavity. The crab-creature waves its legs frantically. I am still uncertain
about what to do with the spirit forms once they have been carefully removed from the dream bodies. Suddenly an answer comes
to me in the form of an odd phrase: "transformation through increased vibratory activity." I wonder where that came from and
what it means when I see one of the things it means—the golden
light is "vibrating" with increasing speed and intensity around
and in the spirit-illness forms. It has become a kind of all-consum-
ing golden fire.

The forms disintegrate and disappear, but I have a sense of
"ashes" still suspended in the light. I decide that I do not want *any*
"toxic residues" from these illness-forms around my house, so I
hold the increasing vibratory activity until it is clear that the residues have been completely transformed into pure energy and
evenly distributed throughout the universe in this value-free
form. I am pleased. I look at the three people. At the level of the
dream corresponding to consensual waking reality, none of them
are directly aware of my "shamanizing." I watch them look mo-
mentarily disoriented and startled as they gather around the car. I
perceive them all to be experiencing odd bodily sensations associated with the removal of the spirit-illness-forms. I am also pleased
as I perceive that much, if not all, of their momentary disorienta-
tion is coming from experiencing their surroundings with "new
eyes," suddenly free of the habitual, pre-conscious distortions resulting from their mental and emotional disturbance. The thought
comes to me that these subtle signs bode well for their full recov-
ery. I relax in the knowledge that even though I have not fully
comprehended the experience, I have been able to act in the
dream with greater consciousness and creative response than I
usually have. I slip into seemingly dreamless sleep . . .

In the morning, I awoke with another dream. As I began to
make notes on it, I suddenly recalled the lucid portion of the
dream.

I lived and worked with this dream for more than a week before I realized that, at one vitally important level, it was telling me
that I was neglecting my daughter in favor of my work—most particularly the work of writing this book. That knowledge has al-

lowed me to consciously choose to be with her and play with her more often. Other levels of meaning and significance continue to reveal themselves with continued meditation on the dream.

Let me close this brief discussion of lucid dreams with a dream story that was shared with me in the course of dream work.

A young man, "Dan," dreams he is at a party in a beautiful penthouse apartment. A good jazz band is playing in the corner of the high, carpeted space. The far wall is all glass, and the gigantic city-scape glows and sparkles. The dreamer is sitting in a comfortable chair with a very attractive woman on his lap. There are lots of people around and everyone is having a good time. Suddenly he realizes that he is dreaming—that his physical body is asleep in a cheap rented room in Chicago. At this moment in the dream, the woman on his lap asks him if he is having a good time. He laughs and replies that he is having a great time, but that he will have to leave soon—his alarm is about to go off and wake him up. The woman asks him in surprise what he means, and he replies that all this is a dream and none of it is real.

"You mean you think I'm not real?" the woman asks in some annoyance.

"That's right," he replies.

With this, the woman becomes even more annoyed. "I'll show you who's real or not!" she says, and crushes her lit cigarette out on the back of the dreamer's right hand.

Instantaneously the young man awakens in the rented room with a terrible pain in his right hand. He turns on a light and sees a round burn the size of a cigarette on the back of his right hand. He peers in amazement and sees what appear to be cigarette ashes clinging to the skin around the wound. The young man told the group with whom he shared this dream that he had told his friends about it at the time, and they had all concluded after much debate that he must have walked in his sleep, found a cigarette, burned himself, gone back to bed, and then awakened himself with the dream.

What interests me most is not whether "it really happened that way." I believe the young man was telling us all in the group the truth as he remembered it, but even if the dream and the story of awakening are a conscious fabrication, I still have no reason to

think that such a thing could not happen. It is "impossible" in exactly the same way that it is "impossible" that contemporary non-
technological people can walk through fire and live coals without
burning themselves—yet they do it. Such feats have been so well
documented by such a wide range of anthropological observers
that it is much easier to believe than disbelieve, even though I
have never witnessed it myself.

What I do know to be true is that *all* dreams are seeking to
manifest their energies and images in the world through our conscious experience. If "Dan" had accidentally burned himself with
a cigarette later in the day, no one would think it strange or unusual at all. It is the *speed* with which the burn manifested that
makes the story so eerie and "unbelievable." Yet the ability to
manifest a burn without an external trauma is simply the reverse
of the ability to suppress injury from burning in the presence of
traumatic external heat—something we know many people can
do.

The Hindu-Buddhist tradition with which this discussion began suggests that the level of the unconscious whence come
dreams is also the level at which the Great Dream of waking experience is formed and maintained in its seemingly more stable state
than shifting landscapes of sleeping dreams. If there is any truth to
this notion, then the mechanism of the "spooky" occurrences (like
Dan's dream story and the seeming anomaly of fire-walking) may
be seen as exactly the same as mechanisms that shape all our experiences of waking life. Such a notion also begins to offer a conceptual framework within which other seemingly "miraculous" cures
and "effective" curses may be better understood. At another level
I am also quite sure that even if Dan's dream story is a conscious
fabrication, it is still a very accurate metaphoric representation of
his struggle with his Anima and the ways he tends to deny the "reality" of his intuitive and emotional life, thereby doing himself an
injury.

It is as though every person were an unconscious magician,
creating his or her personal reality and the collective reality simultaneously. "Seth," the archetypal wisdom figure in the works of
Jane Roberts, expands on this theme at great length. Here it is
possible to better understand the odd philosophical history of solipsism. Again, it is simply an aesthetic decision to perceive one

aspect of truth as more important and compelling than others. Solipsism—the belief that all experience is one's own creation and that nothing is real beyond oneself—is, at an archetypal level, a perception of and identification with God the Creator, in much the same fashion as the ancient Egyptian identified himself or herself as Osiris.

The universal experience of guilt for "thought crime" (guilt experienced seeing one's repressed negative desires manifesting in the world, even when one has done nothing conscious to bring them about) makes a different kind of sense in this context. In this framework, such "neurotic guilt" can be understood as a guilty conscience for unremembered dream crimes. It is far from accidental that even people who pay no attention to their dreams will use the phrase, "I wouldn't dream of it," to disavow something strongly. (In fact, no one may say with any certainty what has or has not been dreamed of.)

Indeed, to the extent that we ignore and repress our dream lives, and the life of feeling, thought, and intuition that our dreams embody, we have every reason to feel guilty when our worst imaginings manifest in the world. Here we are approaching the realm of the Original Sin of separating individual consciousness from the unconscious in the first place.

With all this in mind, there is no reason not to cultivate lucid dreaming for whatever reasons one wishes. Often, focusing on lucid dreams and the incubation of lucid dreams in a group will have the effect of increasing the incidence of lucidity in group participants. Here, as in all meditative exercises it is the attitude of openness as against premature closure that makes the exercise a success.

It is the attitude or state of mind that makes any meditation productive. Indeed, it is the attitude or state of mind alone which can transform any mere activity into a meditation. Any activity undertaken with the spirit of openness will tend to turn into a meditation if pursued, while even the best and most proven meditation or ritual will turn barren and unproductive if the attitude of openness is absent from its practice. This is true of the efforts to incubate particular dreams and particular kinds of dreams, just as it is true of all other waking activities.

And even the most horrific and dramatic nightmare has the

ironic and humorous twist of being only a dream when we awaken.

Summary: LUCID DREAMING AND DREAM YOGA

When we become conscious that we are dreaming in the midst of the dream experience, the dream is said to be "lucid." In the Hindu-Buddhist and Taoist traditions, lucid dreaming has been cultivated for religious reasons for more than twenty-five hundred years. In the West, there are some who disparage lucid dreaming as an unwarranted and potentially ominous intrusion of waking consciousness into the natural and spontaneous experience of the dream. In my experience, this attitude is in error—the level of unconsciousness from which the dream itself springs is the foundation of waking consciousness as well. The dreaming unconscious is a center in our being which is so much older, wiser, stronger, and more far-seeing than waking consciousness that to imagine it could be dominated or "controlled" by even the most adept lucid dreamers is to misunderstand its basic nature. The tradition of lucid dreaming and the accounts of lucid dreamers, both Eastern and Western, is clear—the dreaming unconscious can withstand even the most aggressive triviality in the lucid dreamer.

The process whereby the energies and images of our dreams come to be manifested and constellated into the experiences of waking life is complex and ultimately mysterious to me. However, I do know that all dreams are at a deep level associated with the inherent tendency of unconscious, archetypal energies to manifest themselves in our waking experience. Dreaming lucidly provides an arena where human consciousness may examine itself and transform itself in dramatic, exciting, and important ways. The relationship between what we dream on the one hand, and who we are and what we do in waking life on the other, is multiple, deep, subtle, and profound. To enter the realm where the dreams are experienced with a self-awareness normally restricted to waking life allows us to awaken great creative energies.

In experimenting with ways of incubating lucid dreams, and ways of behaving in lucid dreams once they are entered into, it is important to remain as open to new ideas, feelings, emotions, and experiences as possible. Indeed, it is this essential attitude of openness which alone can transform any mere activity into meditation, while even the most tried and true method or meditative practice will turn barren and unproductive if the spirit of openness is absent from its practice.

Chapter XVII
NURTURING THE
CREATIVE IMPULSE

> If one advances in the
> direction of his dreams he
> will meet with success
> unsuspected in common
> hours.
>
> *Thoreau*

As long as consciousness is partial, irony is inevitable (so we might as well cultivate a taste for it).

This might be called the "Law of Irony." Viewed from another perspective, it might also be called the "Law of the Trickster's Revenge." The archetypal Trickster serves two primary functions. It is one of the functions of the Trickster to deliver "comeuppance" (or "just desserts," or "karma") to those who exhibit hubris. It is also one of the functions of the Trickster to deliver the inspirations and energies of the creative impulse. Both of these functions are accomplished in the same way—the revelation of intimate relatedness and interconnection between and among things and events which were previously thought to be separate and unrelated.

To illustrate further, here is a story from Tivland, in what is now Nigeria (I am indebted to Charles Keil for sharing this story with me).

The King of the World decides that there are too many desert and barren places everywhere. He decides that all creation should be summoned to attend a Great Planting Festival, so that the whole world may be turned into a garden. The message is carried forth, and the clouds, the sun, the moon, the rain, the earth, and all the plants and animals come with their seed-bags to celebrate the Great Planting Festival.

Everything proceeds with great pomp and ceremony until the King notices that Hare is absent.

"Where is Hare?" he demands, and his messengers tell him that Hare is still in his burrow, preferring to sleep in the heat of the day.

The King flies into a rage and orders his men to drag Hare from his hole and bring him to face judgment. The guards bring Hare before the King, but Hare is obstreperous and tells the King that his Great Planting Festival is silly, and that he, Hare, could put on a better and more prestigious festival without half-trying.

The King says, "Oh, really! Well, you have my permission to try, but if you fail, I will have you skinned alive, although your pelt is so mangy it's hardly worth the trouble!"

Hare leaves the King's presence and is immediately filled with fear and remorse. His alligator mouth has run away with his humming-bird brain *again,* and this time he is going to have to pay painfully, with his *life.* He considers begging for mercy, but in his heart he knows that begging for mercy is useless.

Later, he returns to the Great Planting Festival and climbs a tree nearby, carrying a sack on his back. When he is settled up in the tree, he opens the sack and takes out a drum—the First Drum—and begins to play. At first he beats the drum slowly and solemnly in time to the ceremonial planting. Then he slowly begins to introduce new rhythms and syncopations, beating faster and faster until all the others have discovered the joys of dancing the First Dance to the First Drum. In their ecstasy their seed-bags lie trampled and unnoticed in the dust beneath their dancing feet. At this point, Hare leans down out of the tree and calls to the King of the World who is dancing along with everyone else. "See? *Everyone* came to my Dancing Festival, but *nobody* came to your old Planting Festival!"

Many parallels to the Hermes myth are clear. In one important way the two stories are the same in that they both represent the paradoxical quality of human consciousness and self-aware-ness—the Trickster from which the disasters of self-deception and the triumphs of creativity both stem. The creative impulse itself is given shape in both dreams as the birth of music. As William Blake said, "Energy is Pure Delight."

As Apollo and the King of the World are transformed by the sound of the First Musical Instrument, so we are each and all transformed by the creative impulse and the surge of energy in creative expression.

Hubris (arrogance, insolence, overweening pride, the inflat-ed self-importance of prematurely closed ideas and world views) is also the Trickster's own primary "character flaw." In the Her-mes myth and the Hare myth, both are lowly and despised fig-ures. Their hubris comes from the spontaneous expression of interior life rather than their perception of themselves as socially important personages. It is the hubris of power that both Apollo and the King of the World exhibit, and are punished for. The punishment is delivered simultaneously with gift of the creative impulse, symbolized in the two myths by the invention of music and "harmony." In my dream of murdering Clint Eastwood, my own hubris is both punished and rewarded by the realization that he is intimately and permanently related to the most positive and nurturing elements in the dream and in myself. In this way the Trickster always performs the necessary task of rebuking prema-ture closure and delivering the message of the creative impulse, by revealing the unexpected, previously unimagined, unper-ceived, subtle, but nonetheless real interconnections among all things. The Trickster always reminds us of the fact that all really is one in the largest view. The Trickster both releases the creative impulse—the spark of imagined possibility and the surge of as-yet-formless energy from within—and punishes the arrogance of pre-mature closure simultaneously. It is this release of creative energy that both chastises hubris and manifests amazing, previously uni-magined possibility.

The most pervasive form of hubris in Western, male-domi-nated culture is that the rational, "objective," logical mode of thought and experience is the yardstick against which all other ex-periences must be measured and valued. The exclusive reliance on the "rational" mind-set is itself the height of irrationality, given what we know to be true about the unconscious and the extent to which we human beings are unconscious about ourselves and the world at every moment. "Objectivity" is, at best, a useful fiction—an impossible ideal which inspires us to greater efforts at creative self-awareness. At worst, it is the source of all the most dangerous and cosmically threatening technological dilemmas and self-deceptions we have manufactured for ourselves so industriously.

To solve and transform the problems we face, both individual and collective, we must cultivate an attitude of openness to all our experience, awake and asleep. This attitude of openness requires an ability to contemplate the paradoxical unity of apparent opposites. In this contemplation, both the overthrow of prematurely closed attitudes, opinions and beliefs and the mobilization of the creative impulse are simultaneously accomplished.

This is one immensely important level at which all the Trickster myths and stories from around the planet are one story—the story of the evolution of human consciousness. To those who have become complacent and callous amidst their prematurely closed visions of their own power and importance—those for whom real growth and development have ceased—the Trickster always brings ironic self-destruction, but to those who remain open to their interior unconscious life, no matter how lowly, unimportant or ineffectual they may appear to be, the Trickster brings the Great Gift of creative energy.

This archetypal drama lends curious appeal to Melvin Dummar's story of picking up the ragged stranger in the middle of the desolate desert night, and then later supposedly being remembered in Howard Hughes' will. This is another Trickster story, and at some level we recognize that it is true—whether it actually took place in waking life or not.

Another story, this time from the heritage of Jewish folklore: Word is brought to the Grand Inquisitor of Seville that a little Christian child has disappeared. The Grand Inquisitor becomes convinced after hearing the story that the child has been abducted and murdered by the Jews so that his blood can be used to make the Passover matzos. He sends his men forth to arrest the Head Rabbi of the Seville ghetto and bring him before the Inquisition.

The Rabbi is arrested and brought before the Inquisition,

and the legal debate that ensues for the following six days is frustratingly inconclusive. Finally, the Grand Inquisitor goes into executive session and tells the other officers that it is obvious that merely human means are insufficient to reach the truth in this matter. God himself must be called upon to make a sign. The Inquisitor proposes that two pieces of paper, one blank and one with the word "guilty" written on it, be placed in a leather bag, and that the Rabbi be forced to pick one without looking. Thus may God reveal the truth. It is agreed. However, the Grand Inquisitor is convinced of the Rabbi's guilt, and since he does not wish God's Will to be contravened by mere chance, he writes "guilty" on both pieces of paper when he prepares the bag.

The Rabbi is brought back in and informed of the decision. He reaches into the bag, draws out a piece of paper, and immediately pops it in his mouth and eats it without looking at it. There is an uproar in the court, and the Rabbi calls out that he acted on an inspiration from God to cleave to his innocence, and if there is any question about which paper he chose, all you have to do is open the bag and see what's left.

Here is another Trickster story where the creative impulse both delivers ironic, self-created revenge on the one possessed by the hubris of power and also inspires action which is previously unimagined, but which turns out to be perfect for the complete transformation of the seemingly hopeless situation. The inherent Trickster quality of the process of dreaming itself means that every dream exemplifies this archetypal story of evolving self-awareness at some deep level, and often in the obvious content of the dream as well.

Increasing openness to the realm of the unconscious is a Trickster's game, and dreams themselves are a Trickster's illusions, revealing endless depths in even the most seemingly unlikely corners.

When we engage in dream work—paying creative attention to our own dreams and to the dreams of others, sharing them and working on them when and where it seems appropriate to do so—we are dancing to Hare's drum. The irony is that everyone dances to Hare's drum, and only a few are aware of it. This is the only choice available to partial, intermittent, individual consciousness—to be aware of Hare's drumming while we dance, or simply to dance to it unawares.

Nightly we stand before the Magic Mirror of the Dream Which Never Lies. Often, like the Wicked Queen in Snow White, we look into the mirror only to discover that we are not "the fairest in the land." Often, like the Wicked Queen, we repress and project this information about ourselves and attempt to "kill" those around in waking life upon whom we project our repressed "ugliness."

However, another alternative is always available. We can accept our interior knowledge that we are in the midst of change, psychic death and rebirth and act creatively and imaginatively on the information in the mirror. It is ancient wisdom that Fortune does not change people—it unmasks them. The same might be said of revolution. In our efforts to change ourselves and our world we will succeed only in creating ironic metaphors of the very things we are trying to alter and overcome unless we realize this. It is the basic problem of consciousness, of "original sin," and it remains basically unchanged, despite the exaggerated forms created by our increasingly powerful, sophisticated, and dangerous technologies.

The solutions to our difficulties will come from the exercise of imagination, and dream work is one of the best methods I know of to nurture and honor the life of the imagination. It is an obvious but insufficiently appreciated fact that everything we have accomplished, both as individuals and as a species, was born first in the imagination, and only manifested in action later, "after the fact." The history of innovation and invention from the making of fire to landing on the moon and sharing the view with those who remained behind is a history of imagination. The history of religion from the worship of the Great Mother to the proliferation of beliefs today is also a history of imagination and creative experience. Imagination is primary. As the ancient wisdom has it, "To know is nothing—to imagine is everything." Albert Einstein echoed this ancient truth when he said, "Imagination is more important than knowledge." Mark Twain said in a different way, "You can't depend on your judgment when your imagination is out of focus."

I believe that reflection will demonstrate that where the imagination and its "pointless," playful products are disparaged and held in low regard, there you will also find an inevitable sense of grimness and despair, action born of desperation, and a subjective sense of having only a severely limited range of choice among relative evils dictated by all-powerful circumstances far beyond our influence or control. Conversely, where the life of the imagination is celebrated and the products of imagination are valued and enjoyed, there you will find the sense of life as an evolving drama of creative expression where the individual is constantly striving for more felicitous forms of communication, and where the sense of self and other is constantly enriched by meaningful individual choice and action.

The disparagement of imagination is the single most powerful of oppressions known to humankind. At this deep and important level, all forms of individual and collective oppression, from the most personal and "psychological" to the most collective and "historical," from the most conscious, manipulative, and cynical to the most unconscious and "sincere," reveal themselves to be varieties of disparagement of "native" and "spontaneous" imagination. By the same token, awakening the imagination and cultivating the attitude of openness to the creative impulse and the interior life is the single most effective means of liberation available to us, both individually and collectively.

Yet another example of the Law of Irony at work in our collective life is the state of the national forests. For almost fifty years the Forest Service has been putting out forest fires whenever they occur, impeding on the natural process of forest ecology where occasional fires clear out the dead brush and kill off crowded saplings without "topping out" and destroying the older trees. The cumulative result of this fifty-year effort is that now virtually every fire that is not controlled immediately feeds on the unnaturally large amount of dead wood and "tops out," destroying even the biggest and oldest trees and raging out of control over vast tracts of land.

This is also a Trickster story. The hubris of the assumption that a "managed forest" where all fires are put out will be "more productive" than a natural forest, where the ecology is dynamically balanced, is punished by the grotesque exaggeration of the very thing we are trying to control by the very means our prematurely closed minds chose to control it.

Once again, the only real choice available to human consciousness is between the attitude of premature closure and the attitude of basic openness. This attitude of openness characterizes early childhood. Children come into the world open, and even battered and brutalized children retain that openness, for a while at least. When you consider that every child who learns to speak at all demonstrates an intellectual ability to learn and make use of the most complex and abstract system of mental/symbolic activity, it seems impossible to call anyone "stupid." The appearance of "stupidity" is inevitably a late development, resulting from the imposition of premature closure on the inherently open mental/conceptual abilities of the young child.

"And a little child shall lead them . . ." "Only as ye become a child again . . ."—these Christian admonitions refer at one important level to this attitude of openness. It is also this attitude to basic openness to interior experience to which Jesus refers when he says things like "The Kingdom of God is within," and "The Kingdom is here among us—it is at hand . . ."

At this important level, the basic message of radical Christianity—"Love your enemies"—is an affirmation of the ultimate unity of all phenomena. At the level of individual psychology, the admonition "Love your enemies" is the only practical solution to the universal problem of repression and projection. All of those whom we perceive to be our enemies (both awake and asleep) are at this vitally important level simply images of our own capacity for evil which we have denied and repressed, and are thus perceiving in others. In this crucial sense, whether we are Christians or not, we must learn to love our enemies because it is the only thing that works.

Remember Telly Savalas playing Pontius Pilate? Word is brought to him that this is the basic message of the preacher from Nazareth about whom everyone is so concerned. He laughs his best disbelieving, decadent, military individualist laugh and says, "Love your *enemies?*" Imagine for a moment what actually loving an enemy would entail—thinking and caring about that person with tenderness and concern and excitement and trying to come up with ways of communicating that love across the barriers of hostile behavior.

This paradoxical act of loving our supposed enemies is what is required of us if we are to evolve and grow as individuals and survive as a species. Here dream work can be of immense practical value. Let me demonstrate another dream of my own:

I am with a group of other men participating in an ancient religious ceremony. We are outdoors, in a wood. It is night. We are dressed in long, light colored robes, standing singly among the trees praying and meditating. The only light comes from the moon, which is full and casts deep shadows and pools of silvery luminescence among the ancient oaks.

Suddenly a wild-looking man dressed in skins with long, unkempt black hair and beard leaps into my field of view. He pauses at the gnarled roots of a gigantic and ancient tree in the middle distance in front of me. From the tree hangs a perpetually whirling circular metal blade attached to a wooden handle. The whole device is suspended from the tree by a live vine with leaves growing on it.

The wild man seizes the handle of the whirling blade in his left hand and grasps his long, dark hair with his right. He brings the whirling blade to his throat and severs his own head from his shoulders. As the head separates from the body, he holds it aloft in triumph, uttering a blood-curdling, demonic laugh.

I am deeply moved, impressed, and shaken by his self-decapitation. I understand that the "wild man" is mocking "the priests," of which I am one. I also understand that at another level the "wild man" is simply demonstrating the depth of his art and the mastery of his meditation. I also know that he is a "Celtic forest yogi." We are all Celts in the wood this night, but the "wild man" is pursuing an ancient tradition of independent shamanizing, while I am part of a somewhat more recent collective, priestly tradition.

At some other point in the same dream, perhaps before the self-decapitation, I am with another group of people, both men and women. It is just before sunset. We are all feasting at tables set up under the trees. There is an atmosphere of gaiety and celebration—a harvest festival in a voluntary religious community.

We are dressed in clothing from different periods in history. Someone hands me a beautifully carved and crafted spherical wooden puzzle, about the size of a tennis ball. Its pieces join together so smoothly and intricately that I find it hard to believe that it is carved out of a single piece of wood, yet clearly it is—the grain matches perfectly everywhere. It has several openings in its surface which afford views of its intricately carved interior. I think to myself in the dream that it is like a sculptural rendition of an M.C. Escher illusion—the interior perspectives are three-dimensional and endless, even though I hold it in my hand. I also have the thought that this is a piece of art and craft out of the Celtic tradition of mandala meditation, rather than the Hindu. I look from the object in my hand to the larger scene in the wood and am filled with great joy in a community filled with great joy and creative ferment. It is an experience of great love. I look around to thank whoever it was who handed me this beautiful gift, but he or she is gone amidst the groups of people and the trees.

This was a very moving and significant dream for me, and it continues to reveal new insights and levels of meaning as I re-experience it again, even years later. At the time it was initially very difficult for me to "love my enemy" in the figure of the "wild man"—to accept him emotionally as an aspect of my own being. Intellectually I recognized him as a Shadow image with whom I was grappling in waking life around the question of whether to seek ordination into the Unitarian Universalist ministry. However, it was a full week of exploring other aspects of this dream, and the dreams that followed it, before I undertook the exercise of actively imaging myself as the "wild man" himself, of attempting to love and acknowledge him fully, not only as an example of an archetype, but as a part of myself.

The following poem was the result.

Dream Yoga

The time of the full moon!
I will show them all—
Old men at their practiced prayers,
Young ones straining to learn the magic,
All standing among the ancient trees.
I have been alone so long,

Living so close to the Divine,
It has burned away my fear.
For me
The Tree blooms and bears a meat-saw
Like an extra-heavy fruit,
Blade perpetually whirling.
Look at me!
You are so startled.
Oh, this is a good show—
You will remember it!
See? I grab my hair
Thus,
And saw right through the neck
So quickly!
I can feel the whirling teeth dividing
The skin, the muscles, bones, and vessels—
All sliced through fast and clean!
I hold my head aloft
To see you stare,
Looking down into your awe-struck faces!
I laugh at your wonderment—
All your books and talking
Never brought you to this!
It takes a wild man
Without a Master
To show the possibilities
Of fearlessness.
I cannot brag—
For me, it is easy.
And being done
I leave you
To your plodding worship—
So correct,
So clearly resonant
With the highest truths!
If only you knew the prayer of praise
My demonic laughter is,
But you do not,

Which makes it even funnier!
When I am out of sight
I will use my two hands
To settle my head back
Upon my shoulders
And knit the severed organs
With the knowledge
That all is one.

In many ways, this Gestalt exercise revealed the same archetypal blend that was revealed in the active imagination of "Clint
Eastwood" in the earlier dream—a shaman-figure combining
Shadow, Willing Sacrifice, Trickster and Universal Love (for all
and each in particular) into one consciousness. In a most paradoxical way, both pieces of expressive meditation took the form of a
variety of love for one's "enemies," who are simply part of the
All that is One. It is my perception that this conscious reconciliation with Shadowy aspects of my own makeup through expressive
work was instrumental in achieving more clarity and taking more
responsibility for relations with others in waking life.

As Heraclitus pointed out, "There is nothing permanent except change." Embracing the inevitability of change (and death) is
a scary business, but *the creative impulse overcomes fear.* Nurturing
the creative, expressive impulse in ourselves whenever we encounter it, and particularly in our dreams, can make it fun-house-
scary, rather than menaced-by-evil-enemies-scary. The creative
impulse, like the dream, bridges the gap between consciousness
and the unconscious and reunites and reconnects that which was
initially perceived as separate. In the sense of inextricably intertwined ecology and psychology, every expression offered to the
creative impulse has a political dimension because it impacts upon
our routine and unquestioned, prematurely closed notions about
ourselves and the world. Poets are, in this vitally important sense,
indeed the "unacknowledged legislators of the world."

In this same sense, every expression offered to the creative
impulse also has a religious dimension, in the oldest and most radical sense of *re-ligio*—to ligate again, to rejoin and reconnect in a
natural and organic fashion. Our word "ligament" is another ex-

ample of the root sense of *ligio.* It has always been the ritual task of religion, and the joyous pleasure of art, to demonstrate and celebrate the deep, organic connection of self with other and each with all—a connection that is as basic and as functionally real as the connection between muscle and bone.

Freud and others have amply demonstrated the sexual nature of the creative impulse, and of dreams, so in paying attention to dreams and nurturing the creative impulse in ourselves and others, we find we are in the realm of the three great taboos of "polite conversation"—sex, religion and politics. Being serious, good-humored, and open with each other regarding our evolving ideas and experiences in these areas has the effect of nurturing the creative impulse.

In this context, it becomes clear that all forms of censorship (especially interior self-censorship and repression) are metaphors of premature closure and thus are also invitations to ironic self-deception and counter-productive efforts. Whenever a book is banned from libraries, its sales inevitably increase in book stores, especially among the young in whose name the censorship is most often invoked. This is ironic, but not accidental.

The tragedy of our nation's (and indeed the world's) criminal justice and penal systems stems from the same archetypal drama of hubris, premature closure and Trickster's revenge. The jails and prisons of this world could hardly be better designed if their purpose was to train criminals and prepare them for further lives of crime, and yet the cry for more money for more prisons and more police and legal apparatus to put people in jail grows ever louder. It is ironic, but far from accidental.

The paradoxical unity of apparent opposites is the source of this irony. It is also the source of the popular opinion that "creative people" are all at least a little bit "crazy," particularly the most unorthodox and productive ones, who are then called "geniuses." This is a comedy with tragic consequences. It is the continued failure to better understand the unconscious source of both creativity and insanity that allows us to continue to squander the planet's limited resources on gigantic engines of horror and destruction whose only use is the painful obliteration of life on that same planet. This behavior is truly insane, and yet it comes to us dressed in the white coat of the lab technician and the top-hat of business and government, and masquerades as the highest expression of hard-headed rationality and "sanity."

It is only when we understand the nature of our problems as exterior manifestations of interior life that we can even begin to imagine their creative solutions. Jung's relationship with James Joyce is interesting in this regard. Joyce is reported to have consulted Jung in Switzerland under the patronage of Mrs. Mellon. Among other things, Joyce apparently consulted Jung regarding Joyce's troubled daughter. Jung is reported to have said to Joyce words to this effect: "The only difference I can see between you and your daughter is that you go into the unconscious like a diver, and she drowns."

Here in this story it is clear once more that the only meaningful difference resides in the attitude of openness and courage with which we face that which is unconscious within us, not the nature or content of the unconscious itself which is essentially the same for all human beings.

Jung is also reported to have advised Mrs. Mellon to terminate her financial patronage of Joyce, lest the secured income rob Joyce of an important incentive to write, and thus hasten Joyce's untimely demise due to alcoholism. But once again, as Joyce himself joyfully testifies, this is all too heavy and somber a way to approach the creative impulse and the evolution and development of consciousness. The creative impulse overcomes fear and brings us closer to the center of the paradoxical unity of opposites. There joy and agony are aspects of a single experience, an experience which we each participate in each time we dream, and each time we give creative expression to our deepest energies.

When we remain open and fully engaged with the whole range of our experience, awake and asleep, we grow and change. We pass through a series of deaths and rebirths, often experiencing our transformations as death in our dreams. Each time we risk ridicule and the loss of security and affection by following our own heart's path, we touch the source of renewal and revitalization within. Sooner or later, the grim suspicion that life is meaningless at best, a set-up, a rigged game in favor of misery at worst, gives way to other perceptions and intuitions. The deck is stacked,

but only in favor of change and against premature closure. Not
only is it actually possible that we come out all right in the end,
but the expression of the creative impulse can actually transform
any situation. All really is one, and the universe actually is a safe
place to play after all.

Newton in his rational passion,
Spinning star-struck
From his meeting with Eve's apple,
Invested everything with the dignity
Of numbers.
Playing on the shores of fathomless oceans,
Riding on the shoulders of giants,
He called the force that binds the universe
In its energetic dance
"The Force of Gravity,"
But in his seriousness, he forgot
That even clothed in numbers
And the shining certainties of thought
The attraction of all things
For one another and themselves
Is another metaphor of love.

(This poem first appeared in *INWARD LIGHT—The Friends' Journal of Psychology and Religion,* Vol. 39, Winter, 1976–1977.)

Summary: NURTURING THE CREATIVE IMPULSE

As long as consciousness is partial, irony is inevitable
(so we might as well develop a taste for it).
There is nothing permanent except change.
Opposites are never true contraries.
It is impossible to say where God is not.
Pride goeth before a fall.
What the good person does is always right.

It requires an unusual mind to undertake an analysis of the obvious.

These aphorisms and fairy tale morals are all born out of the fact that the energy that animates all things is one. Our problems (from the purely personal to the Divine) are the caused effect of consciousness. For this reason, the solutions to our problems are to be found in consciousness as well.

Ultimately, loving others and loving self are one and the same act. The converse is also true: the fear/dislike of our own interior being creates the world of human misery. All expressions offered to the creature impulse are both religious and political because they alter habitual consciousness and open up prematurely closed systems of thought and experience. In this vitally important sense, consciousness is the only thing worth changing. All other efforts to remake the world are successful only to the extent that they succeed in altering consciousness unintentionally, while at worst such efforts result in creating ironic self-defeating metaphors of the very things we are attempting to change and control.

Opening to the creative impulse overcomes fear. When fear is overcome and we give creative expression to our deepest energies, we are renewed and made whole again, and we can bring our best energies to the transformation of our individual and collective lives.

Chapter XVIII
AN ANNOTATED
BIBLIOGRAPHY
ON DREAMS AND DREAMING

> You can learn things from
> books.
>
> *Ringo Starr*

What follows represents virtually everything I have ever read regarding dreams and dreaming. I have derived much pleasure and learned a great deal from the works noted here. It is my hope that the organization of these materials into working categories with brief descriptive notes will be useful to people wishing to explore the world of dreams further. The comments on the books, articles, periodicals and other resource materials are intended wholly and solely as an aid in selecting further reading. The ideas presented in this book are not final formulations, and must be validated and tested against the increasing experience of each individual dreamer.

The categories into which the bibliography is divided are formulated with a particular bias toward facilitating the use of dream work in a wide range of settings with widely diverse groups. There is, unfortunately, no section on dream work with the elderly and the dying, although gerontology and thanatology are fields which seem to me to be most likely to make productive and increasing use of dream work. The dream work that I have done with the old and the dying, although not sufficiently diverse to warrant firm conclusions, certainly does suggest that dreams can be as important and dramatically insightful and transformative of feeling in dealing creatively with the issues of old age, infirmity, and death as with the issues of earlier stages of life. There is a section devoted to dream work with children and young adults. I have had sufficient experience doing dream work with children and young adults to say that dream work with young people can be immensely rewarding for all concerned. Intergenerational dream work is one of the most rewarding activities to grow out of sharing dreams.

There is a section devoted to "Dream and Symbol Dictionaries." By and large, the popular dream dictionaries that purport to list the meanings of dreams all fail to acknowledge the subtlety and complexity of individual dream experience. The nature of dream imagery is always deeply personal and individual and thus can never be adequately codified or routinized. However, the archetypes do manifest themselves in essentially the same ways everywhere they appear around the world, so there is merit to looking up particular archetypal images and examining the ways they have appeared in different cultures at different times. Once again, the touchstone of reliability is the "tingle" or "aha" of the dreamer himself or herself. When an entry in a dream dictionary provokes a felt shift, then you can be sure that the material is true and on-the-case (but always only partially so, since there is no way to say when the metaphoric possibilities of any image have been exhausted). With this important fact borne in mind, even the popular dream dictionaries can be of interest and use. Some of their "definitions" of the meanings of dream imagery are traceable back over four thousand years (to the Chester Beatty papyrus and beyond). Many of the mechanical definitions in the dream dictionaries have an archetypal resonance, and for that reason they may well awaken tingles of recognition in dreamers from time to time.

Far more useful, however, are the dictionaries of symbolism and traditional imagery which do not purport to tell you what your dreams mean, but rather offer succinct accounts of the worldwide incidence and evolution of the most archetypally resonant and recurrent images. Exploring these collective, archetypal resonances to individual dream images is the heart of the Jungian method of "amplification." In this method, the collective associations of a particular image are pursued outward into history and world culture. This is a particularly useful procedure, particularly when combined with the more familiar method of personal association pioneered by Freud. When pursued simultaneously, it is often the case that material revealed by both methods will turn out to be resonant and mutually illuminating.

There are separate categories for "Metaphysical and 'Occult' " and for "Medical and Other Scientific Research." In both categories, the majority of things I have read have struck me as silly, pretentious, and prematurely closed to a high degree. However, some of the finest things I have read which have enriched both waking and dreaming life the most have also been drawn from these distinctly complementary categories. Curiosity and openness in examining the accounts of both scientific researchers and occultists is (once again) greatly rewarded in my experience. In addition, there are categories focusing on separate styles of dream work (Jungian, Freudian, Christian, etc.). As I have said elsewhere, there is much to be gained from looking at all the various styles and approaches to dream work, provided one is not put off by the irrelevant, intensive warfare among competing perspectives and schools of thought.

There is a special section set aside for work relating to lucid dreaming. This is a field which is gaining in interest to large and diverse segments of the population. Just in the course of preparing the manuscript for the publishers, I have become aware of four new and separate periodicals devoted to accounts of lucid dreamers and research at various levels of sophistication into the phenomenon of lucid dreaming. (These are listed under "Resource Guides and Periodicals.") It is clearly the case that when you realize you are dreaming in the midst of the dream, you become free to explore yourself and the relationship between dreams and waking life in dramatic and exciting new ways.

By rights there should also be a section devoted to fictional and poetic accounts of the dream experience, but the task is monumental and beyond the scope of this work. Clearly there should also be sections on "Shamanism," "Journal Keeping," and "Creative Process," but there are already good bibliographies in these areas, and the task of annotating these resources must wait for another occasion.

Finally, there is a brief bibliography of books on world mythology. The experience of mythology is deeply rewarding and can serve to illustrate in fascinating and compelling detail the ways in which each one of us is one with all other human beings (past, present, and presumably future). A knowledge of the world's mythology is not required for good, exciting, and rewarding dream work, but such a knowledge can enrich dream work immeasurably.

Indeed, a growing awareness of how the same essential dramas of inter-relation among the archetypes reflect themselves again and again in the myths and religious visions of all human beings has many beneficial and therapeutic effects in waking life as well. The energies that manifest themselves in archetypal patterns of myth and history are very real. A growing understanding of mythology can both extend and intensify the responsibility we take for shaping our waking lives more creatively, while at the same time allowing us to more fully appreciate the extent to which external events have transpersonal, archetypal significance. Such an appreciation can then begin to re-echo in the mythic dramas of personal life. We each can begin to recognize our own transpersonal essence and allow our feelings and emotions to transform as we continue to face our recurrent life dilemmas and struggles.

For these reasons, I would like to urge everyone who does not already have some knowledge of the world's mythology to peruse the last section of the bibliography for the most attractive doorways into that important and most enjoyable realm of archetypal literature.

For a long time, it was fashionable to codify anthologies of mythology by ethnic and geographical/linguistic boundaries. More recently, scholars have begun to codify and present the myths of the world in terms of the archetypal themes, rather than their geopolitical location. I find this way of organizing anthologies and critical presentations of myth most enjoyable and rewarding, and my selection of introductory materials on world myth under "The Myth Connection" reflects this obvious bias.

In the interests of making the following resource guide as useful and accessible to the greatest number of people as possible, I have foregone formal, correct bibliographical style (which requires that all entries be listed alphabetically by author) and have chosen to list titles first with the idea that for most people it is the title that conveys the most immediate and useful meaning.

A FEW GOOD BOOKS TO BEGIN WITH

1. *Dream Power* and *The Dream Game* by Ann Faraday—two of the best books for getting a sense of dream work, its possibilities and diversity of techniques.

2. *The New World of Dreams* edited by Woods & Greenhouse—the most representative and complete anthology of writings on dreams, culled from all historical periods.

3. *The Understanding of Dreams* by Raymond de Becker—the best general historical survey of attitudes toward dreams and styles of dream work from around the world.

4. *Man and His Symbols* by Carl Jung *et al.*—the best introduction to Jung's work. (Look for the larger format, hard cover edition—the impact of the many beautiful illustrations is greatly reduced in the smaller, black and white reproductions in the paperback edition.)

5. *Creative Dreaming* by Patricia Garfield—the best introduction to possibilities and practices of lucid dreaming in different cultures and different periods.

6. *Working With Dreams* by Ullman and Zimmerman—the best introduction to group-work with dreams.

7. *The Handbook of Dreams* edited by Wolman—the best anthology to date of research, theories, and applications, including contributions from the perspective of medical, psychoanalytic, and consciousness/cognition research. Many diverse and thought-provoking presentations.

8. *Dreams—Visions of the Night* by Coxhead and Hiller—the best picture book of dream art with an extremely good text as well.

9. *Altered States of Consciousness* edited by Tart—a good anthology of modern essays on various altered states of consciousness including dreams; particularly interesting is Kilton Stewart's seminal essay, "Dream Theory in

Malaya," where he describes the dream rituals of the *Senoi* people.

10. *The Inner World of Childhood* by Francis Wickes—an excellent book on therapeutic work with children by one of Jung's pupils.

11. *The Dictionary of Symbols* by Cirlot—perhaps the best one-volume reference to the global occurrence and ritual significance of a number of the most prominent archetypal symbols, particularly useful in pursuing the "amplification" method of dream work.

12. *Myth* by Eliot *et al.*—a very good and well illustrated introduction to world mythology organized by theme rather than nationality. Another excellent book in the same vein is Campbell's *The Mythic Image*.

INTRODUCTIONS AND GENERAL SURVEYS

✓*Dream Power* by Dr. Ann Faraday, Berkeley Publishing Corp., New York, 1972. This book is a broad but thorough overview of the primary issues of dream interpretation and working with dreams in groups. It is written in lucid prose by a woman who has devoted her life to the study of dreams and who is not afraid to talk about her own growth and development in that process.

✓*The Dream Game* by Dr. Ann Faraday, Harper & Row, New York, 1974. Dr. Faraday's second book, pursuing and amplifying the questions raised in *Dream Power,* and acknowledging her debt to Fritz Perls and the Gestalt movement.

Do You Dream? by Tony Crisp, E.P. Dutton, New York, 1972. A broad overview, somewhat spottily written, but with some nice passages—particularly the verbatim and narrative examples of active group work on dreams and "Gestalting."

Dream Worlds: The Complete Guide to Dreams & Dreaming by June and Nicholas Regush, Signet, New York, 1977. An interesting and well written little book touching many of the most important issues of individual and group work with dreams. Notable especially for the experiential exercises for generating and integrating dream insights.

Getting It Together—A Guide to Modern Psychological Analysis by Robert B. Ewen, Franklin Watts, New York, 1976. An extremely rudimentary but admirably clear and conservative survey of contemporary techniques of analysis and therapy, notable primarily for the chapter on "Dream Interpretation" which is simplistic but accurate.

Working With Dreams by Ullman and Zimmerman, Delacorte, New York, 1979. An *excellent* introductory book on the theory and practice of working with dreams in groups, as well as undertaking personal dream work.

Dreams—Visions of the Night by David Coxhead and Susan Hiller, Avon (Flare), New York, 1976. A beautifully illustrated, large format, inexpensive paperback with unusually clear and informative text. Notable also for its effort to present the information and the art in a non-sexist fashion.

The Dream—Mirror of Conscience by Werner Wolff, Grune & Stratton, New York, 1952. A very interesting overview of dream interpretation since 2000 B.C. with an attempt to synthesize the insights of the various schools into a single coherent theory of "dream synthesis."

Exploring the Inner World by Tolbert McCarroll, New American Library, New York, 1976. A practical guidebook to techniques, unusually free of "preachiness," particularly noteworthy for the chapters on journal keeping and dreams.

Savage and Beautiful Country—The Secret Life of the Mind by Alan McGlashan, Hillstone, New York, 1967. An interesting and well written book exploring the nature of imagination and dreams and proposing a return to dreaming and creative expression as a response to political and social turmoil.

The Natural Depth in Man by W. Van Dusen, Perennial Library, New York, 1977. Informed by a close study of the Christian mystic Swedenborg, this offers a coherent view of the nature of consciousness—particularly notable for the comprehensive but somewhat superficial chapter on "Dreams."

The Psychology of Dreaming by R.L. Van De Castle, General Learning Press, Morristown, 1971. An excellent booklet offering a comprehensive survey of the history of dream interpretation, major contemporary schools of thought, current physiological research, and an extensive bibliography.

The Understanding of Dreams by Raymond de Becker, Bell Pub. Co., New York, 1965. This book surveys the history of attitudes toward and methods of dream interpretation from the Epic of Gilgamesh to Jung and includes the texts of many historically important dreams which are discussed in some detail.

Exploring Your Unconscious Mind by Mambert & Foster, Cornerstone, New York, 1977. A very interesting introduction to archetypal self-understanding using dreams as the primary "doorway to your unconscious."

Dreams & Other Manifestations of the Unconscious by Harold Kluger, Analytical Psychology Club of Los Angeles, 1960. A compact and dynamic survey of dream theory and practice in recorded history with a simple explanation of Jungian approaches.

Centering—Your Guide to Inner Growth by Laurie and Tucker, Warner Books, New York, 1978. A charming and well written primer of Jungian, Gestalt, and Body Work methods of enhancing self-awareness—particularly interesting for the final three chapters where dreams and dreaming are dealt with at some length.

Dreams & Dreaming by Normal MacKenzie, Vanguard Press, New York, 1965. A profusely illustrated overview of the history of dream interpretation and dream research touching most major issues and personalities.

Dreams—Messages from Myself by Ruth Kramer, Celestial Arts, Millbrae, 1973. A charming little book with simple graphics illustrating some of the basic truths Ruth Kramer culled from paying attention to her dreams with some examples of her style of dream work.

Your Bedside Dreambook by Nancy Shiffrin, Major Books, Canoga Park, 1977. An interesting effort to introduce several styles of dream work emphasizing the importance of overcoming fear and awakening a wide range of human potentials through dream work.

Sleep On It!—The Practical Side of Dreaming by Janice Baylis, De-Vores & Company, Marina del Rey, 1977. Charming and clear—comprehensively covers methods of generating understanding focused on the relevance to immediate, practical waking concerns.

Dreams: Their Mysteries Revealed by Geoffrey Dudley, Aquarian Press, London, 1969. A cogent, brief book emphasizing the validity of eclectic, multiple approaches to the understanding of dreams and offering thumbnail sketches of the different schools of thought.

How To Understand Your Dreams by Geoffrey Dudley, Wilshire, Hollywood, 1969. A cogent little book offering a broad overview of the material with a special emphasis on practical techniques of interpretation.

Dreams by Walter Gibson, Grosset & Dunlap, New York, 1969. An overly simplistic but nevertheless interesting little book covering a wide range of dream foci from the occult to modern psychology.

An Introduction to Dream Interpretation by Manly Hall, Philosophical Research Society, Los Angeles, 1955. A cogent introductory piece with emphasis on the pitfalls of self-deception in independent work, while still supporting it.

How To Work With Your Dream Life—A Basic Resource Guide (With Some Procedures To Increase Dream Recall) edited by Harmon & June Bro, 1978, Edgar Cayce Foundation, Virginia Beach. An inexpensive ($.75) mimeographed collection of sound, applicable advice with a minimum of pitch for the Cayce trip—succinct and useful.

The Dream Guide by Marie Fay, Center for the Healing Arts, Los Angeles, 1978. A good little introductory guide to Gestalt and expressive dream work with structured exercises and an emphasis on techniques drawn from traditional cultures.

Dreams: A Guide to Interpretation by Aura C. Edwards, Anthelion Press, San Francisco, 1978. A brief, pithy, but somewhat simplistic attempt to make general principles of dream work available to the solitary person for self-study.

The Fabric of Dreams—Dream Lore and Dream Interpretation, Ancient and Modern by Katherine T. Craig, Kegan Paul, Trench, Trubner, & Co., London, 1918. A charming and open-minded presentation of a wide variety of information about dreams from various traditions.

How To Understand Your Dreams by Geoffrey Dudley, Wilshire Book Co., North Hollywood, 1957. An interesting little book, particularly because of the large number of dream accounts offered to illustrate the general points and guidelines.

Nightmare—The World of Terrifying Dreams by Sandra Shulman, Macmillan, New York, 1979. A general introduction to the phenomenology and theoretical understanding of nightmares and other "bad" dreams, made even more appealing by the inclusion of lithographs by John Spencer.

Sleep, The Gentle Tyrant by Wilse Webb, Prentice-Hall, Englewood Cliffs, 1975. A general introduction to sleep and contemporary research on the physiology of sleep, including a chapter on dream research entitled "Sleep and Dreams."

The Complete Book of Sleep—How Your Nights Affect Your Days by Dianne Hales, Addison-Wesley, Reading, 1981. An excellent survey of material regarding the phenomenon of sleep with special emphasis on techniques for dealing with sleep disorders, particularly interesting for the chapter "The Dreaming Mind."

ANTHOLOGIES OF VARIOUS SORTS

The New World of Dreams edited by Woods & Greenhouse, Macmillan, New York, 1974. An extensive anthology bringing together in one place representative examples of practically every school of thought on dreams, including ancient texts, and modern dream research. (This is the current edition of *The World of Dreams* edited by Woods in 1947.)

The Gates of Horn & Ivory edited by Brian Hill, Taplinger Pub. Co., New York, 1968. This is an anthology of dreams (with no analytical raps). It is also published in another edition entitled *Such Stuff as Dreams,* but this edition has no index which limits its usefulness.

Myths, Dreams, and Religion edited by Joseph Campbell, E.P. Dutton, 1970. A collection of lectures delivered in a series of the same name sponsored by the Society for the Arts, Religion, and Contemporary Culture in New York City in the late 1960s exploring archetypal connections and resonances in world myth and religion.

Dreams—The Language of the Unconscious, by Cayce, Clar, Miller & Petersen, A.R.E. Press, Virginia Beach, 1976. An interesting collection of essays and accounts of dream incubation research by followers of Edgar Cayce.

Dreams and Dreaming edited by Lee and Mayes, Penguin, Harmondsworth *et al.* 1973. An interesting collection of readings designed for the "Modern Psychology" series—very good selection, heavy on empirical studies, and includes some historical and symbolic material.

Altered States of Consciousness edited by Charls Tart, Doubleday, Garden City, 1972. A fine anthology covering drugs and hypnosis as well as dream and hypnogenetic phenomena, it reprints Kilton Stewart's important piece on the *Senoi,* "Dream Theory in Malaya."

Handbook of Dreams—Research, Theories and Applications edited by Benjamin Wolman, Van Nostrand, New York, 1979. The best anthology to date of research and theory of dreams and dreaming. The heart of Ullman's pioneering efforts to facilitate lay-led dream groups is included in his essay "The Experiential Dream Group." Richard Jones' essay "Dreams and Education" suggests methods for taking dream group activity into further realms of creative expression.

DREAMS AND SYMBOL DICTIONARIES

A Dictionary of Symbols by J.E. Cirlot, Philosophical Library, New York, 1962. This is an invaluable reference work if you get into the Jungian method of "amplification" as a means of understanding dreams. Cirlot has compiled a massive compendium of references for specific symbols and images. The introductory essays by Cirlot and Herbert Read are brilliant.

An Illustrated Encyclopedia of Traditional Symbols by J.C. Cooper, Thames & Hudson, London, 1978. A very useful resource for work in amplification. Like Cirlot this allows the researcher to survey a global list of cultural and religious phenomena manifesting a particular image.

How To Interpret Your Own Dreams (In Less Than One Minute) by Tom Chetwynd, Syden, New York, 1972. Despite its aggressively simplistic title, this book offers an interesting discussion of the archetypes and a sophisticated multiple reference system for the dream "dictionary."

Zolar's Encyclopedia and Dictionary of Dreams by "Zolar," Zolar, New York, 1973. The classic popular American dream "dictionary" useful primarily for comparative purposes.

The Complete Dream Book by Edward Allen, Warner, New York, 1966. A popularized "dream dictionary" of limited value because of its mechanical definitions, but notable for its extensive quotes from Astrampsychus, Artemidorus, and other ancient dream sagas.

Mystic Dream Book—25,000 Dreams Explained distributed by Foulsham & Co., London (no date). This is a classic popular "dream dictionary" full of racial slurs, ominous warnings, and smug prophecies, useful to the serious student of dreams primarily for comparative purposes.

The Interpretation of Dreams by "Zolar," Sphere Books, London, 1971. Like Zolar's other books, full of bald assertions about the meaning of particular dream images, but often resonant with archetypal meanings.

10,000 Dreams Interpreted by Gustavus Miller, Rand McNally, Chicago, 1979. Originally published in 1931 the book contains a compilation of Miller's automatic writings on the meanings of particular dream images. It was reprinted in a lavishly and charmingly illustrated edition.

FREUD AND THE SEXUALISTS

The Interpretation of Dreams by Sigmund Freud, Avon Books, New York, 1965. First published in 1899 (although dated 1900) this book marks the beginning of modern, "psychological" dream interpretation. It is of immense importance, but its prose is turgid and it is heavy going.

On Dreams by Sigmund Freud, Norton, New York, 1952. Published a year after *The Interpretation of Dreams,* this much shorter and more accessible work concentrates on Freud's own theories and eliminates most of the lengthy arguments with nineteenth century medical pundits which take up so much space in the larger work.

The Secret of Dreams—A Key to Freudian Dream Analysis by W.A. Stewart and Lucy Freeman, Macmillan, New York, 1972. Well written and engaging introduction to Freudian principles of dream work.

The Gates of the Dream by Geza Roheim, International Universities Press, New York, 1972. Roheim is an eminent anthropologist, one of the first to apply psychoanalytic ideas to anthropology. In this, his last book, he argues for a universal and exclusive application of the Oedipus complex to all dreams, and to the process of dreaming itself. It is a massive and compelling work, but a trifle single-minded and rigid.

Dreaming and Memory by Stanley Palombo, M.D., Basic Books, New York, 1978. Palombo, a committed Freudian, examines dreaming as a function of the processes whereby memory is "recorded" and "distorted and repressed" in line with Freud's theoretical model. Convoluted and narrow, but with fascinating dream series related.

The Innocence of Dreams by Charles Rycroft, Hogarth Press, London, 1979. Rycroft, a Freudian, comes to many of the same conclusions that Jung came to regarding the unconscious as the source of creative, healing energies, and he examines various ancient and modern traditions of dream-inspired creative work.

Dream Interpretation—A New Approach by Thomas French and Erika Fromm, Basic Books, New York, 1964. An aggressively Freudian but carefully researched and interesting work, emphasizing the importance of disciplined examination of intuitive insight over the course of therapy to validate interpretations.

Fundamentals of Psychoanalysis by Franz Alexander, Norton, New York, 1963. A cogent textbook of Freudian principles, very clearly written, particularly interesting for the chapter, "The Psychology of Dreaming."

Neurotic Distortion of the Creative Process by Lawrence Kubie, Noonday, New York, 1961. An aggressively Freudian but interesting attempt to develop a theory of creative activity and derive therapeutic strategies to free and enhance creativity. Dreams enter the theory as a minor point.

Dreams Are Your Truest Friends by Joseph Katz, Simon & Schuster, New York, 1975. A simple introduction to dream interpretation (mostly Freudian), notable for the divisions of the material by age and sex groupings, and for the wealth of individual dreams.

The New Psychology of Dreaming by Richard Jones, Viking Press, New York, 1974. Jones, a neo-Freudian has compiled accounts of the most recent laboratory and theoretical work on dreams and draws them into a single, neo-Freudian perspective.

The Psychoanalysis of Dreams by Angel Garma, Dell, New York, 1966. Originally published in 1940, this book is to Freudian dream interpretation what Maria Mahoney's work is to Jungian efforts.

On The Nightmare by Ernest Jones, Liveright, New York, 1971. A reissue of the famous work of Freud's biographer, it includes a lot of scholarly analysis of medieval superstition and the relation of nightmares to childhood fantasy.

Nightmares and Human Conflict by J. Mack, Houghton Mifflin, Boston, 1974. A careful but aggressively Freudian survey of the whole field of nightmare studies, particularly nightmares in children and their relation to the family drama.

A Grammar of Dreams by David Foulkes, Basic Books, New York, 1978. A cumbersome, doctrinaire, and rather silly book attempting to develop a system of mathematical symbolic logic operations for discovering the meaning of dreams. Interesting primarily for the detailed accounts of personal associations of clients to their dreams.

"I Had the Craziest Dream Last Night" by M. Steele and R. Armstrong, Nelson-Hall, Chicago, 1971. A turkey. Freudian dream interpretation techniques are superficially introduced, notable only because of the dream accounts presented.

Dream Analysis by Ella Sharpe, Hogarth, London, 1937. A classic; one of the first sustained presentations of Freudian dream work, with carefully detailed accounts of dreams to illustrate the theoretical arguments.

Symbol, Dream, and Psychosis by Robert Fliess, International Universities, New York, 1974. A monumental re-examination of Freud's pioneering work from the perspective of Fliess' experience as an analyst—detailed, intricate, heavy, and interesting.

The Dream in Psychoanalysis by Leon Altman, International Universities, New York, 1975. A very interesting book addressed to the community of Freudian analysts in an effort to persuade them to return to dream work as a central activity in analysis.

JUNG AND THE ARCHETYPALISTS

Man and His Symbols edited by Carl Jung, Doubleday, Garden City, 1964. Almost his final work, Jung intended this book to be the general reader's introduction to his work. It includes essays by his most trusted pupils on every broad aspect of archetypal psychology. It is also available in an inexpensive paperback edition from Dell, but much of the beauty and impact of the many illustrations is lost in the smaller format.

A Primer of Jungian Psychology by Calvin Hall and Vernon Nordby, New American Library, New York, 1973. A short, lucid, and succinct introduction to Jung's work by two of America's most eminent laboratory dream researchers. Hall and Nordby's *Primer of Freudian Psychology* has become a classic, and the recent publication of the companion volume on Jung reflects some major developments in attitude toward dreams and dreaming on the part of laboratory experimentalists.

Dreams by C.G. Jung, Princeton University Press, Princeton, 1974. A compendium of Jung's work on dreams drawn from his collected works and brought together in one illustrated volume.

Dream Analysis (2 vols.) by C.G. Jung, Psychological Club of Zurich, Zurich, 1958. Notes and transcripts reconstructed from shorthand accounts of the training seminars Jung led in dream analysis between 1928 and 1930—some of the finest material on dream work ever written (but limited for "private use" because the transcripts were never reviewed or approved by Jung himself).

Dreams, The Unconscious, and Analytical Therapy by William Alex, C.G. Jung Institute of San Francisco, 1971. A very brief but very cogent introduction to Jungian dream work—often used as compulsory reading for Jungian analysands.

The Meaning in Dreams and Dreaming by Marie Mahoney, Citadel Press, New York, 1966. This is an introduction to archetypal and depth analytical dream interpretation, written lucidly by one of Jung's pupils.

Experiment in Depth by P.W. Martin, Routledge & Kegan, London, 1976. First published in 1955, this book combines a study of the work of Jung, T.S. Eliot, and Toynbee with a passionate appeal for dream work and increased understanding of the nature and function of the archetypes in the search for religious and social solutions to world problems.

The Psychotherapy of C.G. Jung by Wolfgang Hochheimer, C.G. Jung Foundation, New York, 1969. An excellent survey of the therapeutic styles and interventions developed by Jung, particularly interesting for the chapter "The Dream and Its Treatment."

Clinical Uses of Dreams—Jungian Interpretations and Enactments by James Hall, M.D. Grune and Stratton, New York, 1977. A marvelous textbook of Jungian dream work, including a survey of historical practices and a venture into the domain of "enactments" as creative and therapeutic dream work.

Dreams and the Growth of Personality by Ernest L. Rossi, Pergamon, New York, 1972. A very exciting and extensively researched book dealing with the evolution of dream imagery as a cause and reflection of the growth and development of individual personality.

Applied Dream Analysis: A Jungian Approach by Mary Mattoon, Winston Wiley, Washington, 1978. Focusing on the discursive and interpretive mode, this book provides a text for a detailed survey of techniques of archetypal dream analysis—a fine book.

Dream and Waking Consciousness in the Drama of Authority—A Personal Account of Creative/Archetypal Dream Work by Jeremy Taylor, Dream Tree Press, Sausalito, 1978. A collection of journal entries, poems, drawings, and brief essays on the nature of the archetypes and their influence on waking life.

Jung's Analytical Psychology and Religion by Carl A. Meier, Southern Illinois University, Carbondale, 1977. A collection of four major essays based on lectures given by Meier, the Director of the Jung Institute in Zurich, at the Andover Newton Theological School. Particularly notable for the essay "Interpretation of Dreams."

The Symbolic and the Real by Ira Progoff, McGraw-Hill, New York, 1974. A detailed explanation of Progoff's "intensive journal" technique for recording dreams and working with unconscious material from his Jungian, archetypal point of view.

The Dream—The Vision of the Night by Max Zeller, Analytical Psychology Club of Los Angeles, 1975. This is a memorial volume of papers by a pupil of Jung's who was a founder of the Jungian movement on the West Coast; broad and wide-ranging concerns beyond an exclusive focus on dreams, but with much to say about the play of archetypes in dreams and in therapeutic situations.

Boundaries of the Soul by June Singer, Anchor, Garden City, 1973. An excellent overview of the practice of psychotherapy from a Jungian point of view, particularly notable for the chapter on "Understanding Our Dreams" and the chapter "Dreaming the Dream Onward: Active Imagination."

Awakening Intuition by Frances Vaughan, Doubleday Anchor, Garden City, 1979. A cogent and well written approach to the intuitive function and its value for modern life problem solving and enhancement of creativity, particularly noteworthy for the chapter "Dreams and Intuition."

Dream Psychology by Maurice Nicoll, Samuel Weiser, New York, 1979. Originally published in 1917, the book surveys early scientific research in dreaming and presents a synthetic theory of dream formation based in great measure on Jung's early work.

On Initial Dreams by Kate Marcus, Analytical Psychology Club of Los Angeles, 1954. A monograph on understanding the heightened significance of the first dream shared in a therapeutic or other growth and transformation situation.

The Dream and the Underworld by James Hillman, Harper & Row, New York, 1979. A strange and annoying book inveighing against dream interpretation, and then offering muddled suggestions about how to do it—notable primarily for the quotes from ancient authors.

Success and Failure in Analysis edited by Gerhard Adler, G.P. Putnam's Sons, New York, 1974. An interesting collection of papers from the Fifth International Congress for Analytical Psychology, notable particularly for Diekmann and Blomeyer's presentation on theoretical and clinical aspects of "The Constellation of the Countertransference in Relation to the Presentation of Archetypal Dreams."

Jungian-Senoi Dreamwork Manual by Strephon Williams, Journey, Berkeley, 1980. An interesting but somewhat garbled handbook of techniques and philosophical thoughts developed in the course of dream work with a wide variety of people. This book is the development of ideas in Williams' two previous booklets, *Jungian-Senoi Dreamwork* (Journey, 1977) and *The Principles and Practices of Jungian-Senoi Dreamwork* (Journey, 1978).

Dreams and Other Manifestations of the Unconscious by Harold Kluger, Analytical Psychology Club, Los Angeles, 1960. Dynamic and amusing introduction to Jungian concepts and modes of analysis and therapy with particular emphasis on dreams and dream work.

Basic Hints for Dream Work, and *Nurturing the Creative Impulse With Special Reference to the Energies of Dreams and Dreaming* by Jeremy Taylor, Dream Tree Press, San Rafael, 1980 and 1982 respectively. Two works upon which the present volume is based.

Dream—A Portrait of the Psyche by Stewart McLeod, Century Twenty One, Saratoga, 1981. A curious and interesting but rigid attempt to "verify" Jung's approaches to dream work with a blind study of a series of 145 dreams from the same person, a woman not in analysis who simply agreed to report her dreams without comment to the researcher.

Waking Dreams by Mary Watkins, Harper & Row, New York, 1976. An excellent work focusing on techniques of active imagination and the psychotherapeutic uses of fantasy and imagination throughout history. The connection with sleep dreams is explored in some detail and a number of practical techniques are offered.

Methods of Treatment in Analytical Psychology edited by Iak Baker, Verlag Adolf Bonz, Fellbach, 1980. The Proceedings of the Seventh International Congress for Analytical Psychology. Of particular interest are the papers of Diekmann, Kirsch, Kambert, and Moreno.

Apparitions—An Archetypal Approach to Death Dreams and Ghosts by Aniela Jaffe, Spring, Irving, 1978. An interesting analysis of letters responding to an inquiry requesting accounts of warning dreams, visions, and encounters with ghosts experienced by readers of the *Schweitzer Besbachter*.

CHRISTIAN DREAM WORK

Dreams—God's Forgotten Language by John Sanford, Lippincott, Philadelphia, 1968. A classic in the field of clinical/pastoral counseling offering a synthesis of Christian and Jungian insights constellated around the premise that "dreams and their interpretation can heal the sick soul."

Dreams: The Dark Speech of the Spirit by Morton Kelsey, Doubleday, New York, 1968. Very interesting and detailed discussion of the Judaeo-Christian tradition of dream interpretation. Includes extensive appendices of translations of the most important church documents relating to dream interpretation from Tertullian through Benedict Pererius.

The Gift of Dreams by Kathryn Lindskoog, Harper & Row, 1979. An excellent book. As the author asserts, it is "a Christian view" but very open to metaphors of other religions. Many moving moments of personal insight through dream work.

Dreams—A Way To Listen to God by Morton Kelsey, Paulist Press, New York, 1978. An introduction to dream work for the Christian lay person, following the style of his earlier books and emphasizing the direct experience of spiritual realities in the dream state.

God, Dreams, and Revelation by Morton Kelsey, Augsburg, Minneapolis, 1974. A revised paperback edition of his earlier work, *Dreams—The Dark Speech of the Spirit,* with the appendices translating major statements of the early church fathers on dreams and dream interpretation removed.

Dreams in the Life of Prayer by Harmon Bro, Harper & Row, New York, 1970. An interesting book stressing the incubation of dreams through prayer and meditation—strong emphasis on Edgar Cayce's approaches and teachings.

Edgar Cayce on Dreams by Harmon Bro, Warner, New York, 1976. A compendium of the famous "Sleeping Prophet's" utterances on the process of dreaming itself and hints about a coherent theory of dreams and dreaming.

Dreams, Hallucinations, Visions by Ernst Benz, The Swedenborg Foundation, New York, 1968. An interesting little pamphlet by a noted European Historian of Religion emphasizing the religious validity of dreams and visions, particularly those of Swedenborg.

Dreams and Healing by John Sanford, Paulist Press, New York, 1978. An excellent little book outlining the basics of individual dream work with a sensitive discussion of the nature of the archetypes; particularly interesting for the detailed accounts of two dream series that comprise the last half of the book.

Dreams—Our Judge and Jury by William Petersen, A.R.E. Press, 1951. One of the first A.R.E. publications on dreams—very sober and intense and doctrinaire, but quite interesting.

Dreams—Your Magic Mirror by Elsie Sechrist, Warner Paperback Library, New York, 1974. Sechrist is a student and follower of Edgar Cayce. She includes many of his dream interpretations along with her own. Heavy emphasis on seeking practical guidance from dreams in living "a Christian life" productively and happily.

The Secret of Dreams by Pedro Meseguer, Newman, Westminster, 1960. A selection of the Catholic Book Club, this examination of dreams and dreaming from the point of view of Catholic Church history and current dogma is very interesting.

OTHER STYLES OF DREAM WORK

"I Dreamt Last Night . . ." by Medard Boss, Gardner Press, New York, 1977. The famous Swiss psychiatrist develops his "phenomenological" approach to dreams, arguing that the remembered text of the dream is itself the "interpretation." Cranky and amusing in its insistence on "logic" in approaching dream work.

The Third Reich of Dreams by Charlotte Beradt, Quadrangle, Chicago, 1966. This is an interesting collection of dreams had by people living under Nazi domination. The analytical raps are a trifle polemic and shortsighted, but this is made up for by a sensitive analytical essay by Bruno Bettelheim which is included at the end of the book. Heavy stuff, on the case of psychological aberration associated with political and economic oppression.

New Approaches to Dream Interpretation by Nandor Fodor, University Books, New Hyde Park, 1951. A broad and rambling work chronicling Fodor's life as a dream therapist and concentrating on a number of important dream themes, including numbers in dreams and symbolic representations of the birth trauma and intrauterine states.

Journey of a Dream Animal by Kathleen Jenks, Julian Press, New York, 1975. The autobiographical account of a young woman who begins to work with her dreams with only a stolen copy of the Modern Library edition of Jung's basic works for guidance. Poignant and fascinating.

Seeing With The Mind's Eye—The History, Techniques, and Uses of Visualization by M. and N. Samuels, Bookworks/Random House, New York, 1975. A fascinating overview of visualization treating dreams and dreaming along with healing techniques, meditation, etc. Lives up to its comprehensive title.

Creative Process in Gestalt Therapy by Joseph Zinker, Vintage, New York, 1978. A fascinating book focused on the practice of Gestalt Therapy, utilizing dreams and individual and group dream work among other strategies and techniques of awakening creativity.

The Dream Makers by Corriere and Hart, Funk & Wagnalls, New York, 1977. A popularization of their more scholarly work, *The Transformation of Dreams* written with Woldenberg and Karle, recounting the authors' "rediscovery" of the ancient tradition of group dream work carried out by the Iroquois, *Senoi*, Eskimo, *et al.* and their efforts to forego a modern therapeutic technique for group dream work stressing the activation of the archetype of the Self which they call "the Dream Maker."

Dream Dynamics and Decoding—An Interpretative Manual by Janice Baylis, Sun, Man, Moon, Huntington Beach, 1976. A charming and well thought out series of fifteen lesson plans designed to develop skills and learn specific techniques for working alone with your own dreams.

Studies in Dream Symbolism by Manly Hall, Philosophical Research Society, Los Angeles, 1965. A vaguely interesting book which unfortunately does not live up to the promise of its title—very theoretical with no examples and applications.

The Handbook of Dream Analysis by Emil Guthiel, Washington Square Press, New York, 1967. Detailed analysis of over six hundred individual dreams with discussion of the general issues and principles of symbolic language.

The Interpretation of Dreams by Wilhelm Stekel, Washington Square, New York, 1967. Stekel was a pupil of Freud's in Vienna and a teacher of Guthiel. His work is wide-ranging and includes analyses of many individual dreams which serve as examples of the principles of "active analysis" (the Stekel school).

The Voice of the Symbol by Martin Grotjahn, Dell, New York, 1971. Grotjahn was a pupil of Groddeck's (a contemporary of Freud's and inventor of the term "id"). In this book he discusses general problems of symbolic analysis, dreams and offers some nice work on Hieronymus Bosch as dream-artist.

Dreams and Symbols—Man's Unconscious Language by Leopold Caligor and Rollo May, Basic Books, New York, 1968. An account of a clinical training experience where May received dream accounts from one of Caligor's patients and maintained his own analytical interpretation, which is here published side by side with Caligor's in an attempt to develop "objective" validation for symbolic interpretation.

Book of Dreams by Jack Kerouac, City of Lights, San Francisco, 1976. Verbatim accounts from Kerouac's dream journals over the years he was writing *On the Road, The Subterraneans,* and *The Dharma Bums,* particularly revealing of the process whereby "raw" dream material is translated into "literary" work.

The Forgotten Language by Eric Fromm, Grove Press, New York, 1957. Fromm explores the inter-relationships between dreams, myths, fairy tales, and other folk art and illuminates many basic issues in the understanding of unconscious symbolism.

Dreams and Nightmares—A Book of Gestalt Therapy Sessions edited by Downing and Marmorstein, Perennial Library (Harper & Row), New York, 1973. Verbatim accounts of Gestalt dream groups led by Downing, together with raps about how and why insights and feeling changes are generated with those techniques.

The Sexual Dream by Natterson and Gordon, Crown, New York, 1977. A very interesting survey of sexual dreams from a wide range of people with accounts of interpretive work done with the dreamers and suggestions regarding working with one's own sexual dreams.

1,001 Erotic Dreams Interpreted by Graham Masterton, Warner Books, Anderson, Indiana, 1977. An interesting approach to sexually explicit imagery in dreams using insights from many different schools. Despite its title, it is not a "dictionary" but a serious attempt to help the reader develop a unique and individual understanding of his or her own erotic dreams.

How To Interpret Your Dreams—Practical Techniques Based on the Edgar Cayce Readings by Mark A. Thurston, A.R.E. Press, Virginia Beach, 1978. An interesting attempt to build a single dynamic theory of dreaming from the Cayce readings—very interesting but a trifle doctrinaire.

Women's Erotic Dreams by Graham Masterton, Warner Books, New York, 1976. A pot-boiler—a barely rewritten version of his earlier book, *1,001 Erotic Dreams Interpreted,* notable mainly for the dream accounts presented.

The Clinical Use of Dreams—A Practical Handbook for Analyst and Patient by Walter Bonime, Basic Books, New York, 1962. The first practical handbook of eclectic approaches to dreams and dream work in a clinical setting—a classic in the field.

Waking Dream Therapy—Dream Process as Imagination by Gerald Epstein, Human Sciences, New York, 1981. An interesting survey of contemporary techniques of active imagination as therapeutic tools with a focus on the similarities between sleeping and waking dreams.

Dreaming and Waking—The Functional Approach to Dreams by Corriere, Karle, Woldenberg, and Hart, Peace Press, Culver City,

1980. Despite the "franchise" quality of the style of dream work espoused by this group, their eclectic techniques for both individual and group dream work are most interesting and rewarding.

The Language of the Dream by Emile Gutheil, Macmillan, New York, 1939. An extremely interesting and useful book—one of the earliest attempts to broaden the rigidly Freudian stance toward dreams to include the further researches and insights of his students, most particularly Wilhelm Stekel, Gutheil's mentor.

The Analysis of Dreams by Medard Boss, Philosophical Library, New York, 1958. Stressing the phenomenological approach which honors the dream as a reality in itself, Boss offers telling critiques of all the other major schools of dream work and emphasizes the importance of spontaneous symbolization in philosophical thought—a classic.

Neptune's Plummet by Katherine West, Amata Graphics, Lake Oswego, 1977. A charming blend of spiritualist, feminist, and analytical insights into the dream process including many useful suggestions for solitary work with dreams.

Dreams—Secret Messages from Your Mind by Lois Seldon, Dream Research, Tacoma, 1981. An engaging but overly simplistic and unevenly written introduction to the basic principles of dream "interpretation."

Living Your Dreams by Gayle Delaney, Harper & Row, San Francisco, 1979. A lively and charming "14 week study manual" stressing active involvement with dream incubation and suggesting basic ground rules for group work with dreams.

Total Mind Power—How To Use the Other 90% of Your Mind by Donald Wilson, Berkeley, New York, 1978. Another "franchised" method of self-development stressing active involvement with bringing unconscious material to consciousness. Filled with meditative exercises. Particularly interesting is the chapter "Increasing the Benefits of Total Mind Power While You Sleep and Dream."

Dreams Beyond Dreaming by Jean Campbell, Donning, Virginia Beach, 1980. A charmingly enthusiastic introduction to eclectic techniques of solitary dream work, emphasizing the importance of taking the energies of dreams "beyond dreaming" into waking meditation and creative activity.

Understanding Your Dreams by Katherine West, Amata Graphics, Tacoma (no date). An earlier and less poetic version of Ms. West's larger work, *Neptune's Plummet,* emphasizing the possibilities of dream work with children and adults in alternative educational settings.

Interpret Your Dreams from a Macro View! by Thea Alexander, Macro, Tempe, 1971. An aggressively simplistic guide to dream work by the author of *2150.* Another "franchise."

Dream Voyages by John-Roger, Movement of Spiritual Inner Awareness, Los Angeles, 1979. An interesting blend of spiritualist and psychological insights combined with a blank dream log. Another "franchise."

METAPHYSICAL AND "OCCULT"

An Experiment With Time by J.W. Dunne, Faber & Faber, London, 1927. A classic in the field, often quoted by others. Dunne uses pre-cognitive dreams as an experimental reality to examine the perceived nature of time in the waking and dream state.

Adventures in Consciousness by Jane Roberts, Prentice-Hall, Englewood Cliffs, 1975. Subtitled "An Introduction to Aspect Psychology" the book integrates Ms. Roberts' experience as the medium for "Seth" with her understanding of academic psychology in an effort to broaden the universe of discourse about dreams and related phenomena.

The Psychology of the Esoteric by Bhagwan Shree Rajneesh, Harper & Row, New York, 1978. Rajneesh is a spiritual teacher who argues that "unconscious evolution ends with [us] and conscious evolution begins." Particularly interesting for the chapter "The Psychology of Dreams."

Knowledge of the Higher Worlds and Its Attainment by Rudolf Steiner, Anthroposophic Press, Spring Valley, 1945. A classic work by a famous modern spiritual leader, particularly interesting for the chapter "The Transformation of Dream Life."

Beyond Telepathy by Andrija Puherich, Anchor Doubleday, Garden City, 1973. A fascinating theoretical work on the telepathic phenomenon and the implications for biology and physics. Discusses the dream state from many points of view.

The Second Ring of Power by Carlos Castaneda, Simon & Schuster, New York, 1977. Like the other Castaneda books, this one is an examination of the conscious manipulation of altered states of consciousness through the tradition of Yaqui shamanism. This volume is particularly interesting for the chapter on "The Art of Dreaming."

Psychic Dreamology by Norvell, Barnes & Noble, New York, 1977. A clearly written but aggressively simplistic presentation of the "occult" possibilities of dream work, particularly pre-cognition and the improvement of health and finances.

The Twilight Zone of Dreams by Andre Sonnet, Chilton Co., Philadelphia, 1961. This book sold over a million copies in its original German edition. It offers a compendium of opinions from European intellectuals about the nature and significance of dreams, as well as a number of dream accounts from famous artists and others.

The Hermetic Dream by Robert Thibodeau, Hermes Press, Detroit, 1978. Styled "an astrological tool," this little book attempts to place modern dream work into the context of ancient traditions of astrology and occultism. Particularly interesting is that it reprints old essays by Madame Blavatsky and Francis Mayer, both of which have many practical hints for dream work.

Dreams by C.W. Leadbeater, Theosophical Publishing House, Madras, 1970. A brief exposition of the theosophical perspective on dreams and dreaming.

Joy's Way by W. Brugh Joy, M.D., J.P., Tarcher, Inc., Los Angeles, 1978. An excellent, cogent, clear introduction to the art of psychic and wholistic healing by one of America's leading practitioners—particularly interesting for the chapter "Dream Analysis, Telepathy, The Tarot and the *I Ching*."

Dream Reality by James Donahoe, Bench Press, Oakland, 1974. An ambitious and fascinating effort to discuss and offer practical hints about the ability to develop unusual states of consciousness in dreams and waking life.

ESP and Dream Analysis by Katharine Sabin, Henry Regnery, Chicago, 1974. An eclectic and serious attempt to integrate contemporary experiments in ESP and other "occult" phenomena in dreams with psychological theory, particularly the theory of archetypes.

The Night Voyagers: You and Your Dreams by Sybil Leek, Ballantine, New York, 1975. The famous occultist offers a charming introduction to dreams and dreaming with a special emphasis on pre-cognition; the book includes Ms. Leek's own "dictionary" of symbols and their meanings based on her experience as a dream interpreter.

The Conquest of Time—How You Too Can Dream True by Harold Horwood, Fowler & Son Ltd. (no date) London. A curious account of an incubation technique with claims to great success for predicting the results of horse and dog races. The author dedicates the book to Mary Baker Eddy and speaks of the necessity to use one's winnings for charity and ministry if the technique is to work.

The Mystery of Dreams by William Oliver Stevens, Allen and Unwin, London, 1950. Another compendium of prophetic, pre-cognitive, and other curious dream experiences, presented in a rapid-fire, journalistic style with serious attempts to corroborate claims.

Enigma by James J. Donahoe, Bench Press, Oakland, 1979. A very interesting survey of the literature and contemporary experimental data, discussing the dream state as the central metaphor of self-transformation and the cultivation of seemingly paranormal states.

The Psychic Reality of Dreams by Iyonne Barber, Exposition, Hicksville, 1976. A survey of the more famous and well documented cases of "psychic" and "occult" circumstances surrounding dream experiences by a researcher who has devoted his life to such study.

Chain of Reasoning by C. Gretter, Exposition Press, Hicksville, 1978. An interesting but highly idiosyncratic book detailing the author's efforts to "decipher" his dream life through synchronous encounters with an old encyclopedia and a "counselor"—often very moving.

Sun Signs and Dreams by Doris Kaye, Signet, New York, 1977. An engaging but somewhat mechanical attempt to correlate the basic sun-sign character studies to dreaming and generalized tendencies of personality manifested in dreams.

The Mystery of Dreams by William Stevens, Allen & Unwin, 1950. A very interesting book offering a wide selection of prophetic, prodromic dream accounts from all periods in history, but concentrating on contemporary examples. Well written.

Dream Cycles by Dusty Bunker, Para Research, Rockport, 1981. An intriguing exploration of cyclic patterns of dreaming, with emphasis on a nine year cycle. Her style is very warm and chatty but bespeaks a big vision.

The Book of Secrets by Bhagwan Rajneesh, Harper & Row, New York, 1974. Sixteen talks by a leading exponent of the Tantric tradition, particularly interesting for the chapter "Devices To Transcend Dreaming."

Watch Your Dreams by Ann Colton, ARC, Glendale, 1973. An awkwardly doctrinaire but interesting presentation of "laws" governing different aspects of dream experience. "The Phoenix Fire of the Self-Genesis Mind" section is particularly on-the-case.

The Wisdom of the Overself by Paul Brunton, Samuel Weiser, New York, 1943. A most interesting presentation of "mentalist" philosophy. Particularly interesting are the chapters "Studies in Dreams" and "The Yoga of the Discerning Mind."

Dreamer Awake—A Dream Study Guide by Street and Dupree, Lotus Ashram, Miami, 1971. A series of twelve lessons in Spiritual Dream Yoga. The tone is friendly but firm.

MEDICAL AND OTHER SCIENTIFIC RESEARCH

The Functions of Sleep by Ernest L. Hartmann, Yale University Press, New Haven, 1973. An interesting survey of laboratory studies of sleep and dreaming emphasizing the restorative function of sleep and dreaming in the preservation of general health.

Experimental Studies of Dreaming edited by Witkin and Lewis, Random House, New York, 1967. An interesting collection of research reports focusing on issues of factors influencing dream recall, the psychological functions of sleep, and the influence of daily experiences on dream imagery.

The Psychology of Sleep by David Foulkes, Scribner's, New York, 1966. An interesting compendium of results of research during the first fifteen years after the REM experiments with an exclusive emphasis on laboratory studies and the tiniest tip-of-the-hat to psychoanalysis.

Some Must Watch While Some Must Sleep by William Dement, Stanford Alumni Association, 1972. One of the discoverers of REM sleep, Dement reviews laboratory data and the major issues of dream research with care and passion. A series of reproductions of Picasso prints make this book beautiful as well as informative.

The Anatomy of Sleep distributed by Roche Laboratories, Nutley, N.J., 1966. This book is essentially an expensive advertisement for Roche's sleeping pills and related drugs, but since it was prepared to persuade doctors to prescribe Roche products, there is a great deal of readable information on the chemistry and pharmacology of sleep, together with some amusing history of dream interpretation.

Dream Telepathy by Ullman, Krippner, Vaughn & Murphy, Macmillan, New York, 1973. Fascinating account of controlled laboratory experiments measuring telepathic and other "occult" phenomena in dreams.

Dreams and Nightmares by J.A. Hadfield, Pelican Books, Baltimore, 1971. A general survey of research and contemporary arguments about dreams, with a heavy emphasis on physiological elements influencing the dream process. The book makes a nice corrective to purely "psychological" approaches to dreaming.

Sleep by Ian Oswald, Penguin, London, 1972. A lucid compendium of contemporary sleep research in biology, biochemistry, etc.

together with a serious effort to draw inferences from this body of material regarding dreams and dreaming.

The Science of Dreams by Edwin Diamond, Macfadden, New York, 1968. A detailed overview of the various avenues of dream and sleep research in the mid-1960's with a nice historical chapter on the evolution of dream interpretive techniques.

The Meaning of Dreams by Calvin Hall, McGraw-Hill, New York, 1974. Originally published in 1953 and revised in this new edition, the book outlines Hall's statistical and other researches into the content and structure of dreams in "normal" people from his neo-Freudian and experimentalist perspective.

The Individual and His Dreams by Calvin Hall and Vernon Nordby, Signet, New York, 1972. Hall and Nordby talk about their research and stress the importance of observing patterns over large numbers of dreams and offer statistical methods for discovering and understanding broad patterns of development in an individual's dream symbolism.

Song of the Siren by Stanley Krippner, Harper & Row, San Francisco, 1975. Perhaps the foremost laboratory experimenter with dreams recounts his experiences over a period of several years of exciting breakthroughs.

Sleep by Luce and Segal, Arena Books, New York, 1977. A very interesting survey of the laboratory dream research carried out, primarily in the U.S., primarily in the late 1960's—particularly interesting for the reports of LSD dream research.

Night Life—Explorations in Dreaming by Rosalind D. Cartwright, Prentice-Hall, Englewood Cliffs, 1977. Detailed account of Dr. Cartwright's life as a dream researcher and the broad range of issues related to dream recall and the relationships among dreams of a single night.

Current Research on Sleep and Dreams, Public Health Service Publication #1389 (no date). Put together primarily by Gay Luce, this report codifies research efforts and results prior to 1964.

Dreams, Images, and Fantasy—A Semantic Differential Casebook by C. Moss, University of Illinois, Urbana, 1970. A lumbering but interesting study of "hypnotic investigation of dream symbolism."

DREAMS IN OTHER CULTURES

The Interpretation of Dreams—The Oneirocritics of Artemidorus translated by Robert White, Noyes Classical Studies, Park Ridge, 1975. A full, annotated translation of the famous work composed around 175 A.D.

The Dream and Human Societies edited by von Grunebaum and Caillois, University of California Press, Los Angeles, 1966. A heavy duty anthology of papers delivered by twenty-five leading scholars at the conference of the same name held near Paris in 1962. The conference drew leaders in separate fields as diverse as neurophysiology and comparative religion. Because the original conference was sponsored by the Near Eastern Center at U.C.L.A. there is a disproportionate representation of Islamic Studies, but many other cultures are represented as well.

The Dream In Primitive Cultures by J.S. Lincoln, Johnson Reprint, New York, 1970. This is a reprint of Lincoln's classic study of the role and content of dreams in "primitive" cultures, particularly Native American cultures (originally published in 1935).

Strange Superstitions and Magical Practices by William Fielding, Blakiston Co., Philadelphia, 1945. An interesting and charming little book cataloguing metaphors of unconscious manifestations from many cultures and societies—useful in amplification. Also of particular interest is the chapter "Dreams and the Dream World."

Ancient Incubation and Modern Psychotherapy by C.A. Meier, Northwestern University Press, Evanston, 1967. A fascinating account of the Hellenic traditions of dream incubation for the purpose of healing and promoting health. Meier claims this tradition in continuity with archetypal dream work.

Lacandon Dream Symbolism I by Robert Bruce, Ediciones Euroamericanas, Perugino, 1975. A fascinating account of participant observation anthropology among the Lacandon peoples of Chiapas, "the least acculturated, the most traditional and conservative, of the Peninsular Mayas."

Reality and Dream by George Devereux, International Universities Press, New York, 1951. An interesting account of a course of therapy with a Sioux/Wolf Indian using dreams as the central focus. Aggressively Freudian, but sensitively aware of the problems of cultural relativism and cross-cultural therapy.

Dreams, Culture and the Individual by Carl O'Nell, Chandler & Sharp, Corte Madera, 1976. An overly simplistic but interesting survey of anthropological work with dreams emphasizing Freudian approaches.

Culture and Personality in Two Primitive Groups by Kilton Stewart, Stewart Foundation for Creative Psychology [144 East 36th St., NYC 10016]. A fascinating paper on Stewart's anthropological and psychological field work among the *Senoi* and a comparative study of *Senoi* culture with *Yami* culture (a subject people of the Japanese).

The Fabric of Dreams by Katherine Craig, Kegan Paul, Trench, Trubner, & Co., London, 1918. A very interesting compendium of archaic, folk, and other beliefs and practices related to dreaming from around the world, gathered by an open-minded woman who writes well.

Egyptian Magic by E. Budge, Dover, New York, 1971. A republication in abridged form of Budge's original 1901 work, particularly interesting for the descriptions of ritual practices related to dream incubation and dream interpretation related in Chapter 7.

Open Secrets—A Western Guide to Tibetan Buddhism by Walt Anderson, Viking, New York, 1979. An engaging introduction to Tibetan Buddhist faith and practice, particularly interesting for the chapter "Dream Analysis, Tibetan Style."

Warriors of the Rainbow—Strange and Prophetic Dreams of the Indian People by Willoya and Brown, Naturgraph, Healdsburg, 1962. A beautifully written and illustrated recounting of great prophetic dreams from the Native American tradition, comparing them with great prophetic dreams and visions from other cultures and focusing on the vision of global human reconciliation.

Dreams in Greek Tragedy—An Ethno-Psycho-Analytical Study by George Devereux, University of California, Los Angeles, 1976. A very interesting study of the "psychological validity" of the dreams of characters in ancient Greek tragedy, despite its vituperative anti-Jungian bias.

Basic Problems in Ethno-Psychiatry by George Devereux, University of Chicago, Chicago, 1980. A collection of Devereux's principal papers on "culturally non-relativistic psychoanalytic [Freudian] ethnopsychiatry." Many of the papers refer to specific pieces of dream work in a cross-cultural setting.

LUCID DREAMING

Creative Dreaming by Patricia Garfield, Simon & Schuster, 1974. A dynamite book dealing with the techniques for developing lucid consciousness while dreaming, reviewing techniques from Tibetan Yoga, *Senoi* techniques, historical lucid dreamers, and Dr. Garfield's own extensive experience.

Lucid Dreaming by G.S. Sparrow, A.R.E. Press, Virginia Beach, 1977. A very interesting booklet outlining Sparrow's personal research into the incubation of lucid dreams. Emphasizes the importance of meditation and the focus on spiritual ideals as keys to lucid dreaming.

Lucid Dreams by Celia Green, Institute for Psychophysical Research, Oxford, 1968. Offers extensive examples of lucid dream accounts and analyzes them with an eye to developing a general theory and practice of lucid dreaming. Very interesting.

Studies in Dreams by H.O. Arnold-Foster, Allen & Unwin, London, 1921. A fascinating book chronicling the author's successful efforts to induce lucid dreaming—the primary source for much of the material quoted by Celia Green.

Pathway to Ecstasy—The Way of the Dream Mandala by Patricia Garfield, Holt, Rinehart & Winston, New York, 1979. A very good book, outlining her successes in incubating lucid dreams over a period of several years. A worthy successor to her first, fine book.

Tibetan Yoga and Secret Doctrines edited by W.Y. Evans-Wentz, Oxford, London, 1968. A fascinating collection of Tibetan texts and recordings of oral teachings, particularly notable for the "Yoga of the Six Doctrines" including discussions and practices for "yoga of the dream state."

Dream Your Way to Happiness and Awareness by David Graham, Warner Books, New York, 1975. Despite its title and some strange mechanical metaphors for the dreaming process, an interesting little book with great anecdotes and at least two very interesting chapters on the development of lucid dreaming techniques.

The Life and Teaching of Naropa translated and analyzed by Herbert Guenther, Oxford University Press, Oxford, 1963. A collection of manuscript and oral teaching from the esoteric schools of Tibetan Buddhism, particularly interesting for the philosophical discussions and descriptions of yogic practices for achieving lucidity in the dream state for the purpose of transforming character and experience.

How To Educate Your Dreams To Work for You by Kilton Stewart, Stewart Foundation for Creative Psychology. A compilation of practical techniques culled from Stewart's other publications on the *Senoi* and strung together in a single place. Particularly valuable for the complete bibliography of Stewart's work.

Tantra—The Yoga of Sex by Omar Garrison, Causeway, New York, 1964. A fascinating and detailed introduction to this "underground" tradition of yogic practice, particularly notable for the chapter on "yoga in the dream state."

WORKING WITH CHILDREN AND YOUNG ADULTS

Windows to Our Children by Violet Oaklander, Real People Press, Moab, 1978. A Gestalt therapist and teacher examines and explores a wide range of creative, engaging, and therapeutic approaches to both one-on-one counseling and group work. Particularly interesting for the chapter "Dreams" which includes ideas for and accounts of work with children.

A Child's Library of Dreams by Sheri Clyde, Celestial Arts, Millbrae, 1978. An interesting little book designed "to help children explore their dreams and cope with their nightmares" using the "library" of "typical" children's dreams to encourage attention to children's dreams.

Build Your Own Dream House by Paula M. Craig, A.R.E. Press, Virginia Beach, 1974. An interesting little book for working with children and their dreams—set up as a workbook so the child can record and work on several dreams.

Theater of the Night—What We Do and Do Not Know About Dreams by S.C. Hirach, Rand McNally, New York, 1976. An excellent book offering a comprehensive overview of the field designed to speak to teenagers.

How To Make Your Dreams Work for You by Dian Buchman, Scholastic Book Service, New York, 1977. A succinct and serious attempt to present the basic issues of dream work to an adolescent audience. Inexpensive—a good possibility to use with beginning groups.

The Dream Collector by Arthur Tress and John Minahan, Avon, New York, 1967. Tress is a photographer who is interested in dream imagery, particularly children's dream imagery. The book is a collection of the photos created out of conversations with children about their dreams. Minahan's text is sensitive and to the point.

Dreams by Stephen Dunning, Scholastic Book Services, New York (no date). An excellent resource for teachers reprinting a wide variety of stories, articles and poems together with exercises for evaluating reading and comprehension skills.

Crystallizing Children's Dreams by Katherine West, Amata Graphics, Lake Oswego, 1978. An interesting work recounting a wide experience working with children and their dreams and including several exercises and games.

Dreams in Your Life—Scientific and Occult Interpretations by Howard Smith, Doubleday, Garden City, 1975. An excellent introduction to the world of dreams written for adolescents and including many black and white illustrations.

RESOURCE GUIDES AND PERIODICALS

Welcome to the Magic Theater—A Handbook for Exploring Dreams by Dick McLeester, Food for Thought Press (P.O. Box #331, Amherst, MA 01002), 1976. An excellent book on the order of the *Whole Earth Catalogue* listing and discussing a wide range of resources including books, other periodicals, and a directory of dream workers in the U.S. and Canada.

Sundance Community Dream Journal originally published quarterly by Herbert Read and others associated with the Edgar Cayce Association for Research and Enlightenment (P.O. Box #595, Virginia Beach, VA 23451). An ambitious and exciting journal emphasizing group dream work, lucid dream incubation, and spiritual awareness, unfortunately now defunct, although back issues may still be available.

GATES—A Sausalito Waterfront Community Dream Journal published by John Van Damm, Dream Tree Press (P.O. Box #1123, Sausalito, CA 94966). Publishing dreams related to the houseboat community of Sausalito (see Chapter 10). An exemplary publication demonstrating the creative vitality of dreaming shared on a community-wide basis.

Dream Journal published briefly by Carl Levinson in connection with his dream workshop focusing on creativity at the San Francisco Jewish Center in 1976. Notable particularly for the presentation of dream accounts side by side with the poems and stories they inspired. Some back copies may still be available from Carl Levinson, 2760 Sacramento Street, San Francisco, CA 94115.

Io #8—Dreams/Oneirology published by Richard Grossinger (370 Mitchell Road, Cape Elizabeth, ME 04107) in 1971. A full issue of this venerable "little magazine" devoted to dreams with contributions from a wide range of artists and scholars—a marvelous collection.

The Sleep Book by Lind and Savory, Harper & Row, New York, 1974. A large-format paperback collection of quotes, research reports, folklore, yoga exercises, and other materials related to dreams and dreaming, enhanced by dream inspired photographs by Murray Riss.

"Dream Works"—a special issue of *Voices,* the Journal of the American Academy of Psychotherapists, Vol. 14 #1, Spring 1978, edited by Mark Stern. All the articles are devoted to the place of dream work in the wide range of therapies falling under the rubric of "humanistic psychology"—fascinating.

Dreamworks—An Interdisciplinary Quarterly devoted to the "art of dreaming," edited by Kenneth Atchity and Marsha Kinder, Human Sciences Press (72 Fifth Avenue, New York, NY 10011). An excellent journal including dream reports, poems, stories, and critical, interpretive work. Often the items in *Dreamworks* transcend the ordinary boundaries of both art and scholarship.

Dreamweaver edited by Harry Posner and Nick Trusolino (172 Rushton Road, Toronto, Canada, M3G 3J1). A quarterly serving the burgeoning dream work movement in Canada including dream accounts, art, poetry, stories, and regular columns devoted to interpretation of readers' dreams.

Dream Network Bulletin (rotating editorship) coordinated by Bill Stimson at the Dream Community of New York (333 West 21st Street, #2FW New York, NY 10011). An effort to coordinate information regarding the dream work movement in North America, including listings and calendars of upcoming events, articles, and interviews with prominent dream workers.

Rainbow Flicker Dream Journal published by Molly Willard. A sporadic publication sharing dreams among members of the Rainbow Flicker Clan between their yearly gatherings.

So Let It Be Written published by Brad Erikson. A community dream journal serving the New College of California (777 Valencia Street, San Francisco, CA 94110).

Paths published by Charlotte Brown and Frances Day. A community dream journal serving the Starr King School for Religious Leadership (2441 LeConte Ave., Berkeley, CA 94709).

Lucidity Letter edited by Jayne Geckenbach. This journal is devoted to review of controlled research into lucid dreaming and regularly includes listing and reviews of scholarly papers on the subject (Department of Psychology, University of Northern Iowa, Cedar Falls, Iowa 50614).

Lucidity and Beyond published by Sally Shute. A sporadic publication devoted to popular interest in lucid dreaming emphasizing techniques for incubating lucid dreaming and accounts of lucid dreams.

Coordinate Point International—A Talk Magazine published by Jim Cook (P.O. Box #151, Clarcona, FL 32710). A publication devoted to popular exploration of the work of Jane Roberts, emphasizing the precepts of "Seth" and the idea that people "create their own reality" particularly through lucid dreaming. Chatty and energetic.

"Dreams and Seeing," a special issue of *Parabola—Myth and the Quest for Meaning* edited by D. Dooling, Volume 7, #2, Spring 1982. An issue of this interesting and ambitious quarterly devoted to dreams and dreaming in the context of world myth and religious belief (150 Fifth Ave., New York, NY 10011).

The Dream Theater by Hammel and Marshall, Harper & Row, San Francisco, 1970. An interesting and very good-humored large format paperback with many exercises and games designed to increase awareness and understanding of dreams.

MAGAZINE AND JOURNAL ARTICLES

"Lucid Dreaming as an Evolutionary Process" by G. Sparrow, *A.R.E. Journal,* Vol. X, #3, May 1975. An article describing Sparrow's incubation techniques developed over a period of years with theoretical speculations about the evolution of consciousness.

"In Search of the Dream People" by Jeremy Taylor, *East/West Journal,* Vol. 7, #5, May 1977. A review of the scanty first-hand sources of information about the *Senoi* people with emphasis on the archetypal influences contributing to popular interest in their dream work practices.

"Dream Incubation" by Henry Reed, *A.R.E. Journal,* Vol. X, #2, March 1975. A description of Reed's incubation techniques for group dream work emphasizing spiritual development.

"Once Upon a Dream" by Ann Faraday, *Voices,* Spring 1978. A fascinating account of work with one of Ann Faraday's own dreams discussing the impact of the dream work on waking life and decisions and contrasting various styles of dream work.

"Cancer in Myth and Dream" by Russell Lockhart, *Spring* 1977.

A very interesting article outlining research done with cancer patients and their dreams with emphasis on archetypal elements at work in confronting cancer.

"Jung and Politics . . ." by Jeremy Taylor, *East/West Journal,* Vol. 7, #1, January 1977. A review of the literature on the social and political implications of Jung's work emphasizing the importance of understanding the archetypes in developing productive strategies for social and political change.

"Toward a Theory of Dream Recall" by David Cohen, *Psychological Bulletin,* Vol. 81, #2, February 1974. An exhaustive review of the literature on dream recall with emphasis on other elements besides repression as major factors in forgetting dreams.

"Sleep, Unease, and Dreams" [four articles grouped together by theme] by Berger, Van de Castle, Krippner, Hughes and Ullman, *Psychology Today,* Vol. 4, #1, June 1970. A classic series of articles including an early account of Krippner and Ullman's research on dream telepathy.

"Dreams" and "Dream Messages" by Betsy Blackwell, *et al., The Sun—A Magazine of Ideas,* Issue #35, February 1978. An interesting article and accompanying readers' letters and dream accounts focusing on the increasing importance of dreams in their waking lives.

"Putting Your Dreams To Work" by Gayle Delaney, *New Realities,* Vol. 1, #4, October 1977. An interesting outline for incubating helpful dreams and analyzing them when they come, including a transcription of a dream work session conducted on the long-distance telephone.

"Exploring Mutual Dreaming" by James Donahoe, *Psychic,* November/December 1975. A very interesting article by Donahoe (author of *Dream Reality*) outlining his research with varieties of cross-dreaming and increasing consciousness in the "mutual dream" where two dreamers are aware of each other in their respective dreams.

"Martial Artists Use Dream Techniques" by John Moody, *Singularities,* Vol. 2, #3, March 1978. A preliminary report of the use of lucid dream states by practitioners of the martial arts to develop and experiment with further "unification of mind and body."

"The Mystery of Sleep" (anonymous staff writers) *Newsweek,* July 13, 1981. An interesting and snappy survey of sleep and dream research around the U.S. focusing to a large degree on research into sleep disorders.

"Dream Weavers" by Mike Edelhart, *TWA Ambassador,* August 1981. A report on lucid dream research concentrating on Keith Hearne's work at Hull University in England developing a biofeedback device to promote lucid dreaming by signaling the dreamer when REM periods occur without awakening him/her.

"Dream Interpretation" by Dan Gollub, *Mensa Bulletin,* #250, October 1981. A curiously rigid system for interpreting dreams is described and dream accounts solicited from readers for ongoing study.

"Terror in the Night" (anonymous staff writers) *Science Digest,* March 1981. A brief survey of the scientific hypotheses regarding nightmares and the sleep disorder known as "night terrors," concluding, "In some ways, the data are consistent with the ancient notion of a relationship between artistic creativity and psychosis."

"Lucid Dreaming—Directing the Action as It Happens" by Stephen LaBerge, *Psychology Today,* Vol. 15, #1, January 1980. A fascinating article outlining LaBerge's work at Stanford developing methods to verify the occurrence of lucid dreams objectively, including a number of interesting techniques for incubating lucid dreams. (There was also a most interesting reply in the "Letters" section of the April issue from Peter Fellows suggesting another most productive technique.)

"Lucid Dreams" by Douglas Colligan, *Omni,* Vol. 4, #6, March 1982. A fascinating update on Stephen LaBerge's work, including the report of his success in signaling to observers while in the midst of a lucid dream, and fascinating speculations about the possibilities of future research and therapeutic applications.

"Dreams That Saved Lives" by Marc McCutcheon, *Science Digest,* May 1982. A charming little article speculating about the evolutionary function of dreaming and the association of dreams with the earliest creative inspirations of the species.

"Sleep and Dreams" (a special section of *Science Digest,* July 1981) including articles by Cherry, Glassman, Swerdloff, Batten, and Koral. A most interesting and charmingly illustrated survey of various fields of dream research and the various approaches to dreams and dreaming currently fashionable in the scientific world.

"New Dream Research" [three articles grouped around this theme] by McCarley, Cartwright, and Foulkes, in *Psychology Today,* December 1978, Vol. 12, #7. Not nearly so interesting as the first revelations of the research on telepathy in dreams but still an interesting group of articles.

THE MYTH CONNECTION

Mythology by David Leeming, Newsweek Books, New York, 1971. A very good, profusely illustrated survey of world myth with discussions of the psychological connections.

The Illustrated Golden Bough by Frazer, edited by Mary Douglas, Doubleday, New York, 1978. A profusely illustrated condensation of Frazer's master work, exploring themes and structural meanings in world myth. Very readable.

The Greek Myths by Robert Graves (2 vols.), Penguin Books, Baltimore, 1955. The best reference work on the Greek tradition. Very useful for the copious notes relating archeological information related to the myths which are rendered with a care for their many various versions.

The World's Mythology in Colour by Veronica Ions, Hamlyn, London, 1974. A well written, well illustrated survey of world myth collected and rendered by geographical and cultural connection.

Larousse Encyclopedia of Mythology by Guirand *et al.,* Prometheus Press, New York, 1960. Somewhat dry but meticulous collection of surveys of mythology from around the world—useful reference, good index.

Encyclopedia of World Mythology (no authors cited), Galahad Books, New York, 1975. Another beautifully illustrated and reasonably well-written survey of world myth.

Myths by Eliot *et al.,* McGraw-Hill, New York, 1976. An excellent collection of surveys of world myth by type (rather than by geography), beautifully illustrated, good index.

The Mythic Image by Joseph Campbell, Princeton University Press, Princeton, 1974. A magnificent book, beautifully illustrated, well conceived and written by one of the greatest living archetypal scholars.

Mystery Religions in the Ancient World by Joscelyn Godwin, Harper & Row, San Francisco, 1981. A fascinating and well illustrated survey of the ancient mystery religions suggesting archetypal patterns persistent in contemporary times.

The Goddesses and Gods of Old Europe—6500–3500 B.C. by Marija Gimbutas, University of California, Los Angeles, 1982. A comprehensive outline of the religious cult images and inferred ritual practices of the matrilinear societies of Old Europe prior to the arrival of the patriarchal Indo-Europeans.

. . . and a very good series:

The Two Hands of God—Myths of Polarity by Alan Watts, Collier, New York, 1969.

The Wisdom of the Serpent—The Myths of Death, Rebirth, and Resurrection by Henderson & Oakes, Collier, New York, 1963.

Lord of the Four Quarters—Myths of the Royal Father by John Perry, Collier, New York, 1966.

Alpha—The Myths of Creation by Charles Long, Collier, New York, 1963.

AND ESPECIALLY FOR YOUNGER PEOPLE, BUT USEFUL FOR ANYONE . . .

Greek Gods and Heroes by Robert Graves, Dell Books, New York, 1960. A clear, cogent, poet's retelling of some of the most famous Greek myths.

Tales of the Greek Heroes, Myths of the Norsemen, Tales of Ancient Egypt by Roger Green, Puffin Books, Harmondsworth, 1958, 1960, and 1967 respectively. Very well-crafted retellings of the significant stories from these vitally important traditions.